T0212438

Lecture Notes in Computer Science   12004

More information about this series at http://www.springer.com/series/7409

Fu Lee Wang · Haoran Xie ·
Wai Lam · Aixin Sun · Lun-Wei Ku ·
Tianyong Hao · Wei Chen ·
Tak-Lam Wong · Xiaohui Tao (Eds.)

Information Retrieval Technology

15th Asia Information Retrieval Societies Conference, AIRS 2019
Hong Kong, China, November 7–9, 2019
Proceedings

Springer

Editors
Fu Lee Wang
Open University of Hong Kong
Hong Kong, China

Haoran Xie
The Education University of Hong Kong
Hong Kong, China

Wai Lam
Chinese University of Hong Kong
Hong Kong, China

Aixin Sun 🄳
Nanyang Technological University
Singapore, Singapore

Lun-Wei Ku
Institute of Information Science
Academia Sinica
Taipei, Taiwan

Tianyong Hao
South China Normal University
Guangzhou, China

Wei Chen
Chinese Academy of Agricultural Sciences
Beijing, China

Tak-Lam Wong
Douglas College
New Westminster, BC, Canada

Xiaohui Tao
University of Southern Queensland
Toowoomba, QLD, Australia

ISSN 0302-9743   ISSN 1611-3349 (electronic)
Lecture Notes in Computer Science
ISBN 978-3-030-42834-1   ISBN 978-3-030-42835-8 (eBook)
https://doi.org/10.1007/978-3-030-42835-8

LNCS Sublibrary: SL3 – Information Systems and Applications, incl. Internet/Web, and HCI

This Springer imprint is published by the registered company Springer Nature Switzerland AG
The registered company address is: Gewerbestrasse 11, 6330 Cham, Switzerland

Preface

Welcome to the proceedings of the 15th Asia Information Retrieval Societies Conference (AIRS 2019). AIRS is the premier Asian regional conference in the broad area of information retrieval (IR). Following the successes of IROL 1996 (International Workshop on IR with Oriental Languages) and IRAL 1997–2003 (International Workshop on IR with Asian Languages—), the first AIRS (Asia IR Symposium) was held in 2004 in Beijing. In 2010, the first edition of AIRS was held in Taipei. AIRS 2019 was held during November 7–9, 2019, at the Open University of Hong Kong, Hong Kong, China.

The acceptance rate for AIRS 2019 was 70% (14/20) for full papers and 43% (3/7) for short/demo papers. Each paper was peer reviewed by three Program Committee (PC) members and the final decisions were made by the PC chairs.

AIRS 2019 featured the keynote speech "Event Modeling and Mining: Towards Explainable Events with a Plank Road" by Prof. Qing Li (The Hong Kong Polytechnic University, Hong Kong).

As conference chairs and PC chairs of AIRS 2019, we extend our sincere gratitude to all authors and contributors to this year's conference. We are also grateful to the PC for the great reviewing effort that guaranteed AIRS a quality program of original and innovative research in IR. Special thanks go to our sponsor, Croucher Foundation, for their generosity. We also thank the Special Interest Group in Information Retrieval (SIGIR) for supporting AIRS by granting it in-cooperation status and sponsoring the SIG-friends funding.

November 2019

Fu Lee Wang
Haoran Xie
Wai Lam
Aixin Sun
Lun-Wei Ku
Tianyong Hao
Wei Chen
Tak-Lam Wong
Xiaohui Tao

Organization

General Co-chairs

Fu Lee Wang Philips   The Open University of Hong Kong, Hong Kong
Haoran Xie   Lingnan University, Hong Kong

Honorary Co-chairs

Ching Ping Kwan Reggie   The Open University of Hong Kong, Hong Kong
Qing Li   Hong Kong Polytechnic University, Hong Kong

Program Co-chairs

Wai Lam   Chinese University of Hong Kong, Hong Kong
Aixin Sun   Nanyang Technological University, Singapore
Lun-Wei Ku   Academia Sinica, Taiwan

Publication Co-chairs

Tianyong Hao   South China Normal University, China
Louise Luk   The Open University of Hong Kong, Hong Kong

Tutorial Chair

Xiaohui Tao   University of Southern Queensland, Australia

Web Chair

Wei Chen   Chinese Academy of Agricultural Sciences, China

Poster Chair

Tak-Lam Wong   Douglas College, Canada

Local Arrangement Co-chairs

Lee Lap Kei   The Open University of Hong Kong, Hong Kong
Au Tat Sheung Oliver   The Open University of Hong Kong, Hong Kong

Secretariats

Tingting Li	The Education University of Hong Kong, Hong Kong
Susie Liu	The Open University of Hong Kong, Hong Kong

Program Committee

Ting Bai	Renmin University of China, China
Paheli Bhattacharya	Indian Institute of Technology Kharagpur, India
Chien Chin Chen	National Taiwan University, Taiwan
Wei Chen	Chinese Academy of Agricultural Sciences, China
Pu-Jen Cheng	National Taiwan University, Taiwan
Koji Eguchi	Hiroshima University, Japan
Jialong Han	Nanyang Technological University, Singapore
Xianpei Han	Chinese Academy of Sciences, China
Tianyong Hao	South China Normal University, China
Yoshihiko Hayashi	Waseda University, Japan
Ben He	Chinese Academy of Sciences, China
Hen-Hsen Huang	National Chengchi University, Taiwan
Jizhou Huang	Baidu Inc., China
Masashi Inoue	Tohoku Institute of Technology, Japan
Adam Jatowt	Kyoto University, Japan
Jyun-Yu Jiang	University of California, Los Angeles, USA
Zhuoren Jiang	Sun Yat-sen University, China
Makoto P. Kato	University of Tsukuba, Japan
Atsushi Keyaki	Denso IT Laboratory, Inc., Japan
Lun-Wei Ku	Academia Sinica, Taiwan
Wai Lam	The Chinese University of Hong Kong, Hong Kong
Yanyan Lan	Chinese Academy of Sciences, China
Lung-Hao Lee	National Central University, Taiwan
Chenliang Li	Wuhan University, China
Jing Li	Inception Institute of Artificial Intelligence, UAE
Piji Li	Tencent, China
Xinshi Lin	The Chinese University of Hong Kong, Hong Kong
Peiyu Liu	Shandong Normal University, China
Ying-Hsang Liu	The Australian National University, Australia
Kuang Lu	University of Delaware, USA
Cheng Luo	Tsinghua University, China
Muhammad Kamran Malik	University of the Punjab, Pakistan
Cunli Mao	Kunming University of Science and Technology, China
Jiaxin Mao	Tsinghua University, China
Seung-Hoon Na	Chonbuk National University, South Korea
Yifan Nie	University of Montreal, Canada
Xi Niu	University of North Carolina at Charlotte, USA
Liang Pang	Chinese Academy of Sciences, China
Dae Hoon Park	Yahoo Research, USA

Zhaochun Ren	JD.com, China
Haggai Roitman	IBM Research Haifa, Israel
Tetsuya Sakai	Waseda University, Japan
Li Su	Academia Sinica, Taiwan
Kazunari Sugiyama	Kyoto University, Japan
Aixin Sun	Nanyang Technological University, Singapore
Fu Lee Wang	The Open University of Hong Kong, Hong Kong
Yuanyuan Wang	Yamaguchi University, Japan
Tak-Lam Wong	Douglas College, Canada
I-Chin Wu	National Taiwan Normal University, Taiwan
Haoran Xie	Lingnan University, Hong Kong
Takehiro Yamamoto	University of Hyogo, Japan
Lina Yao	The University of New South Wales, Australia
Jui-Feng Yeh	National Chia-Yi University, Taiwan
Masaharu Yoshioka	Hokkaido University, Japan
Liang-Chih Yu	Yuan Ze University, Taiwan
Xin Zhao	Renmin University of China, China
Xiaofei Zhu	Chongqing University of Technology, China

Steering Committee

Hsin-Hsi Chen	National Taiwan University, Taiwan
Zhicheng Dou	Renmin University of China, China
Wai Lam	The Chinese University of Hong Kong, Hong Kong
Alistair Moffat	University of Melbourne, Australia
Hwee Tou Ng	National University of Singapore, Singapore
Dawei Song	The Open University of Hong Kong, Hong Kong
Masaharu Yoshioka	Hokkaido University, Japan

Contents

Question Answering

Towards Automatic Evaluation of Reused Answers in Community Question Answering

Hsin-Wen Liu[1]($\boxtimes$), Sumio Fujita[2]($\boxtimes$), and Tetsuya Sakai[1]($\boxtimes$)

[1] Waseda University, 3–4–1, Shinokubo, Tokyo 169–0072, Japan
`stephanie1125@toki.waseda.jp`, `tetsuyasakai@acm.org`
[2] Yahoo Japan Corporation, 1–3, Kioityo, Tokyo 102–8282, Japan
`sufujita@yahoo-corp.jp`

Abstract. We consider the problem of reused answer retrieval for community question answering (CQA): given a question q, retrieve answers a_i^j posted in response to other questions $q_i (\neq q)$, where a_i^j serves as an answer to q. While previous work evaluated this task by manually annotating the relationship between q and a_i^j, this approach does not scale for large-scale CQA sites. We therefore explore an automatic evaluation method for reused answer retrieval, which computes nDCG by defining the gain value of each retrieved answer as a ROUGE score that treats the original answers to q as gold summaries. Our answer retrieval experiment suggests that effective reused answer retrieval systems may not be the same as effective gold answer retrieval systems. We provide case studies to discuss the benefits and limitations of our approach.

Keywords: Answer retrieval · Community question answering · ROUGE

1 Introduction

In community question answering (CQA), questions that seek the same or similar answers are posted repeatedly. Instead of making people respond to these similar questions every time, the CQA site should ideally retrieve useful existing answers from the repository and provide them to the questioner. This is the task of reused answer retrieval: given a question q, retrieve answers a_i^j posted in response to other questions $q_i (\neq q)$, where a_i^j serves as an answer to q. Here, a_i^j denotes the j-th answer to q_i, and q_i is the i-th question in the repository that has at least one answer that can be reused for q. While previous work evaluated reused answer retrieval by manually annotating the relationship between q and a_i^j [6], this approach does not scale for large-scale CQA sites. We therefore explore an automatic evaluation method for reused answer retrieval, which computes nDCG (normalised discounted cumulative gain) [4] by defining the gain value of each retrieved answer as a ROUGE [5] score that treats the original answers to q as

© Springer Nature Switzerland AG 2020
F. L. Wang et al. (Eds.): AIRS 2019, LNCS 12004, pp. 3–9, 2020.
https://doi.org/10.1007/978-3-030-42835-8_1

gold summaries. While our measure, R-nDCG, is not applicable to newly posted questions in an online environment (since gold answers initially do not exist), it is potentially useful for offline tuning of CQA answer retrieval systems where we can utilise not only the gold answers but also answers that are similar to the gold answers. Our answer retrieval experiment, in which we utilise Yahoo! Chiebukuro questions that contain an image, suggests that effective reused answer retrieval systems may not be the same as effective gold answer retrieval systems. We provide case studies to discuss the benefits and limitations of our automatic evaluation method.

2   Related Work

Several CQA tasks, including the *Question-External Comment Similarity* subtask, have been evaluated at SemEval [6]. This subtask is defined as follows. Given a question q with 10 related questions $\{q_1, \ldots, q_{10}\}$, and their associated comments $\{c_1^1 \ldots, c_1^{10}, \ldots, c_{10}^1, \ldots, c_{10}^{10}\}$, rank the comments according the relevance to q. The relevance of each comment c_i^j with respect to q is manually annotated in SemEval. Note that only up to 100 comments are assessed for each q; this approach does not scale for large-scale CQA data.

nDCG [4] (actually, its Microsoft variant [8]) is a widely used evaluation measure for ranked retrieval with graded relevance. When graded relevance measures such as nDCG are used, it is usually assumed that there are discrete relevance levels, and we predefine a gain value for each level, e.g., 3 for relevant and 1 for partially relevant. However, it is possible to handle *continuous* gain values: we can simply sort all documents by the continuous gain values to define an ideal ranked list, and then compute nDCG and other measures based on it [9]. Specifically, we give a continuous gain value to each retrieved answer in the form of a ROUGE score [5]: this approach can potentially reward systems that can retrieve answers that serve as good responses to q even though they were originally posted for other questions, without requiring manual relevance assessments.

3   Proposed Automatic Evaluation Method: R-nDCG

We consider a CQA answer retrieval experimental setting in which we have a repository of questions $\{q_i\}$ and their answers $\{a_i^j\}$, and the answers are indexed as the search target corpus. In gold answer retrieval, we take a question q_i as the input q, and see if its gold answers $\{a_i^j\}$ can be retrieved successfully from the repository. To evaluate this, we simply use binary-relevance nDCG, by giving a gain value of 1 to each a_i^j and 0 to each non-gold answer $a_{i'}^j$ where $i' \neq i$. As for reused answer retrieval, we propose to evaluate it as discussed below.

Given the input question q, we let a system search the target corpus to retrieve an answer list. From the list, all gold answers of q are removed[1], since

---

[1] This approach is similar to the classical *residual collection* method for evaluating relevance feedback in IR [3].

we want useful answers that were posted in response to questions other than q. We then apply nDCG to the answer list, by treating the gold answers of q as the gold summaries and computing a ROUGE score for each retrieved answer and treating it as its gain value. More specifically, given the set $A^* = \{a^*\}$ of gold answers, the gain value of a retrieved answer a is computed basically as a *word unigram recall* that takes into account unigram frequencies:

$$ROUGE\text{-}1(a, A^*) = \frac{\sum_{a^*} \sum_{w \in gram_1(a) \cap gram_1(a^*)} Count_{match}(w, a, a^*)}{\sum_{a^*} \sum_{w \in gram_1(a^*)} Count(w, a^*)}, \quad (1)$$

where $gram_1(a)$ denotes the set of unigrams from answer a, $Count(w, a)$ denotes the number of occurrences of word w in a, and $Count_{match}(w, a, a^*) = \min(Count(w, a), Count(w, a^*))$ [8].

For a given q, we compute the above ROUGE score for every non-gold answer a in the repository such that $gram_1(a) \cap gram_1(a^*) \neq \phi$ for at least one gold answer a^*. These answers will have a positive ROUGE score, while others in the repository will have a zero. Hence, the ideal list for R-nDCG is obtained by sorting the former in decreasing order of ROUGE scores.

4   Experiments

To compare gold answer retrieval evaluation in terms of binary-relevance nDCG and reused answer retrieval in terms of the proposed R-nDCG, we experimented with an evaluation setting similar to Tamaki et al. [10], who addressed question classification rather than answer retrieval, where each question contains not only text but also an image. Thus, our experiment uses 67,538 questions and 439,808 answers from the 2013–2014 Yahoo Chiebukuro (Japanese Yahoo Answers) data, with a 8:1:1 split for training, development, and testing; our test data contains 6,754 questions and 43,905 answers. Answer retrieval with this dataset is a hard task, since systems are required to process questions that contain an image.

We experimented with six deep learning-based systems [10]:

text-only A 3-layer CNN (Convolutional Neural Network) that uses question and answer text features but ignores the image part;

image-only A 5-layer CNN that uses the question image features only;

SP Combines the text and image features by taking the sum and elementwise product and then concatenating the results;

MCB Generates a joint text and image representation using Multimodal Compact Bilinear pooling [1];

DualNet Computes the sum and element-wise product of a pre-trained ResNet [2] with the image and text features [7].

More details can be found elsewhere [10]; note that retrieval approaches are not the focus of the present study.

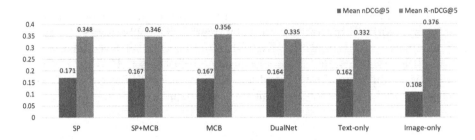

Fig. 1. Experimental results on the test set. The systems have been sorted by Mean nDCG (gold answer retrieval) scores shown in blue. (Color figure online)

Table 1. nDCG@5 (gold answer retrieval): Tukey HSD p-values. P-values smaller than 5% are shown in bold.

	Image-only	SP	MCB	SP+MCB	DualNet
Text-only	**0.000**	0.088	0.632	0.679	0.949
Image-only	–	**0.000**	**0.000**	**0.000**	**0.000**
SP	–	–	0.886	0.855	0.497
MCB	–	–	–	0.999	0.986
SP+MCB	–	–	–	–	0.992

Table 2. R-nDCG@5 (reused answer retrieval): Tukey HSD p-values. P-values smaller than 5% are shown in bold.

	Image-only	SP	MCB	SP+MCB	DualNet
Text-only	**0.000**	**0.000**	**0.000**	**0.000**	0.914
Image-only	–	**0.000**	**0.000**	**0.000**	**0.000**
SP	–	–	**0.039**	0.985	**0.000**
MCB	–	–	–	**0.004**	**0.000**
SP+MCB	–	–	–	–	**0.002**

5   Results and Discussions

5.1   System Ranking Results

Figure 1 compares the mean nDCG@5 (i.e., gold answer ranking) scores of six systems, as well as the mean R-nDCG@5 (i.e., reused answer ranking) scores of the same systems. Tables 1 and 2 show the Tukey HSD test results. The results can be summarised as follows:

- In gold answer retrieval (as measured by nDCG), Image-only statistically significantly *underperforms* the other five systems;
- In reused answer retrieval (as measured by R-nDCG), Image-only statistically significantly *outperforms* all other systems; MCB statistically significantly

outperforms all other systems except Image-only; Both SP and SP+MCB statistically significantly outperform Text-only and DualNet;
- Other differences are not statistically significant.

What is most remarkable about the above results is that while Image-only is the worst system in gold answer retrieval (nDCG), it is rated the best in reused answer retrieval as measured by R-nDCG. Moreover, R-nDCG, which utilises ROUGE weights, appears to be much more statistically discriminative than the binary nDCG. While the fact that Image-only performs very poorly in gold answer retrieval is not surprising since the method ignores the input question text completely, the fact that the Image-only is considered the best by R-nDCG suggests that this system manages to retrieve reused answers a_i^j that have high vocabulary overlaps with the gold answers of q. Whether the answers rated highly by R-nDCG are *actually* often relevant to q needs to be verified by manually assessing them, which is beyond the scope of the present short paper. Instead, Sect. 5.2 provides some case studies, and discuss the possible usefulness and shortcomings of our approach.

5.2   Case Studies

Table 3 shows some examples of $\langle q, a_i^j, q_i \rangle$ triplets from our experiments, with the ROUGE-based gain value for each answer a_i^j. Example (a) is a relatively successful case, in that R-nDCG managed to give a high ROUGE score to a_i^j, which actually is an acceptable response for q. The question q is "Do you like Natto Rolls?" and the retrieved answer a_i^j is "Yes, I do eat them," which was actually a response to a different question q_i: "Can you eat these right after getting up from bed?" where "these" refers to the food in the accompanying image. Example (b) is an unsuccessful case, where a good answer for q is given a very low ROUGE score by R-nDCG. The question q is "What do you think of my haircut?" and the a_i^j shown here is "Would look pretty on baby faces and round faces," which was a response to a q_i which is actually very similar to q. The ROUGE score is low because the gold answers to q were completely different from a_i^j. This example suggests that we should utilise not only answer-answer similarity but also question-question similarity [6] to compute the gain value for each a_i^j; this approach will be explored in our future work.

The above two examples concern questions where the questioner is seeking communication; a good reused answer retrieval system may serve as a kind of chatbot to satisfy that need. In contrast, Example (c) in Table 3 concerns a factual question. Although this is an unsuccessful case since an irrelevant answer was given a high ROUGE score, the example suggests that a single CQA answer may be appropriate for multiple *factual* questions with related but different information needs. The question q is "Is Subaru 'Sambar' a regular car?" and the answer shown was a response to a related question q_i: "Is 'Pleoplus' a Subaru compact car?" The ROUGE score for a_i^j is high because it actually contains a large list of Subaru cars with their specifications. Since the list does not cover regular cars, a_i^j is not relevant to q; however, if the list did cover both car types,

Table 3. Examples of relatively successful ((a)) and unsuccessful ((b)(c)) cases from our experiments, with English translations.

Example (a)
q:
(Do you like Natto Rolls?)
a_i^j: . . .(ROUGE=0.750)
(Yes, I do eat them.)
q_i:
(Can you eat these right after getting up from bed?)
Example (b)
q:
(What do you think of my haircut?)
a_i^j. . . (ROUGE=0.056)
(Would look pretty on baby faces and round faces.)
q_i: . .
(Male, hairstyle, I'm in high school. What do you think about this haircut?)
Example (c)
q:
(Is Subaru "Sambar" a regular car?)
a_i^j. . .(). . . (ROUGE=0.718)
(. . .It's actually a Daihatsu E-s (OEM car))
q_i:
(Is "Pleoplus" a Subaru compact car?)

this example would have been a successful case. It is possible that reused answer retrieval may be useful even for factoid questions, especially when there are answers that potentially cover multiple factual information needs.

6   Conclusions

We explored an automatic evaluation method for reused answer retrieval, which computes nDCG by defining the gain value of each retrieved answer as a ROUGE score that treats the original answers to q as gold summaries. Our answer retrieval experiment suggests that effective reused answer retrieval systems may not be the same as effective gold answer retrieval systems. We provided case studies to discuss the benefits and limitations of our automatic evaluation method. Our future work includes incorporating question-question similarity into R-nDCG (See Sect. 5.2), and manually evaluating the usefulness of reused answers rated highly by our method in order to quantify the effectiveness of our automatic evaluation approach (See Sect. 5.1).

References

1. Fukui, A., Park, D.H., Yang, D., Rohrbach, A., Darrell, T., Rohrbach, M.: Multimodal compact bilinear pooling for visual question answering and visual grounding. arXiv:1606.01847 (2016)
2. He, K., Zhang, X., Ren, S., Sun, J.: Deep residual learning for image recognition. In: 2016 IEEE Conference on Computer Vision and Pattern Recognition (CVPR), pp. 770–778 (2016)
3. Hull, D.: Using statistical testing in the evaluation of retrieval experiments. In: Proceedings of ACM SIGIR 1993, pp. 329–338 (1993)
4. Järvelin, K., Kekäläinen, J.: Cumulated gain-based evaluation of IR techniques. ACM Trans. Inf. Syst. (TOIS) **20**(4), 422–446 (2002)
5. Lin, C.Y.: Rouge: a package for automatic evaluation of summaries. Text Summarization Branches Out (2004)
6. Nakov, P., et al.: SemEval-2017 task 3: community question answering. In: Proceedings of SemEval-2017, pp. 27–48 (2017)
7. Saito, K., Shin, A., Ushiku, Y., Harada, T.: Dualnet: domain-invariant network for visual question answering. In: 2017 IEEE International Conference on Multimedia and Expo (ICME), pp. 829–834. IEEE (2017)
8. Sakai, T.: Metrics, statistics, tests. In: Ferro, N. (ed.) PROMISE 2013. LNCS, vol. 8173, pp. 116–163. Springer, Heidelberg (2014). https://doi.org/10.1007/978-3-642-54798-0_6
9. Sakai, T.: Unanimity-aware gain for highly subjective assessments. Proc. EVIA **2017**, 39–42 (2017)
10. Tamaki, K., Togashi, R., Fujita, S., Kato, S., Maeda, H., Sakai, T.: Classifying community qa questions that contain an image. In: ICTIR (2018)

Unsupervised Answer Retrieval with Data Fusion for Community Question Answering

Sosuke Kato[1]([⊠]), Toru Shimizu[2], Sumio Fujita[2], and Tetsuya Sakai[1]

[1] Waseda University, Tokyo, Japan
sow@suou.waseda.jp, tetsuyasakai@acm.org
[2] Yahoo Japan Corporation, Tokyo, Japan
{toshimiz,sufujita}@yahoo-corp.jp

Abstract. *Community question answering* (cQA) systems have enjoyed the benefits of advances in neural information retrieval, some models of which need annotated documents as supervised data. However, in contrast with the amount of supervised data for cQA systems, user-generated data in cQA sites have been increasing greatly with time. Thus, focusing on unsupervised models, we tackle a task of retrieving relevant answers for new questions from existing cQA data and propose two frameworks to exploit a Question Retrieval (QR) model for Answer Retrieval (AR). The first framework ranks answers according to the combined scores of QR and AR models and the second framework ranks answers using the scores of a QR model and *best answer* flags. In our experiments, we applied the combination of our proposed frameworks and a classical fusion technique to AR models with a Japanese cQA data set containing approximately 9.4M question-answer pairs. When best answer flags in the cQA data cannot be utilized, our combination of AR and QR scores with data fusion outperforms a base AR model on average. When best answer flags can be utilized, the retrieval performance can be improved further. While our results lack statistical significance, we discuss effect sizes as well as future sample sizes to attain sufficient statistical power.

Keywords: Community question answering · Question Retrieval · Answer Retrieval · Unsupervised model · Data fusion

1 Introduction

Community question answering (cQA) systems have enjoyed the benefits of advances in neural information retrieval, some models of which need annotated documents as supervised data. There are some cQA-related competitions [1,4,9] that distribute supervised data for development and evaluation. However, in contrast to the amount of supervised data for cQA systems, the large amount of user-generated data in cQA sites has been increasing greatly with time. We

© Springer Nature Switzerland AG 2020
F. L. Wang et al. (Eds.): AIRS 2019, LNCS 12004, pp. 10–21, 2020.
https://doi.org/10.1007/978-3-030-42835-8_2

therefore focused on unsupervised models that exploit only user-generated data. Compared to the publicly available data sets such as English Yahoo QA Data set[1], and SemEval cQA Data set[2], the Yahoo Chiebukuro data, which we handle in our experiments, is substantially larger. Yahoo Chiebukuro[3] is the well-known Japanese cQA site equivalent to Yahoo Answers[4].

Much cQA-related research using publicly available cQA data has leveraged particular cQA tasks, such as answer selection, question retrieval (QR), and answer retrieval (AR). We define the problem as ensuring that cQA systems retrieve relevant answers when new questions are posted, and we addressed the AR task using the Yahoo Chiebukuro data set containing approximately 9.4M QA pairs. Given an input question, in order to find relevant answers in the cQA data, not only the answer texts but also the corresponding question texts are useful user-generated data. In addition, in the case of cQA data, the type of user-generated data depends on the cQA site. For example, in Yahoo Answers and Yahoo Chiebukuro, a *best answer* flag can be used by the questioner to label an answer, indicating that it is the most satisfying answer for their question. This study explores the use of QR models and best answer flags in an AR task with massive cQA data.

In this paper, we propose two frameworks to exploit a QR model for AR. The first framework ranks answers according to the combined scores of the QR and AR models, and the second framework ranks answers by the scores of the QR model and best answer flags. We also applied data fusion techniques [14] on top of these frameworks. For evaluation, we performed crowdsourcing to add relevance labels to answers for test questions, Finally, we compared the final models for practical retrieval tasks using the Yahoo Chiebukuro data. When best answer flags in the cQA data cannot be utilized, our combination of AR and QR scores with data fusion outperforms a base AR model on average. When best answer flags can be utilized, the retrieval performance can be improved further. While our results lack statistical significance, we discuss effect sizes as well as future sample sizes to attain sufficient statistical power.

2 Related Work

2.1 cQA-related Work

NTCIR OpenliveQ Task [4] has handled the Yahoo Chiebukuro data for QR. They evaluated systems using evaluation metrics such as nDCG (normalized discounted cumulative gain) [2,11], ERR (expected reciprocal rank), and Q-measure were used for their offline evaluation. In contrast to the OpenliveQ Task, the SemEval cQA Task [9] (described later in this section) includes QR and AR subtasks. Some cQA research [3,16,18] leveraged the subtasks of the SemEval

---

[1] https://webscope.sandbox.yahoo.com/catalog.php?datatype=l&did=10.
[2] http://alt.qcri.org/semeval2017/task3/index.php?id=data-and-tools.
[3] https://chiebukuro.yahoo.co.jp/.
[4] https://answers.yahoo.com/.

cQA Task using neural networks. Training of neural networks has limitations owing to GPU Memory. For example, Tay et al. [15], where the model was based on a neural network, filtered questions and answers in the English Yahoo QA data set by text length. On the other hand, Okapi BM25 [10], which is usually compared as a baseline model, has no limitation of text length. Not only does the training of neural networks have the limitations, but it also results in difficulty in reproduction [6], although neural network-based models are the state-of-the-art for some tasks with some cQA data sets. In addition to the limitation of text length, apart from the model of Zhang et al. [18], most of neural network-based models exploited supervised data. This model utilized a transformer-based [17] neural network as an auto-encoder, trained it taking and yielding texts of questions, and calculated similarity scores between questions using a hidden representation of this neural network. In addition to the similarity scores, this model utilized lexical mismatch scores and rank orders of retrieved questions with respect to a test question.

In our experiments, we utilized the original transformer[5] instead of the neural network proposed in Zhang et al. [18]. Lexical mismatch scores did not work for Yahoo Chiebukuro data; therefore, we did not utilize lexical mismatch scores. While Zhang et al. [18] utilize the ranks of retrieved questions according to QR, our present study utilizes the relevance scores of BM25 and those of a transformer-based model in data fusion, since scores are more informative than ranks.

The SemEval cQA Task series, including QR and AR subtasks, was organized for three years from 2015, and the organizers made the data set for this task public. In the QR and AR subtasks, given a test question and candidates for possible questions and answers, systems are required to rank these candidates. The systems are evaluated using graded relevance, i.e., "Perfect Match", "Relevant", and "Irrelevant" for the QR subtask and "Good", "Potentially Useful", and "Bad" for the AR subtask. Referring to these subtasks, we created our own evaluation data as described in Sect. 4. However, while data for the QR and AR SemEval cQA subtasks was collected from Qatar Living Forum[6], our data is from Yahoo Chiebukuro.

2.2   Data Fusion

Data fusion techniques are used to combine the results from multiple different algorithms. There are many data fusion techniques, such as supervised, cluster-based, rank-based, and score-based techniques. There are also well-known effects of data fusion, i.e., *skimming effect*, which occurs when systems retrieve different documents; *chorus effect*, which occurs when several systems retrieve many of the same documents; and *dark horse effect*, which occurs when outlier systems are unusually good (or bad) at finding unique documents which other systems do not retrieve [5]. The chorus effect is based on the hypothesis that the overlap

---

[5] https://github.com/tensorflow/models/tree/master/official/transformer.

[6] https://www.qatarliving.com/forum.

of relevant documents in the retrieved lists is higher than that of nonrelevant documents. We focused on the *chorus effect* in the case of QR and AR for cQA systems, and assumed that an answer retrieved by our AR model should be promoted if its original question is retrieved at a high rank by the QR model. Classical unsupervised score-based data fusion techniques such as CombSUM and CombMNZ [14] are consistent with the *chorus effect*. Given retrieved documents L_i by a system i, in CombMNZ, fusion scores are calculated as follows:

$$F_{CombMNZ} = m \sum_{L_i : d \in L_i} s_{L_i}(d), \qquad (1)$$

where $s_{L_i}(d)$ denotes scores of a document d of a system i, and $m = |\{L_i : d \in L_i\}|$. We verified both CombSUM and CombMNZ for our data, and CombMNZ was always better than or equivalent to CombSUM in our preliminary experiment; therefore, we do not show the results related to CombSUM.

When combining multiple scores from different systems, scores should be normalized. We adopted the *standard* normalization [8], which utilizes maximum and minimum scores of scores in each L_i, for all fusion in our experiments.

3   Proposed Frameworks

We propose two frameworks to exploit a QR model for AR; ARQR (described in Sect. 3.1) and BA (described in Sect. 3.2). In our experiments, we apply the combination of our proposed frameworks and a classical fusion technique to AR models (described in Sect. 5.1).

3.1   ARQR: Combining AR Scores and QR Scores

This section describes the combining framework between a QR model and an AR model for the AR task. Given retrieval resources of questions and answers, Q and A, and a test question p, QR and AR models retrieve lists of questions and answers, L_Q and L_A, from Q and A. A combined score for an answer a ($\in A$) for p, $F_{ARQR}(p, a)$, is calculated as follows:

$$F_{ARQR}(p, a) = \begin{cases} S_A(p, a) + S_Q(p, q_A(a)) & (q_A(a) \in L_Q) \\ S_A(p, a) & (q_A(a) \notin L_Q) \end{cases} \qquad (2)$$

where $S_Q(p, q)$ and $S_A(p, a)$ denote scores between the given test question p and the retrieved question q and answer a respectively, and $q_A(a)$ denotes the question which has the answer a. We also normalized scores of questions and answers in L_Q and L_A for all combining in our experiments. This combining framework (without best answer flags) is referred to as ARQR in this paper.

3.2   BA: Best Answer Retrieval via Question Retrieval

This section describes the framework using a QR model and best answer flags. Given a set of best answers B ($\subset A$) and a test question p, a QR model retrieves a list of questions, L_Q. A score of a best answer b ($\in B$) for p, $F_{\mathrm{BA}}(p, b)$, is then calculated as follows:

$$F_{\mathrm{BA}}(p, b) = S_Q(p, q_A(b)). \tag{3}$$

This framework ignores answers other than best answers. This framework (with best answer flags) is referred to as BA in this paper.

4   Data Set and Annotations

In our experiments, we used questions that have more than one answer and their corresponding answers actually posted in Yahoo Chiebukuro from 2009 to 2014. These questions and answers were each classified into a single category that a questioner has to select when they post their question. There are 16 categories in this site, such as "Region, Travel, Outing" (TRAVEL), "News, Politics, International affairs", and "Life and romance, Worries of human relations". In this study, we focus on questions in the TRAVEL category because questions in this category are less time-sensitive and opinionated than other categories. After we extracted the data in the TRAVEL category, we sampled 120 questions randomly for evaluation. We used the remaining questions and corresponding answers as both development data for a neural network-based model and a retrieval resource for BM25. In the 120 test questions, there were some meaningless questions such as those that were simply statements of opinion, and we excluded these meaningless questions from the evaluation data set. Table 1 shows the final statistics of the data set that we used in our experiments.

Table 1. Statistics of Yahoo Chiebukuro data in the TRAVEL category

Data set	# Qs	# QA Pairs
Development & retrieval resource	3.9M	9.4M
Evaluation	103	–

In the SemEval cQA data set, questions and answers were labelled using graded relevance (mentioned in Sect. 2.1), and we labelled questions and answers similarily. The description of our labels for Yahoo Chiebukuro data for the QR and AR task are shown in Table 2. For annotations, we prepared some models in Sect. 5.1, which retrieved the top 10 questions and top 100 answers for the test questions, respectively. To label these questions and answers, we used crowdsourcing via Yahoo Japan Crowdsourcing[7]. After removing duplicated questions and answers, there were 20.4 questions and 469.9 answers per one test question on average. In addition to the labels in Table 2, we allowed crowd workers to label a question pair and a QA pair as "undecidable", and we regarded these undecidable labels as "Not Consistent" and "Not Useful" for each task. Three

---

[7] https://crowdsourcing.yahoo.co.jp/.

crowd workers labelled each pair, and we took the majority label as the final label. When three crowd workers all gave different labels to a pair, we regarded "Partially Consistent" and "Potentially Useful" to be the final labels of the pair for the QR and AR task, respectively.

Table 2. Labels for the QR and AR task in our experiments

Task	Label (translated)	Description (translated)
QR	Match	It is conceivable that an answer exists which satisfies each asker of a question
	Partially match	It is conceivable that an answer exists which satisfies each asker of a question at least slightly
	Not match	It is not conceivable that an answer exists which satisfies each asker of a question
AR	Useful	An answer satisfies the asker of a question
	Potentially useful	An answer possibly satisfies the asker of a question
	Not useful	An answer does not satisfy the asker of a question

5 Experiments

5.1 Setup

We first tokenized questions and answers of Yahoo Chiebukuro data in the TRAVEL category using Mecab[8] and indexed these questions and answers using Elasticsearch[9] for BM25 with $k1 = 1.2$ and $b = 0.75$ (default parameters of Elasticsearch). We did not tune hyperparameters for either BM25 or a neural network-based model. For the unsupervised neural network-based QR models [18] (mentioned in Sect. 2.1), namely the transformer-based QR model, we divided the development data into training and validation data in a ratio of 9:1. We trained a word embedding matrix using word2vec [7] with questions from Yahoo Chiebukuro data in the TRAVEL cetegory, and then trained a transformer [17]. Training of the transformer as an auto-encoder for questions from Yahoo Chiebukuro data in the TRAVEL category took 12 h per one epoch and more than one week until overfitting. We utilized the model that obtained the minimum loss for the validation data. To reduce the calculation cost of the neural network, BM25 retrieved ten thousands candidates for each test question, and the transformer-based QR model reranked these candidates.

For our frameworks with data fusion, as base models, we prepared two QR models, i.e., BM25 for QR (QR-BM25) and the transformer-based QR model (QR-TRAN), and one AR model, i.e., BM25 for AR (AR-BM25). We applied

---

[8] http://taku910.github.io/mecab/.
[9] https://www.elastic.co/jp/products/elasticsearch.

our frameworks and data fusion to these base models at most three times in total, as shown in Fig. 1. First, we fused QR-BM25 and QR-TRAN using CombMNZ (CMNZ) and named this fused model CMNZ(QR-BM25+QR-TRAN). Second, we combined these three QR models and AR-BM25 using our proposed frameworks, i.e., ARQR and BA, and named these models ARQR(①+④), among others. Finally, we fused combinations of all above models and named the final fused models CMNZ(ARQR(①+④)+ARQR(②+④)), among others. The window size used in all combining and fusions was set to 100.

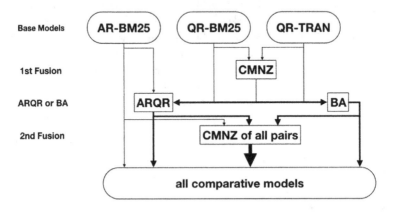

Fig. 1. Process of our frameworks with data fusion

5.2   Results

For evaluating the effectiveness of AR, we adopted nDCG at 10 [2,11]. Tables 3 and 4 show the mean nDCG scores of all QR and AR models for QR and AR tasks, respectively. The maximum scores of models without and with best answer flags are underlined. We conducted randomized Tukey HSD tests using the Discpower tool[10] with $B = 10,000$ trials [11]. Table 5 shows randomized Tukey HSD p-values and effect sizes (i.e., standardized mean differences) of AR model pairs with largest effect sizes as measured as the gain over AR-BM25. The effect sizes are based on two-way ANOVA (without replication) residual variance [13].

For the QR task, all QR models statistically significantly differ from each other. From Table 3, it is observed that CombMNZ did not work to fuse QR-BM25 and QR-TRAN.

For the AR task, no model outperformed AR-BM25 with a statistical significance at $\alpha = 0.05$; therefore, we state our view in terms of effect sizes in Sect. 6. Comparing the combined AR models, i.e., ARQR(①+④), ARQR(②+④), and ARQR(③+④), with AR-BM25, all these combined AR models outperformed AR-BM25 on average. The unfused AR model using BA did not outperform AR-BM25; however, CMNZ(④+BA(①)) outperformed AR-BM25 with a

---

[10] http://research.nii.ac.jp/ntcir/tools/discpower-en.html.

6.3% improvement on average. Note that CMNZ(④+BA(①)) does not exploit scores from neural networks. Overall, CMNZ(ARQR(①+④)+ARQR(②+④)) obtained the best evaluation score on average among the models without best answer flags, and CMNZ(ARQR(②+④)+BA(③)) obtained the best evaluation score on average among the models with best answer flags.

Table 3. Mean nDCG scores for Question Retrieval (# Qs = 103)

Model	Alt	Mean nDCG@10
QR-BM25	①	0.5817
QR-TRAN	①	0.4423
CMNZ(QR-BM25+QR-TRAN)	③	0.5263

6   Discussion

The purpose of the study was to investigate the effect of the use of QR models and best answer flags for the AR task. From Table 5, no model outperformed AR-BM25 with statistical significance at $\alpha = 0.05$; however, the sample size (i.e., the number of the test questions) is only 103. According to a power analysis for the first pair shown in Table 5[11], the sample size required to achieve 80% power for a paired t-test of this system pair is 343; hence we need to more than triple the current sample size. However, our current results shown in Table 5 suggest that some the effect sizes are substantial, and that they may deserve further investigations.

To visualize how the combinations and fusions worked, we chose ARQR(①+④) and CMNZ(④+BA(①)) which have the highest effect size against AR-BM25 among the models using only ARQR and all models, respectively, and show (a) scatterplots and (b) ranked lists in Figs. 2 and 3 to visualize the relationship between these combined models and their component models using a visualization tool that we have developed[12]. The linked nodes denote the same answers (or answers and their original questions). In Fig. 2(a), the points colored in green, red, and yellow denote the test questions for which ARQR(①+④) outperformed AR-BM25, those for which ARQR(①+④) underperformed AR-BM25, and the rest, respectively. In the area below 0.2 on the y-axis (nDCG of AR-BM25), there are 16 green dots but only 7 red dots. That is, when AR-BM25 performs poorly, ARQR tends to be successful. Fig. 2(b) visualizes one such case: the green dot indicated by an arrow in Fig. 2(a). It can be observed that ARQR successfully pulls up a "Useful" answer from rank 21 to rank 1, while also pulling up a "Not Useful" answer from rank 17 to rank 6.

In Fig. 3(a), the points colored in blue, magenta, and cyan denote the test questions for which CMNZ(ARQR(③+④)+BA(③)) outperformed both

---

[11] Sakai's power analysis script `future.sample.pairedt` [12] was used for the analysis.
[12] https://github.com/sosuke-k/simple-fusion-visualization.

Table 4. Mean nDCG scores for Answer Retrieval (# Qs = 103)

Model	Alt	Mean nDCG@10
Base model		
AR-BM25	④	0.2735
Combined model with QR model		
ARQR(①+④)		0.2827
ARQR(②+④)		0.2795
ARQR(③+④)		0.2808
Final fused model		
CMNZ(④+ARQR(①+④))		0.2823
CMNZ(④+ARQR(②+④))		0.2771
CMNZ(④+ARQR(③+④))		0.2799
CMNZ(ARQR(①+④)+ARQR(②+ ④))		<u>0.2843</u>
CMNZ(ARQR(①+ ④)+ARQR(③+④))		0.2822
CMNZ(ARQR(②+ ④)+ARQR(③+④))		0.2821
All models (with best answer flags)		
BA(①)		0.2621
BA(②)		0.1559
BA(③)		0.2560
CMNZ(④+BA(①))		0.2907
CMNZ(④+BA(②))		0.2685
CMNZ(④+BA(③))		0.2898
CMNZ(ARQR(①+④)+BA(①))		0.2853
CMNZ(ARQR(①+④)+BA(②))		0.2690
CMNZ(ARQR(①+④)+BA(③))		0.2883
CMNZ(ARQR(②+④)+BA(①))		0.2909
CMNZ(ARQR(②+④)+BA(②))		0.2717
CMNZ(ARQR(②+④)+BA(③))		<u>0.2921</u>
CMNZ(ARQR(③+④)+BA(①))		0.2859
CMNZ(ARQR(③+④)+BA(②))		0.2669
CMNZ(ARQR(③+④)+BA(③))		0.2855
CMNZ(BA(①)+BA(②))		0.2560
CMNZ(BA(①)+BA(③))		0.2620
CMNZ(BA(②)+BA(③))		0.2275

ARQR(③+④) and BA(③), those for which CMNZ(ARQR(③+④)+BA(③)) underperformed both ARQR(③+④) and BA(③), and the rest, respectively. It can be observed that the magenta points are relatively close to the origin while

Table 5. p-Values and effect sizes of the model pairs with largest effect sizes as measured as the gain over AR-BM25 using the randomized Tukey HSD tests ($ES = \bar{d}/\sqrt{V_E}$ where $\bar{d}$ is calculated by subtracting mean nDCG scores of Model 2 from mean nDCG scores of Model 1 and V_E is the two-way ANOVA residual variance)

Model 1	Model 2	p-value	ES
CMNZ(ARQR(②+④)+BA(③))	AR-BM25	0.9997	0.2150
CMNZ(ARQR(②+④)+BA(①))	AR-BM25	0.9999	0.2011
CMNZ(④+BA(①))	AR-BM25	0.9999	0.1987
CMNZ(④+BA(③))	AR-BM25	1.0000	0.1884
CMNZ(ARQR(①+④)+BA(③))	AR-BM25	1.0000	0.1712
CMNZ(ARQR(③+④)+BA(①))	AR-BM25	1.0000	0.1435
CMNZ(ARQR(③+④)+BA(③))	AR-BM25	1.0000	0.1392
CMNZ(ARQR(①+④)+BA(①))	AR-BM25	1.0000	0.1366
CMNZ(ARQR(①+④)+ARQR(②+ ④))	AR-BM25	1.0000	0.1250
ARQR(①+ ④)	AR-BM25	1.0000	0.1064

the blue points are relatively scattered: that is, when CMNZ works, its positive effect is tends to be large; when it fails, its negative effect tends to be small. Hence CMNZ improves on the components on average. Fig. 3(b) visualises a case where CMNZ was successful: the blue bot indicated by an arrow in Fig. 3(a). It can be observed that a "Useful" answer found in both of the component lists is promoted from ranks 14 and 16 to rank 1, while nonoverlapping answers are mildly demoted.

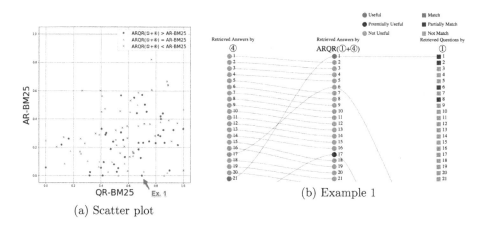

(a) Scatter plot   (b) Example 1

Fig. 2. Combining effects of ARQR(①+④); (a) The x-axis and y-axis are nDCG scores of QR-BM25, i.e., ① and AR-BM25, i.e., ④, respectively. (b) The lists of nodes denote ranked documents by ④, ARQR(①+④), and ① from left to right. (Color figure online)

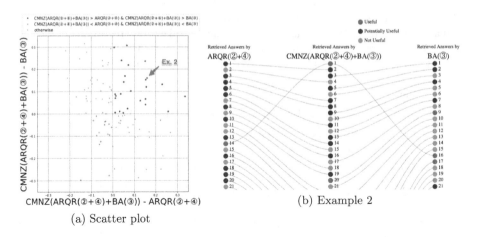

(a) Scatter plot   (b) Example 2

Fig. 3. Fusion effects of CMNZ(④+BA(①)); (a) The x-axis and y-axis are the differences of nDCG scores between CMNZ(ARQR(③+④)+BA(③)) and ARQR(③+④) and BA(③), respectively. (b) The lists of nodes denote ranked documents by ARQR(③+④), CMNZ(ARQR(③+④)+BA(③)), and BA(③) from left to right. (Color figure online)

7 Conclusion

To exploit a QR model for the AR task, we proposed frameworks that calculate scores of answers using a QR model with and without best answer flags. We applied the combination between our proposed frameworks and the classical fusion technique to the AR task using a Japanese cQA data set containing approximately 9.4M QA pairs. To summarize our results, our ARQR combining framework improved the base AR model regardless of the choice of the QR model on average; therefore, the framework that exploits QR models is useful for AR. The best model among all models with best answer flags outperformed the best model among all models without best answer flags. Best answer flags should therefore be utilized when the target cQA data includes best answer flags. The best AR model (CMNZ(ARQR(②+④)+BA(③))) outperformed the AR-BM25 by 6.8%. The best AR model that does not utilize neural networks (CMNZ(④+BA(①))) also outperformed the AR-BM25 by 6.3%. However, no model outperformed BM25 for AR with a statistical significance using 103 test questions. Power analysis showed that we need to increase the number of the test questions to at least 343. In future work, we will also verify our proposed frameworks for other AR models that utilize only user-generated data.

References

1. Agichtein, E., Carmel, D., Pelleg, D., Pinter, Y., Harman, D.K.: Overview of the TREC 2016 LiveQA track. In: The Twenty-Fifth Text REtrieval Conference (2016)

2. Burges, C., et al.: Learning to rank using gradient descent. In: Proceedings of the 22nd International Conference on Machine Learning, pp. 89–96 (2005)
3. Joty, S., Màrquez, L., Nakov, P.: Joint multitask learning for community question answering using task-specific embeddings. In: Proceedings of the 2018 Conference on Empirical Methods in Natural Language Processing, pp. 4196–4207 (2018)
4. Kato, M.P., Nishida, A., Manabe, T., Fujita, S., Yamamoto, T.: Overview of the NTCIR-14 OpenLiveQ-2 task. In: The 14th NTCIR Conference (2019)
5. Kurland, O., Culpepper, J.S.: Fusion in information retrieval: SIGIR 2018 half-day tutorial. In: The 41st International ACM SIGIR Conference on Research & Development in Information Retrieval, pp. 1383–1386 (2018)
6. Lin, J.: The neural hype and comparisons against weak baselines. SIGIR Forum **52**(2), 40–51 (2019)
7. Mikolov, T., Sutskever, I., Chen, K., Corrado, G.S., Dean, J.: Distributed representations of words and phrases and their compositionality. In: Proceedings of NIPS 2013, pp. 3111–3119 (2013)
8. Montague, M., Aslam, J.A.: Relevance score normalization for metasearch. In: Proceedings of the Tenth International Conference on Information and Knowledge Management, pp. 427–433 (2001)
9. Nakov, P., et al.: SemEval-2017 Task 3: community question answering. In: Proceedings of the 11th International Workshop on Semantic Evaluation (SemEval - 2017), pp. 27–48 (2017)
10. Robertson, S.E., Walker, S., Hancock-Beaulieu, M., Gatford, M., Payne, A.: Okapi at TREC-3. In: Proceedings of TREC-3 (1996)
11. Sakai, T.: Metrics, statistics, tests. In: Ferro, N. (ed.) PROMISE 2013. LNCS, vol. 8173, pp. 116–163. Springer, Heidelberg (2014). https://doi.org/10.1007/978-3-642-54798-0_6
12. Sakai, T.: Statistical significance, power, and sample sizes: a systematic review of SIGIR and TOIS, 2006–2015. In: Proceedings of the 39th International ACM SIGIR Conference on Research and Development in Information Retrieval, pp. 5–14 (2016)
13. Sakai, T.: Laboratory Experiments in Information Retrieval: Sample Sizes, Effect Sizes, and Statistical Power. TIRS, vol. 40. Springer, Singapore (2018). https://doi.org/10.1007/978-981-13-1199-4
14. Shaw, J.A., Fox, E.A.: Combination of multiple searches. In: Proceedings of the Third Text REtrieval Conference (TREC 1994), Gaithersburg, Maryland, USA, 2–4 November 1994, pp. 105–108 (1994)
15. Tay, Y., Phan, M.C., Tuan, L.A., Hui, S.C.: Learning to rank question answer pairs with holographic dual LSTM architecture. In: Proceedings of the 40th International ACM SIGIR Conference on Research and Development in Information Retrieval, pp. 695–704 (2017)
16. Uva, A., Bonadiman, D., Moschitti, A.: Injecting relational structural representation in neural networks for question similarity. In: Proceedings of the 56th Annual Meeting of the Association for Computational Linguistics (Volume 2: Short Papers), pp. 285–291 (2018)
17. Vaswani, A., et al.: Attention is all you need. In: Guyon, I., et al. (eds.) Advances in Neural Information Processing Systems 30, pp. 5998–6008 (2017)
18. Zhang, M., Wu, Y.: An unsupervised model with attention autoencoders for question retrieval. In: Proceedings of the 32nd AAAI Conference on Artificial Intelligence (2018)

A Semantic Expansion-Based Joint Model for Answer Ranking in Chinese Question Answering Systems

Wenxiu Xie[1], Leung-Pun Wong[2], Lap-Kei Lee[2], Oliver Au[2], and Tianyong Hao[3(✉)]

[1] Department of Linguistics and Translation, City University of Hong Kong, Hong Kong, China
vasiliky@outlook.com
[2] School of Science and Technology, The Open University of Hong Kong, Hong Kong, China
{s1243151,lklee,oau}@ouhk.edu.hk
[3] School of Computer Science, South China Normal University, Guangzhou, China
haoty@m.scnu.edu.cn

Abstract. Answer ranking is one of essential steps in open domain question answering systems. The ranking of the retrieved answers directly affects user satisfaction. This paper proposes a new joint model for answer ranking by leveraging context semantic features, which balances both question-answer similarities and answer ranking scores. A publicly available dataset containing 40,000 Chinese questions and 369,919 corresponding answer passages from Sogou Lab is used for experiments. Evaluation on the joint model shows a Precison@1 of 72.6%, which outperforms the state-of-the-art baseline methods.

Keywords: Answer ranking · Synonyms · Word2vec · Joint model

1 Introduction

With the rapid development of community-based question answering (cQA) systems such as Yahoo!, Baidu Zhidao and Quora, millions of questions and posted answers are accumulated over time and accelerate the research of non-factoid question answering [1–3]. A question answering system works in three major steps: (1) question analysis, (2) candidate answer retrieval and extraction, and (3) answer ranking. Answer ranking identifies answer-bearing sentences from candidate answer passages and then ranks these candidate answers according to their relevance [4–6]. Since answer retrieval and extraction may produce erroneous candidate answers, answer ranking involves identifying relevant answers among many irrelevant ones [7], which is a challenging task.

The variance of answer quality and the asymmetry problem of question-answer information make answer ranking crucial to cQA services [3]. Existing research mainly focuses on developing various features [3] (e.g., linguistic, semantic, and syntactic features [8, 9]), or employing machine learning techniques. User-generated contents are

© Springer Nature Switzerland AG 2020
F. L. Wang et al. (Eds.): AIRS 2019, LNCS 12004, pp. 22–33, 2020.
https://doi.org/10.1007/978-3-030-42835-8_3

commonly lack of formal representations. Moreover, semantically similar contents are frequently expressed differently. Thus, answer ranking has two major challenges [4, 7, 10]: (1) Highly semantic relevant candidate passages for a question may not contain correct answers. (2) Correct answers may not directly share the same words with questions. Answer candidates are sometimes noisy (i.e., containing a large amount of irrelevant information) while questions are commonly short and lack of context. To better discover answers for a question, identifying relevant answer fragments from candidate answers and expanding context semantic features of questions are critical.

This paper proposes a joint model for answer ranking in Chinese question answering systems, which addresses the ranking problem in two aspects. The first is question-answer similarity, which evaluates the semantic relevance of co-occurrence terms between a question and a candidate answer. To this end, we propose two kind of semantic features, namely, context-relevant words and synonyms, to expand question context information and increase co-occurrences to tackle the lexical variety issue. After that, a latent semantic index method is utilized to capture the semantic similarity between questions and answers. The other aspect is answer ranking score, which evaluates the common and different features between correct answers and incorrect answers of a question via Ranking support vector machine (Ranking SVM). Finally, these two kinds of answer relevance are aggregated for answer ranking. Evaluating on a publicly available dataset on Sogou Lab with 40,000 Chinese questions and 369,919 corresponding answer passages, our model gains a Precision@1 of 72.6% and a normalized discounted cumulative gain at rank 5 of 77.9%, outperforming a list of baseline methods.

2   Related Work

Researchers have developed answer ranking methods in two main categories: (1) feature engineering-oriented and (2) integrating multiple machine learning techniques. As posted questions in question answering systems are usually short while candidate answers are long and lack of standard expressions, feature expansion helps addressing the issue that a question and its candidate answer are semantically similar but are expressed differently [8]. The most representative QA system IBM Watson [11] explores 354 features for learning the answer-question relevance. Recently, they develop a genetic programming approach for feature selection and learning ranking function, which uses much fewer features but achieves comparable performance [12]. Bilotti et al. [13] presents a general rank-learning framework for answer ranking by leveraging linguistic and semantic features. Their experiments show that a trained ranking model using the composed rich feature set achieves more than 20% improvement over keyword retrieval baseline models in Mean Average Precision. Yang et al. [14] design two kinds of features to assisting the answer retrieving process, i.e. the semantic and context feature. The proposed context features are the semantic features and features that proposed by Metzler and Kanungo [15] of the sentence before and after the candidate sentence. The experiment results demonstrate the effectiveness of the context feature to retrieving answer sentences for non-factoid queries. Similarly, a context-relevant feature is proposed to enrich the context information of both question and answer key words in the proposed question-answer similarity calculation.

Besides using linguistic, semantic, and syntactic features [8, 9, 16–18], cQA researchers also utilize user profile information for answer ranking [3, 19–21], which is assumed to be related to answer quality. There are two most effective methods for engineering features. One is the kernel method such as [22, 23], which naturally maps feature vectors in richer feature spaces and combine heterogeneous answer features [24]. The other is deep learning approaches adopted by more recent work such as [4, 24–26]. Deep learning is successfully applied to various NLP tasks as it automatically learns optimal feature representations for given inputs.

In addition to feature engineering, fusion machine learning methods are applied to answer ranking, which combine the results from multiple ranking lists or aggregate probability of answers from several aspects. Ko et al. [7] apply a probabilistic graphical model for answer ranking, which estimates both the correctness of answers as well as their correlation. Ko et al. [10] propose a language-independent probabilistic answer ranking framework that estimates the joint probability of a candidate answer considering both answer similarity features and answer relevance features, where the answer similarity is calculated by a list of synonyms and the multiple string distance metrics (e.g., cosine similarity), and the answer relevance is a score between a question and an answer by utilizing an extra corpus like gazetteers, WordNet and Wikipedia (e.g., for the answer "Mark Twain" and question "Who wrote the book *Song of Solomon*?", 0.5 is gained for "Mark Twain" has a hypernym "writer" in WordNet). This joint model was shown effective for answer ranking on a standard dataset. Yet, the method only process short answers containing solely a named entity, a date or a noun and not able to rank answers in the style of sentences or passages. Agarwal et al. [5] propose a cascading approach to combine 5 ranking algorithms, where the ranking produced by one ranker is used as input to the next stage. Experiments present that the aggregated method is more robust and effective than the method that relies on a single ranker only.

Instead of exploring rich feature set or applying deep learning as in previous work, our approach proposes two kinds of features to enrich the context semantic information for answer ranking. Besides, we propose to jointly consider both question-answer similarity and answer ranking score for ranking.

3   The Joint Model for Answer Ranking

A semantic expansion-based joint model for answer ranking is proposed to rank candidate answer passages and to return top k answers for a given question. The proposed joint model considers two aspects together: question-answer similarity and answer ranking score. Question-answer similarity estimates the semantic relevance between questions and candidate answers while answer ranking score evaluates the similarity and variance between correct answers and incorrect answers. The framework of the joint answer ranking model, as shown in Fig. 1, consists of four components: preprocessing, Question-Answer Similarity Calculation (QASC), Answer Ranking Score Calculation (ARSC), and rank aggregation. The preprocessing step includes HTML tags filtration and full-width character to half-width character transformation. The other steps are described in Sects. 3.1 and 3.2 in details. The answer relevance to a given question is jointly measured with question-answer similarity and answer ranking score via the proposed joint model.

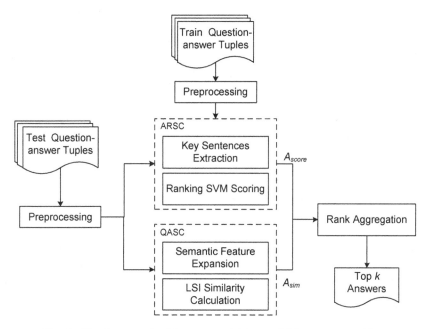

Fig. 1. The framework of the proposed joint model for answer ranking.

3.1 Question Answer Similarity

Question-answer similarity calculation (QASC) consists of two steps: semantic feature expansion and Latent Semantic Indexing (LSI) similarity calculation. QASC is based on an assumption that the relevance of an answer to a given question can be estimated by their semantic similarity and co-occurrence terms. The co-occurrence terms are the words or phrases that exist in both the question and a candidate answer. For instance, for a question "盛—伦的身高是多少?"('*How tall is Sheng Yilun?*'), the answer "盛—伦的身高是180 cm" ('*Sheng Yilun is 180 cm tall.*') is more relevant than answer "李晨的身高是180 cm" ('*Li Chen is 180 cm tall.*') or "盛—伦体重67 kg" ('*Sheng Yilun weighs 67 kg.*'), since the first answer has more co-occurrence terms. Yet, there are two issues. Different background knowledge or linguistic habits can result in different expressions for the same information, which is known as word synonymy and polysemy issue, as addressed in Cohen et al. [27]. Also some high-quality answers may have co-occurrence terms missing, such as an answer "180 cm" to the example question.

To tackle these two issues, we first expand the keywords of questions and answers with context semantic features: context-relevant words and synonyms. Jieba, a Chinese text segmentation tool, is utilized for keyword extraction. Then, Word2Vec and Synonyms are applied for feature expansion. Word2Vec, an efficient tool for transforming words into a distributed representation in a vector space [28], is applied for context-relevant word expansions. To extend the coverage of Word2Vec, Wikipedia is applied to train word vectors. The training parameter "size" is set to "300", "window" is "5" and "min_count" is "3". As for synonym expansion, we utilize Synonyms, a Chinese Synonyms toolkit for natural language processing and understanding [29]. These two kinds of expanded features are helpful to increase the co-occurrence terms of questions and candidate answers. For instance, the extracted keywords of question "苹果官方电话" ('*The official telephone of Apple*') are "苹果" ('*Apple*') and "电话" ('*telephone*'), and the corresponding top 2 context-relevant words are < "apple", "苹果公司"('Apple Inc.') > and < "电话号码"('telephone number'), "拨打"('call') > , respectively. The expanded synonyms for the two keywords are respectively "苹果公司"('Apple Inc.') and "电话号码"('telephone number'), which are the same as the context-relevant words. Therefore, the feature expansion effectively expand the context information. Missing co-occurrence terms may also be recovered to some extent via the feature expansion.

After feature expansion, the expanded questions and candidate answers are sent to LSI for similarity calculation. LSI is effective in capturing higher order co-occurrence semantic information between a question and a candidate answer, and solve the synonymy and polysemy issue to some extent. As LSI approach takes advantage of implicit higher-order semantic structure and matches terms in questions with terms in answer passages, we treat each candidate answer as a short document and detect the most relevant answers. LSI applies Singular-value decomposition (SVD) to construct a semantic space that reflects the major associative patterns in answer passages and ignore less important influences. If terms are consistent with the major patterns of associations, LSI treats them as similar to the answer passages even if they do not actually appear in the answer passages [30].

LSI first measures term weights (word occurrences) and constructs a term-document matrix A and a question matrix Q. Then it decomposes the matrix A and find the U, S and V matrices, where $A = USV^T$ using SVD. In this paper, the latent dimension k is set to "8", which is the optimal value we get in parameter training process. After that, answer document a_m is represented as a k-dimensional vector $(w_{a_m 1}, w_{a_m 2}, \ldots, w_{a_m k})$. Then it finds the question vector coordinates in the reduced k-dimensional space, where $q = q^T U_k S_k^{-1}$. Finally, the similarity of the question and the answer is computed by dot products between question vector w_q and answer vector w_{a_m} coordinates and is divided by the product of query and document vector lengths as shown in Eq. (1).

After QASC, an answer-similarity set $A_{sim} = \{<a_m, a_{m, sim}>\}(m = 1\ldots n)$ is sent to rank aggregation process for further ranking. $A_{m, sim}$ is question-answer cosine similarities of answer passage a_m.

$$Sim(q, a_m) = \frac{\sum_{i=1}^{k} (w_{qi} \times w_{a_m i})}{\sqrt{\sum_{i=1}^{k} w_{qi}^2 \times \sum_{i=1}^{k} w_{a_m i}^2}} \tag{1}$$

3.2 Answer Ranking Score

The answer ranking score mainly learn the fusion weight of common and different features of correct answers and incorrect answers via Ranking SVM method. Ranking SVM formalizes learning-to-rank as a problem of binary classification on instance pairs and ranks candidate answers using implicit relevance feedback [31]. The ARSC process first extracts the key sentences of a candidate answer. Key sentences are the split sentences of answer passage that contains more than two co-occurrence words, which help to filter noise information and reduce feature space in training.

Then, the extracted key sentence of answer passages are sent to Ranking SVM to learn feature weights and compute answer scores. First we build instance pair set $S = \{(a_{i1}, a_{i2}), y_i\}$ on the training data, where a_{i1} and a_{i2} are the candidate answer passages of the same question q_i. The function $y_i (a_{i1}, a_{i2})$ is shown in Eq. (2). Then the Ranking SVM constructs the model for solving the classification problem. The quadratic convex optimization problem in Ranking SVM is defined as Eq. (3) [32], where l is the number of instance pair set S, w is a weight vector used for transformation, ε is the slack variable, and C is a parameter that allows the trade-off between the margin size and the training error. After quadratic convex optimization, the optimal w^* is gained for learning ranking function $score_{rank} (a)$, as shown in Eq. (4). For a given answer instance a, the ranking function outputs an answer score. If $a_{i1} \succ a_{i2}$, $score_{rank}(a_{i1})$ is larger than $score_{rank}(a_{i2})$. The answer-score set $A_{score} = \{<a_i, a_{iscore}>\}$, where answer a_i is paired with corresponding answer scores a_{iscore}, is sent to rank aggregation for further ranking.

$$y_i = \begin{cases} +1, & \text{if } a_{i1} \text{ is ranked higher than } a_{i2}, \text{i.e., } a_{i1} \succ a_{i2} \\ -1, & \text{otherwise} \end{cases} \quad (2)$$

$$minimize \tfrac{1}{2} \|w\|^2 + C \sum_{i=1}^{l} \varepsilon_i \quad (3)$$
$$s.t. \quad y_i <w, a_{i1} - a_{i2} > \geq 1 - \varepsilon_i \quad \forall i : \varepsilon_i \geq 0$$

$$score_{rank}(a) = <w^*, a> \quad (4)$$

The final step of the joint model is rank aggregation. For all answer instance a, the similarity of a_{sim} and the ranking score a_{score} is calculated via LSI-based and Ranking SVM methods, respectively. Then the similarity and ranking scores are aggregated as *relevance* to calculate balanced values of the answer instance to a question. The relevance calculation function is presented in Eq. (5), where $<a, a_{sim}> \in A_{sim}$, $<a, a_{score}> \in A_{score}$. α and β are the weights of a_{sim} and a_{score}, which are set in the training process.

$$relevance(a) = \alpha \cdot a_{sim} + \beta \cdot a_{score} \quad (5)$$

Finally, the joint model ranks all the candidate answers in decreasing order according to answer relevance and return top k answers to users.

4   Evaluation and Results

4.1   Datasets

A publically available standard dataset provided by Sogou Lab[1] is used to test the effectiveness of the proposed joint method. The dataset contains 40,000 Chinese questions-answer tuples (question, <answer-passages>). For each question-answer tuple, it contains one question and an answer-passages set which has more than 10 candidate answer passages (nine candidate answer passages on average). The candidate answer passages are manually annotated with three kinds of relevance scores: "2" (the passage contains the full correct answer), "1" (the passage contains correct but not good enough answer), and "0" (the passage does not contain the answer). Each answer passage has 50 to 500 Chinese characters. The dataset is randomly shuffled into three subgroups as training dataset (70%), developing dataset (20%) and testing dataset (10%).

4.2   Evaluation Metrics

As each question has more than one correct answer, Discounted Cumulative Gain at rank K (DCG@K), Normalized Discounted Cumulative Gain at rank K (NDCG@K) and Precision at rank 1(P@1) are used as evaluation metrics. NDCG@K and P@1 are reported in % in this paper. DCG@K measures the gain of an answer passage based on its position in the ranked answer list. The gain is accumulated from the top of the ranked result list to the top K, with the gain of each result discounted at lower ranks. DCG@K is computed using Eq. (6). rel_i is the relevance score of candidate answer i for the question. For better comparing rank algorithm performance from one question to another, the cumulative gain at each position for a chosen value of K should be normalized across questions. Therefore, NDCG provides a finer granularity for evaluation. NDCG@K is computed in Eq. (7). Q is the test set and $|Q|$ denotes the count of question-answer tuples in Q. IdealDCG@K is simply DCG@K with the ideal ranking.

$$DCG@K = \sum_{i=1}^{k} \frac{2^{rel_i} - 1}{log_2(i+1)} \tag{6}$$

$$NDCG@K = \frac{1}{|Q|} \sum_{i=1}^{|Q|} \frac{DCG@K}{IdealDCG@K} \tag{7}$$

P@1 accesses the performance of ranking algorithm by the proportion of correct answers in top 1 ranked answer by the system, as shown in Eq. (8). $Rel_i = 1$ if the annotated relevance score of top 1 answer is equals to "2" or "1", otherwise it is 0.

$$P@1 = \frac{1}{|Q|} \sum_{i=1}^{|Q|} Rel_i \tag{8}$$

---

[1] http://www.sogou.com/labs/.

4.3 Results

To validate the proposed joint answer ranking model, five experiments are conducted. The first experiment is to verify the effectiveness of the LSI answer ranking method by comparing to four baseline methods, including Doc2vec, Latent Dirichlet Allocation (LDA), Locality Sensitive Hashing (LSH) and docsim[2]. The LSI-based answer ranking method and the baseline methods calculate similarity between questions and candidate answers. The developing dataset is used for accessing the performance as the LSI-based method and baselines are an unsupervised method. The feature used in this experiment is the commonly used bag-of-words. DCG@K, NDCG@K and P@1 are adopted as evaluation metrics, where K is set to 3 and 5, respectively. Table 1 presents the experiment results. For measuring the question-answer semantic similarity, LSI method outperforms other baseline methods on all evaluation metrics and 52.5% of correct answers are ranked in the top of candidate answer list.

Table 1. Evaluation results comparing to the baseline methods on the developing dataset.

Methods	DCG@3	DCG@5	NDCG@3	NDCG@5	P@1
Doc2Vec	2.91	4.05	53.0	59.6	47.8
docsim	3.12	4.30	56.6	63.2	49.7
LSH	3.10	4.27	56.3	62.8	50.3
LDA	3.13	4.34	56.8	63.8	51.3
LSI	**3.21**	**4.42**	**58.4**	**65.1**	**52.5**

The second experiment is to test the effectiveness of the proposed feature expansion for answer ranking. LSH and LDA are selected as baselines as they obtains top 2 ranking performance among the four baseline methods along with LSI. The expanded features as cws_syns contain context-relevant words and synonyms of keywords in questions and candidate answers. The dataset and evaluation metrics are the same to that in the first experiment. The answer ranking performance with expanded features are presented in Table 2. From the results, the features benefits all the ranking methods, e.g., DCG@3 of LSI method improves from 3.21 to 3.34. The performance has 3.26% increasing on average, demonstrating the contribution of proposed features on the answer ranking task.

Table 2. The comparison of LSI with the baseline methods using the proposed features.

Methods	DCG@3	DCG@5	NDCG@3	NDCG@5	P@1
LSH	3.10	4.27	56.3	62.8	50.3
LSH + cws_syns	3.17 (+2.3%)	4.29 (+0.5%)	57.6 (+2.3%)	63.1 (+0.5%)	52.6 (+4.6%)
LDA	3.13	4.34	56.8	63.8	51.3
LDA + cws_syns	3.18 (+1.6%)	4.38 (+0.9%)	57.8 (+1.8%)	64.4 (+0.9%)	52.1 (+1.6%)
LSI	3.21	4.42	58.4	65.1	52.5
LSI + cws_syns	3.34 (+4.1%)	4.54 (+2.7%)	60.6 (+3.8%)	66.8 (+2.6%)	54.1 (+3.1%)

---

[2] http://radimrehurek.com/gensim/similarities/docsim.html.

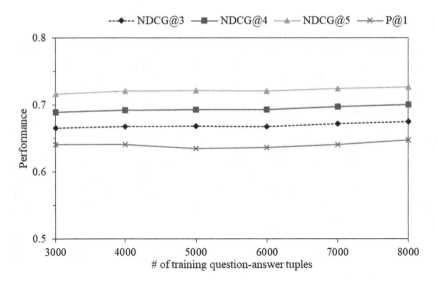

Fig. 2. The performance of our method with the increasing size of training data.

The third experiment is to evaluate the robustness and stability of proposed Ranking SVM method (as *R_SVM*) with different sizes of training data, measuring with NDCG@*K* and P@1 (*K* = 3, 4, 5). Six training subsets are randomly selected from the training dataset, containing 3000, 4000, 5000, 6000, 7000, and 8000 question-answer tuples respectively. The performance is evaluated on the testing dataset containing 4000 question-answer tuples. The feature used in this experiment is the bag-of-words of the extracted key sentences from candidate answer passages. As illustrated in Fig. 2, our method receives a stable performance on all evaluation metrics. Besides, when only 3000 training data is used, the P@1 of answer ranking still achieves 64.1%. Moreover, training with 8000 training question-answer tuples, the P@1 of proposed method is 64.8%, which has 5.5% improvement compared to the baseline (61.4%) without key sentence extraction. This also verifies the effectiveness of the key sentence extraction for answer ranking.

To optimize the question-answer similarity weight α and answer ranking score weight β for effective combination, we randomly select 1000 question-answer tuples as test set from the developing set and 8000 question-answer tuples as training set from the training dataset. The NDCG@*K* (*K* = 3, 4, 5) and P@1 are used as evaluation metrics. The weight α and β are set according to the ranking performance of LSI and Ranking SVM method, where α plus β is equal to 1. Figure 3 presents the parameter training results of ranking performance with different α and β values. From the results, the joint model (LSI + cws_syns + R_SVM) achieves higher ranking performance (P@1) when α is "0.6" and β is "0.4". Considering the P@1 as priority since the correctness of the first answer is more related to user satisfaction, we thus select "0.6" and "0.4" as the optimized value for α and β respectively.

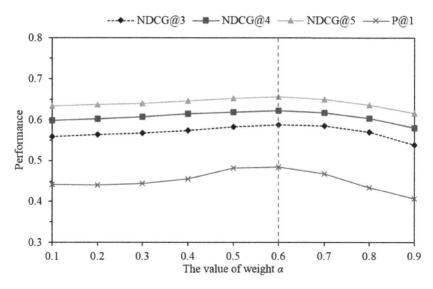

Fig. 3. The performance with different values of weights α and β ($\beta = 1-\alpha$).

The last experiment presents the comparison of the proposed model with six baseline methods. Using the training dataset and the testing dataset, the performance is compared using DCG@K, NDCG@K and P@1 ($K = 3, 5$). From the result presented in Table 3, the proposed model obtains the best performance on all evaluation metrics. For P@1, our method improves 31.8% compared to LSH which has the best performance among baselines. Measured in NDCG@3, our joint model gains an improvement of 15.2% and 3.6% respectively, comparing to our proposed method LSI and Ranking SVM alone.

Table 3. The performance comparison of our model with the 6 baseline methods.

Methods	DCG@3	DCG@5	NDCG@3	NDCG@5	P@1
Doc2Vec + cws_syns	3.23	4.45	56.0	62.2	52.9
LDA + cws_syns	3.42	4.71	59.3	65.8	55.1
docsim + cws_syns	3.36	4.65	58.3	65.0	53.8
LSH + cws_syns	3.39	4.68	58.8	65.3	55.1
LSI + cws_syns	3.71	5.01	64.3	69.9	61.7
R_SVM	4.12	5.46	71.5	76.3	69.4
LSI + cws_syns + R_SVM	**4.27**	**5.58**	**74.1**	**77.9**	**72.6**

5 Conclusions

This paper proposed a joint model for answer ranking based on semantic feature expansion. The proposed semantic features are concise but effective for capturing the semantic information and co-occurrence terms between questions and candidate answers. Using a publicly available Chinese QA dataset, five experiments were conducted for evaluating the effectiveness of the proposed joint model through a comparison with a list of baseline methods. The results showed that our model achieved the best performance on all the evaluation metrics, demonstrating its effectiveness for answer ranking.

Acknowledgements. This work was supported by National Natural Science Foundation of China (No.61772146), the OUHK 2018/19 S&T School Research Fund (R5077), and Natural Science Foundation of Guangdong Province (2018A030310051).

References

1. Zhao, Z., Lu, H., Zheng, V.W., Cai, D., He, X., Zhuang, Y.: Community-based question answering via asymmetric multi-faceted ranking network learning. In: The 31th Conference on Artificial Intelligence, pp. 3532–3538 (2017)
2. Freihat, A.A., Qwaider, M.R.H., Giunchiglia, F.: Using grice maxims in ranking community question answers. In: International Conference on Information, Process, and Knowledge Management. pp. 38–43 (2018)
3. Zhou, Z.-M., Lan, M., Niu, Z.-Y., Lu, Y.: Exploiting user profile information for answer ranking in cQA. In: The 21st International Conference Companion on World Wide Web, pp. 767–774 (2012)
4. Li, Z., Huang, J., Zhou, Z., Zhang, H., Chang, S., Huang, Z.: LSTM-based deep learning models for answer ranking. In: 2016 IEEE First International Conference on Data Science in Cyberspace. pp. 90–97 (2016)
5. Agarwal, A., et al.: Learning to rank for robust question answering. In: The 21st ACM International Conference on Information and Knowledge Management, pp. 833–842 (2012)
6. Yulianti, E., Chen, R.-C., Scholer, F., Croft, W.B., Sanderson, M.: Ranking documents by answer-passage quality. In: The 41st International ACM SIGIR Conference on Research & Development in Information Retrieval, pp. 335–344 (2018)
7. Ko, J., Nyberg, E., Si, L.: A Probabilistic graphical model for joint answer ranking in question answering. In: The 30th Annual International ACM SIGIR Conference on Research and Development in Information Retrieval, pp. 343–350. ACM (2007)
8. Severyn, A., Nicosia, M., Moschitti, A.: Building structures from classifiers for passage reranking. In: The 22nd ACM International Conference on Information & Knowledge Management, pp. 969–978. ACM (2013)
9. Moschitti, A., Quarteroni, S., Basili, R., Manandhar, S.: Exploiting syntactic and shallow semantic kernels for question answer classification. In: The 45th Annual Meeting of the Association of Computational Linguistics, pp. 776–783 (2007)
10. Ko, J., Mitamura, T., Nyberg, E.: Language-independent probabilistic answer ranking for question answering. In: The 45th Annual Meeting of the Association of Computational Linguistics, pp. 784–791 (2007)
11. Ferrucci, D., et al.: Building watson: an overview of the DeepQA project. AI Mag. **31**(3), 59–79 (2010)
12. Bhowan, U., McCloskey, D.J.: Genetic programming for feature selection and question-answer ranking in IBM watson. In: Machado, P., et al. (eds.) EuroGP 2015. LNCS, vol. 9025, pp. 153–166. Springer, Cham (2015). https://doi.org/10.1007/978-3-319-16501-1_13
13. Bilotti, M.W., Elsas, J., Carbonell, J., Nyberg, E.: rank learning for factoid question answering with linguistic and semantic constraints. In: The 19th ACM International Conference on Information and Knowledge Managementm pp. 459–468 (2010)

14. Yang, L., et al.: Beyond factoid QA: effective methods for non-factoid answer sentence retrieval. In: Ferro, N., et al. (eds.) ECIR 2016. LNCS, vol. 9626, pp. 115–128. Springer, Cham (2016). https://doi.org/10.1007/978-3-319-30671-1_9

15. Metzler, D., Kanungo, T.: Machine learned sentence selection strategies for query-biased summarization. In: Sigir Learning to Rank Workshopm, pp. 40–47 (2008)

16. Jeon, J., Croft, W.B., Lee, J.H., Park, S.: A framework to predict the quality of answers with non-textual features. In: The 29th Annual International ACM SIGIR Conference on Research and Development in Information Retrieval, pp. 228–235 (2006)

17. Liu, Y., Bian, J., Agichtein, E.: Predicting information seeker satisfaction in community question answering. In: The 31st Annual International ACM SIGIR Conference on Research and Development in Information Retrieval, pp. 483–490 (2008)

18. Blooma, M.J., Goh, D.H.: A predictive framework for retrieving the best answer. In: The 2008 ACM Symposium on Applied Computing, pp. 1107–1111 (2008)

19. Shah, C., Pomerantz, J.: Evaluating and predicting answer quality in community QA. In: The 33rd international ACM SIGIR Conference on Research and Development in Information Retrieval, pp. 411–418 (2010)

20. Liu, M., Liu, Y., Yang, Q.: Predicting best answerers for new questions in community question answering. In: Chen, L., Tang, C., Yang, J., Gao, Y. (eds.) WAIM 2010. LNCS, vol. 6184, pp. 127–138. Springer, Heidelberg (2010). https://doi.org/10.1007/978-3-642-14246-8_15

21. Bian, J., Agichtein, E., Liu, Y., Zha, H.: Finding the right facts in the crowd: factoid question answering over social media categories and subject descriptors. In: The 17th International Conference on World Wide Web, pp. 467–476 (2008)

22. Severyn, A., Nicosia, M., Moschitti, A.: Learning adaptable patterns for passage reranking. In: The Seventeenth Conference on Computational Natural Language Learning, pp. 75–83 (2013)

23. Severyn, A., Moschitti, A.: Automatic feature engineering for answer selection and extraction. In: Empirical Methods in Natural Language Processing, pp. 458–467 (2013)

24. Tymoshenko, K., Bonadiman, D., Moschitti, A.: Convolutional neural networks vs convolution kernels : feature engineering for answer sentence reranking. In: North American Chapter of the Association for Computational Linguistics: Human Language Technologies, pp. 1268–1278 (2016)

25. Severyn, A., Moschitti, A.: Learning to rank short text pairs with convolutional deep neural networks. In: The 38th International ACM SIGIR Conference on Research and Development in Information Retrieval, pp. 373–382 (2015)

26. Shen, Y., et al.: Knowledge-aware attentive neural network for ranking question answer pairs. In: International ACM SIGIR Conference on Research & Development in Information Retrieval, pp. 901–904 (2018)

27. Cohen, D., Croft, W.B.: A hybrid embedding approach to noisy answer passage retrieval. In: Pasi, G., Piwowarski, B., Azzopardi, L., Hanbury, A. (eds.) ECIR 2018. LNCS, vol. 10772, pp. 127–140. Springer, Cham (2018). https://doi.org/10.1007/978-3-319-76941-7_10

28. Mikolov, T., Chen, K., Corrado, G., Dean, J.: Distributed representations of words and phrases and their compositionality. In: Advances in Neural Information Processing Systems, pp. 3111–3119 (2013)

29. Wang, H., Xi, H.: Chinese synonyms toolkit (2017). https://github.com/huyingxi/Synonyms

30. Garcia, E.: Latent Semantic Indexing (LSI) A Fast Track Tutorial. Grossman and Frieders Information Retrieval, Algorithms and Heuristics (2006)

31. Cao, Y., Huang, T., Tian, Y.: A ranking SVM based fusion model for cross-media meta-search engine. J. Zhejiang Univ. Sci. C **11**(11), 903–910 (2010)

32. Joachims, T.: Training linear SVMs in linear time. In: The 12th ACM SIGKDD International Conference on Knowledge Discovery and Data Mining, pp. 217–226 (2006)

Arc Loss: Softmax with Additive Angular Margin for Answer Retrieval

Rikiya Suzuki[1(✉)], Sumio Fujita[2], and Tetsuya Sakai[1]

[1] Waseda University, Tokyo, Japan
`rikiyasuzuki@ruri.waseda.jp,tetsuyasakai@acm.org`
[2] Yahoo! Japan Corporation, Tokyo, Japan
`sufujita@yahoo-corp.jp`

Abstract. Answer retrieval is a crucial step in question answering. To determine the best Q–A pair in a candidate pool, traditional approaches adopt triplet loss (i.e., pairwise ranking loss) for a meaningful distributed representation. Triplet loss is widely used to push away a negative answer from a certain question in a feature space and leads to a better understanding of the relationship between questions and answers. However, triplet loss is inefficient because it requires two steps: triplet generation and negative sampling. In this study, we propose an alternative loss function, namely, arc loss, for more efficient and effective learning than that by triplet loss. We evaluate the proposed approach on a commonly used QA dataset and demonstrate that it significantly outperforms the triplet loss baseline.

Keywords: Question answering · Answer retrieval · Representation learning

1 Introduction

Answer retrieval (AR) is a crucial component of question answering (QA). The AR problem can be formulated as follows: Given a question q and a candidate answer pool $P = \{a_1, a_2, \ldots, a_p\}$ for this question (p is the pool size), the goal is to retrieve $a \in P$ that correctly answers q. Traditional approaches [5,14] tackle this problem by calculating the cosine similarity of each Q–A pair and using the k-nearest neighbor algorithm (k-NN). To obtain the best Q–A pair by 1-NN, AR models utilize similarity learning for a meaningful distributed representation.

Classical similarity learning for face recognition (FR) in computer vision and passage retrieval in information retrieval (IR) adopts triplet loss, that is, pairwise ranking loss, for the objective function in training. Triplet loss is widely used to push away a negative answer from a certain question in a feature space. However, training by triplet loss is inefficient because it requires two steps: triplet generation and negative sampling. For similarity learning, a triplet loss model should sample a negative answer that violates the triplet constraint in a randomly selected answer pool. Thus, the model should generate triplets in a pool

© Springer Nature Switzerland AG 2020
F. L. Wang et al. (Eds.): AIRS 2019, LNCS 12004, pp. 34–40, 2020.
https://doi.org/10.1007/978-3-030-42835-8_4

of predefined size and calculate the cosine similarity between a question and all candidate answers. Finally, the model selects only one negative answer in the negative answer pool per each Q–A pair as a training target. To resolve this inefficiency, we propose an alternative loss function, namely, arc loss. In arc loss, the model samples negative questions and answers, and then adds an angular margin to the angle between correct Q–A pair representations. Finally, the model learns an adequate metric space according to the loss function using all negative samples. Thereby, we avoid unnecessary calculations (related to unused candidate answers) for triplet loss training targets and improve learning efficiency. In this study, we adopt a straightforward network architecture to focus on the loss performance and improve the versatility. We evaluate the proposed approach on a commonly used QA dataset and demonstrate that it significantly outperforms a triplet loss baseline.

2 Related Work

In this section, we first describe traditional triplet loss and point out its drawbacks. Then, we explain the necessity of triplet generation through negative sampling.

2.1 Triplet Loss

Traditional neural network models in AR, such as QA-LSTM [3], adopt triplet loss to learn only the relative similarity relationship between positive and negative Q–A pairs in triplets. We assume that we are given a set of training Q–A pairs $\{(q_1, a_1), \ldots, (q_K, a_K)\}$, where $q, a \in \mathbb{R}^v$ denote the feature embeddings of questions and answers, respectively. The goal of triplet loss is to push away the negative answer a_n from the anchor question q by a cosine margin $m > 0$ relative to the positive answer a_p, that is,

$$\cos(q, a_p) \geq \cos(q, a_n) + m . \tag{1}$$

To enforce this constraint, a common relaxation of Eq. 1 is the minimization of the following hinge loss:

$$L_{\text{triplet}} = [m - \cos(q, a_p) + \cos(q, a_n)]_+ , \tag{2}$$

where the operator $[x]_+ = \max(0, x)$ denotes the hinge function. In the training phase, a triplet loss model should select negative samples that violate the triplet constraint in Eq. 1. Thus, the model should calculate the cosine similarity between a question and all candidate answers even though only one answer is selected in the candidate pool as a negative sample per Q–A pair.

2.2   Sampling Strategy

In triplet loss, negative sampling can be divided into two types according to the relationship of the samples with correct Q–A pairs. *Hardest* negative sampling is a simple idea: sampling a negative answer with maximum value in L_{triplet} per each correct Q–A pair. This implies that the model samples a negative answer closest to a question. However, this strategy can lead to a collapsed model such as $\cos(q, a_p) = \cos(q, a_n) = 1$ in any task or any dataset. To mitigate this, *semi-hard* negative sampling strategy was proposed in FaceNet [12]. In this strategy, the model selects a negative sample a_n such that

$$\cos(\boldsymbol{q}, \boldsymbol{a}_p) \geq \cos(\boldsymbol{q}, \boldsymbol{a}_n) . \tag{3}$$

In triplet loss, it is necessary to change the sampling strategy flexibly depending on the task or the dataset.

2.3   Triplet Generation

To select negative answers violating the triplet constraint and satisfying the sampling strategy, the model should prepare an answer pool of predefined size. In the triplet generation phase, there are two options: offline or online triplet generation. In offline generation, we randomly select candidate answers per each Q–A pair before training in every epoch. By contrast, in online generation, we select candidate answers from within a mini-batch. In FR [12], offline generation may lead to inadequate training, as mislabeled face images would dominate the *hardest* negative samples. Even in AR, similarity learning by offline triplets is not effective if the answer sampled as a negative is in fact a positive (i.e., happens to be relevant to the question). Thus, we apply online triplet generation for efficient learning.

3   Proposed Method

Inspired by ArcFace [2] in computer vision, we propose arc loss for learning more efficiently and effectively than by triplet loss. Arc loss consists of two parts: softmax loss and additive angular margin. The most widely used classification loss function, softmax loss, is as follows:

$$L_{\text{softmax}} = -\frac{1}{N} \sum_{i=1}^{N} \frac{e^{x_i}}{\sum_{j=1}^{n} e^{x_j}}, \tag{4}$$

where x is scalar, N is the mini-batch size and n is the number of classes. Arc loss uses the cosine similarity of all selected candidate Q–A pairs and adds an angular margin to the angle between correct Q–A representations. We define arc loss as follows:

$$L_{\text{arc}} = -\frac{1}{N} \sum_{i=1}^{N} \log \frac{e^{s\cos(\theta_{q_i a_i}+m)}}{e^{s\cos(\theta_{q_i a_i}+m)} + \sum_{j=1,i\neq j}^{n} \left(e^{s\cos(\theta_{q_i a_j})} + e^{s\cos(\theta_{q_j a_i})}\right)}, \tag{5}$$

where s is a scalar scale for cosine-based softmax loss and θ_{qa} is the angle between Q–A representations. m is an additive angular margin and n means the predefined pool size in this case. In FR, there are several elements in the same class (e.g., the pictures of the same people), and thus the model applies and calculates the center vectors of the same face representations. By contrast, in AR, there are only two elements in the same class (Q–A), and it is not worth calculating the center vectors of the correct Q–A pairs. In this task, there are more classes than in FR. Thus, the arc loss model samples not only negative answers but also negative questions from within a mini-batch and learns a large amount of information regarding the relative similarity relationship between a correct Q–A pair and negative candidate Q–A pairs simultaneously. This method improves learning efficiency.

4   Experiments

4.1   Datasets

InsuranceQA[1] is one of the most widely used large-scale QA datasets from the insurance domain. This dataset provides a training set, a development set, and two test sets. $12,887$ questions with correct answers are included in the training set, whereas the development set has $1,000$ Q–A pairs and the two test sets consisting of $1,800$ pairs. In the experiments, the model is expected to retrieve the one correct answer from 500 candidate answers under the Hit@1 metric [11], that is, Precision@1. We use the first version of the dataset. More details can be found in Feng et al. [5].

4.2   Network Architecture

To evaluate the effectiveness of the proposed method, we use a straightforward NN model [3] based on bidirectional long short-term memory (BiLSTM) [6]. The first layer of each model transforms each input word w into a fixed-size real-valued word embedding $r \in \mathbb{R}^d$. This is then passed to the hidden layer (HL) that performs nonlinear transformation by tanh. The output of the HL is then passed on to a BiLSTM. In Fig. 1, P is the 1-MaxPooling layer that is a dimension-wise Max-Pooling over the hidden states of all time steps, and T is the tanh layer. The result is a vector representation for both question and answer. The final output is the cosine similarity between these vectors.

Fig. 1. Network architecture

---
[1] https://github.com/shuzi/insuranceQA.

4.3 Implementation Details

We set the length of the input words to 60 for InsuranceQA because according to Santos et al. [3], this setting leads to the best performance. We initialized the word embeddings with 300-dimensional GloVe vectors[2] [9] trained on 840 billion words for InsuranceQA. The embeddings are frozen, and unknown words are embedded into zero vectors. The hidden layer size is 200 and the output vector size of BiLSTM is 141×2. These hyperparameters are based on Feng et al. [5] and Santos et al. [3]. We use stochastic gradient descent as the optimization strategy. The initial learning rate λ is 1.1. The additive angular margin m is $\pi/64$ and the scalar scale s is 64. These hyperparameters are tuned for this dataset. Following Santos et al. [4], we set the learning rate λ_t for epoch t to $\lambda_t = \lambda/t$. The mini-batch size is 64 and the pool size n is 50. In triplet selection for triplet loss, we apply *hardest* negative sampling for InsuranceQA.

5 Results and Discussion

Table 1 presents the experimental results for the InsuranceQA dataset, with different loss functions, as well as some previously published scores. It can be seen that the arc loss model outperforms the triplet loss baseline on both Test1 and Test2 sets as well as the development set. Paired t-test p-values [10] comparing the arc loss and the traditional loss baseline demonstrate that the improvements are statistically highly significant. In Fig. 2, we demonstrate the learning curves of triplet loss and arc loss. Training by arc loss is substantially more efficient than that by triplet loss.

Table 1. Experimental results on InsuranceQA under the Hit@1 metric. The first set of results are from published papers. The second set is based on the present implementation with BiLSTM. The p-values indicate statistically significant improvements over the triplet loss baseline.

Model	Dev	Test1	Test2
QA-CNN [5]	0.654	0.653	0.610
QA-LSTM with attention [14]	0.684	0.681	0.622
Attentive LSTM [13]	0.689	0.690	0.648
IARNN-Gate [17]	**0.700**	0.701	0.628
IRGAN [18]		0.644	0.611
Local-global attention [1]		0.701	**0.674**
NN using string kernels [7]		0.541	0.502
SRanker [16]		0.689	0.658
Multihop attention network [15]		**0.705**	0.669
AdvIR_SVAT [8]		0.652	0.613
Baseline(QA-LSTM)	0.667	0.676	0.655
ArcLoss	**0.722**	**0.712** $(p = .000)$	**0.686** $(p = .001)$

---

[2] https://nlp.stanford.edu/projects/glove/.

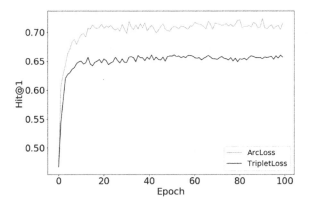

Fig. 2. Learning curves of triplet loss baseline and arc loss model.

6   Conclusions

We studied the AR problem using more efficient and effective similarity learning than that by triplet loss, and we proposed arc loss in the loss function to resolve the inefficiency of previous approaches. Experiments with BiLSTM demonstrated that the proposed method significantly outperforms the triplet loss baseline. The results suggest that arc loss contains a large amount of similarity relationship information, including all negative candidate Q–A pairs, and improves the model's learning efficiency. Since the proposed method only changes the objective function, it can be applied to some models where the matching score is output by 2D convolutions, Neural Tensor Networks or more sophisticated structures and this loss could serve as a general-purpose loss for all pair-wise or group-wise ranking tasks. In future work, we aim to extend the present approach to other IR tasks that involve representation or similarity learning.

References

1. Bachrach, Y., et al.: An attention mechanism for neural answer selection using a combined global and local view. In: 2017 IEEE 29th International Conference on Tools with Artificial Intelligence (ICTAI), pp. 425–432 (2017)
2. Deng, J., Guo, J., Xue, N., Zafeiriou, S.: Arcface: Additive angular margin loss for deep face recognition. In: The IEEE Conference on Computer Vision and Pattern Recognition (CVPR), June 2019
3. Dos Santos, C., Tan, M., Xiang, B., Zhou, B.: Attentive pooling networks (2016)
4. Dos Santos, C.N., Zadrozny, B.: Learning character-level representations for part-of-speech tagging. In: Proceedings of the 31st International Conference on International Conference on Machine Learning - Volume 32 ICML 2014, pp. II-1818-II-1826. JMLR.org (2014)
5. Feng, M., Xiang, B., Glass, M.R., Wang, L., Zhou, B.: Applying deep learning to answer selection: a study and an open task. In: 2015 IEEE Workshop on Automatic Speech Recognition and Understanding (ASRU), pp. 813–820. IEEE (2015)

6. Hochreiter, S., Schmidhuber, J.: Long short-term memory. Neural Comput. **9**(8), 1735–1780 (1997). https://doi.org/10.1162/neco.1997.9.8.1735

7. Masala, M., Ruseti, S., Rebedea, T.: Sentence selection with neural networks using string kernels. Procedia Comput. Sci. **112**(C), 1774–1782 (2017). https://doi.org/10.1016/j.procs.2017.08.209

8. Park, D.H., Chang, Y.: Adversarial sampling and training for semi-supervised information retrieval. In: The World Wide Web Conference WWW 2019, pp. 1443–1453. ACM, New York, USA (2019). https://doi.org/10.1145/3308558.3313416

9. Pennington, J., Socher, R., Manning, C.D.: GloVe: global vectors for word representation. In: Empirical Methods in Natural Language Processing (EMNLP), pp. 1532–1543 (2014)

10. Sakai, T.: Laboratory Experiments in Information Retrieval. TIRS, vol. 40. Springer, Singapore (2018). https://doi.org/10.1007/978-981-13-1199-4

11. Sakai, T., Ishikawa, D., Kando, N., Seki, Y., Kuriyama, K., Lin, C.Y.: Using graded-relevance metrics for evaluating community QA answer selection. In: Proceedings of the Fourth ACM International Conference on Web Search and Data Mining WSDM 2011, pp. 187–196. ACM, New York, USA (2011). https://doi.org/10.1145/1935826.1935864

12. Schroff, F., Kalenichenko, D., Philbin, J.: Facenet: a unified embedding for face recognition and clustering. In: IEEE Conference on Computer Vision and Pattern Recognition CVPR 2015, pp. 815–823. Boston, MA, USA, 7–12 June 2015. (2015). https://doi.org/10.1109/CVPR.2015.7298682

13. Tan, M., dos Santos, C., Xiang, B., Zhou, B.: Improved representation learning for question answer matching. In: Proceedings of the 54th Annual Meeting of the Association for Computational Linguistics (Volume 1: Long Papers), pp. 464–473. Association for Computational Linguistics, Berlin, Germany, Aug 2016. https://doi.org/10.18653/v1/P16-1044

14. Tan, M., Santos, C.d., Xiang, B., Zhou, B.: LSTM-based deep learning models for non-factoid answer selection (2015)

15. Tran, N.K., Niederée, C.: Multihop attention networks for question answer matching. In: The 41st International ACM SIGIR Conference on Research & Development in Information Retrieval SIGIR 2018, pp. 325–334. ACM, New York, NY, USA (2018). https://doi.org/10.1145/3209978.3210009

16. Tran, N.K., Niederée, C.: A neural network-based framework for non-factoid question answering. In: Companion Proceedings of the The Web Conference 2018, WWW 2018, pp. 1979–1983. International World Wide Web Conferences Steering Committee, Republic and Canton of Geneva, Switzerland (2018). https://doi.org/10.1145/3184558.3191830

17. Wang, B., Liu, K., Zhao, J.: Inner attention based recurrent neural networks for answer selection. In: Proceedings of the 54th Annual Meeting of the Association for Computational Linguistics (Volume 1: Long Papers), pp. 1288–1297. Association for Computational Linguistics, Berlin, Germany (Aug 2016). https://doi.org/10.18653/v1/P16-1122

18. Wang, J., et al.: IRGAN: A minimax game for unifying generative and discriminative information retrieval models. In: Proceedings of the 40th International ACM SIGIR Conference on Research and Development in Information Retrieval SIGIR 2017, pp. 515–524. ACM, New York, NY, USA (2017). https://doi.org/10.1145/3077136.3080786

Context-Awareness

Context-Aware Collaborative Ranking

Wei Dai, Weike Pan$^{(\boxtimes)}$, and Zhong Ming$^{(\boxtimes)}$

National Engineering Laboratory for Big Data System Computing Technology,
College of Computer Science and Software Engineering, Shenzhen University,
Shenzhen, China
`daiwei20171@email.szu.edu.cn, {panweike,mingz}@szu.edu.cn`

Abstract. Recommender systems (RS) are being used in a broad range
of applications, from online shopping websites to music streaming platforms, which aim to provide users high-quality personalized services. Collaborative filtering (CF) is a promising technique to ensure the accuracy
of a recommender system, which can be divided into specific tasks such
as rating prediction and item ranking. However, there is a larger volume
of published works studying the problem of rating prediction, rather than
item ranking though it is recognized to be more appropriate for the final
recommendation in a real application. On the other hand, many studies
on item ranking devoted to leveraging implicit feedback are limited in
performance improvements due to the uniformity of implicit feedback.
Hence, in this paper, we focus on item ranking with informative explicit
feedback, which is also called collaborative ranking. In particular, we
propose a novel recommendation model termed context-aware collaborative ranking (CCR), which adopts a logistic loss function to measure
the predicted error of ranking and exploits the inherent preference context derived from the explicit feedback. Moreover, we design an elegant
strategy to distinguish between positive and negative samples used in the
process of model training. Empirical studies on four real-world datasets
clearly demonstrate that our CCR outperforms the state-of-the-art methods in terms of various ranking-oriented evaluation metrics.

Keywords: Preference context · Collaborative filtering · Matrix
factorization

1 Introduction

As an important part of information filtering, recommender systems play a piv-
otal role in the big data era. Many popular applications have deployed recommender systems to boost sales and optimize user experience, such as product
recommendation in Amazon, content in Facebook and music in NetEase. A successful recommender system largely relies on a close cooperation of manifold
functional components, while the most complicated one is the recommendation
algorithms which determine how a recommender system performs in a real-world

© Springer Nature Switzerland AG 2020
F. L. Wang et al. (Eds.): AIRS 2019, LNCS 12004, pp. 43–55, 2020.
https://doi.org/10.1007/978-3-030-42835-8_5

setting. And undoubtedly, collaborative filtering (CF) is one of the most popular techniques which has shown excellent performance both in academia and industry.

Rating prediction and item ranking are two subfields of collaborative filtering methods distinguished by the model objective. Rating prediction aims at estimating the real score of a user to an item through a regression function, whereas item ranking boils down to making the order of items in the candidate list as accurate as possible. Most existing CF methods focus on the task of rating prediction rather than item ranking. However, the ultimate goal of a recommender system is to obtain a candidate list of items for each target user, which means that whether the predicted score of an item is correct or not is less important. It is the relative positions of candidate items that determine the quality of recommender systems, which exactly corresponds to the goal of item ranking. Thus, the research direction has largely turned to the problem of item ranking.

Training data commonly used for the ranking problem includes explicit feedback such as five-star ratings and implicit feedback such as clicks. Previous ranking-oriented works using implicit feedback are more likely to suffer from unsatisfactory performance because of the uniformity of implicit feedback. For example, if user u clicks items A, B and C, the only thing we know is that user u may prefer items A, B and C than other unobserved items. But the relative preference between these three clicked items is not given, which limits further training of the models. In an attempt to compensate for this disadvantage, some works resort to taking the context into consideration such as social connections and geographical locations [21]. However, such auxiliary information is not always available in most real applications and it is challenging to model sometimes. On the contrary, explicit feedback, e.g., rating records, contains rich inherent contextual information that is shown valuable in rating prediction works such as SVD++ [3] and MF-MPC [10], but it is overlooked by a large portion of item ranking methods. Hence in this paper, we pay closer attention to the exploitation of such inherent preference context in explicit feedback for solving the ranking and recommendation problem.

In this paper, we propose a novel solution, i.e., context-aware collaborative ranking (CCR), which utilizes the logistic loss and preference context derived from rating records to improve the ranking performance. Specifically, the definition of preference context in our CCR is the same as that in MF-MPC [10], which is the items that a user has historical interactions with. Besides, we design an elegant strategy to construct positive and negative samples from explicit feedback for the logistic loss by setting a personalized threshold for each user. We perform comprehensive experiments via comparison with the state-of-the-art collaborative filtering methods. Particularly, in order to separately study the effectiveness of logistic function and preference context in the ranking and recommendation task, we conduct independent experiments by considering these two components as variables. Results on four real-world datasets of different scales show that our CCR outperforms the baseline models, and the logistic loss function and preference context contribute substantially to the improvement in recommendation accuracy.

We list our main contributions as follows: (i) we propose a novel method, i.e., CCR, for the task of item ranking; and (ii) we conduct extensive empirical studies to verify the effectiveness of our CCR in particular of the components of the logistic loss function and the inherent preference context.

2   Related Work

Much of the current literatures on recommendation algorithms pay particular attention to collaborative filtering, which generally falls into two categories, i.e., rating prediction and item ranking, respectively. Methods in the branch of rating prediction usually seek a monotonically increasing function to calculate the absolute rating of an item, while those in the branch of item ranking try to generate lists of sorted items that match users' preferences. In this section, we provide a brief overview of related techniques following the above categorization.

2.1   Rating Prediction

There are two main families of methods for solving the problem of rating prediction: neighborhood-based (or memory-based) and model-based methods. Based on the assumption that similar users have similar tastes, the crux of neighborhood-based methods is the similarity matrix which is defined to identify nearest neighbors of users and items [5]. Then the affinity score of the user-item pair is predicted by aggregating the ratings given by the neighbors. The more elaborate the similarity measure is, the better performance the method can achieve. Although neighborhood-based algorithms are simplistic to implement and intuitive to understand, they fail to capture users' characteristics which can yield personalized recommendations. However, model-based methods enjoy the ability of extracting distinctive latent features for each user and thus attract a great deal of attention.

The most attractive advantages of model-based techniques are their effectiveness and flexibility, which benefit remarkable increase of accuracy and easy deployment on online sites. Among multitudinous CF models, matrix factorization (MF) is one of the most popular models designed to decompose the original rating matrix into two low-rank user- and item-specific matrices. Probabilistic matrix factorization (PMF) [7], for example, a widely used MF-based method, assumes that rating scores are generated from a distribution centered around the dot production between users' and items' latent vectors and reconstructs the missing values by narrowing the distance between true and predicted scores. Nevertheless, PMF only models the relationship between a user and the target item, ignoring his/her historical items which also give a clue about the user's preferences. To address this issue, MF-MPC [10] defines the set of items a user rated before as preference context to bridge users and their previous interactions. In particular, MF-MPC alleviates the bias of users rating habits by categorizing contextual items into several groups in accordance with rating values. When contextual items are included in one group without the difference of scores, MF-MPC then reduces to SVD++ [3]. Although MF-MPC achieves desired improvement, when applied to the ranking problem, it still suffers from poor performance because of the un-matching issue [1], that is, there exists a huge gap between accuracy improvements of rating-oriented models and ranking performance lifts of real systems. Even for the promising neural network-based methods like AutoRec [13] and its variant [9], they aim at reconstructing the original input vector through a layered network but still suffer from this problem. Therefore, research on item ranking has been cropping up.

2.2   Item Ranking

Works on the item ranking problem can also be grouped into two categories, i.e., neighborhood-based approaches and model-based approaches. As a pioneer work of item ranking, EigenRank [6] calculates the similarity between users according to the proximity of ordered item lists commonly rated by both two users, in a bid to apply the rating-oriented neighborhood method to the ranking scenario. Similarities between lists of items are indeed more reliable, but when faced with large-scale data, EigenRank may be time consuming. Different from EigenRank that represents a user as an item list, VSRank [15] uses a set of item pairs (i, j) to indicate that user u prefers item i to j, and the similarity is defined on this preference set. All these similarity-based methods requires that users must have common rated items, otherwise their relevance can not be estimated. This issue does not exist in model-based CR methods.

Bayesian personalized ranking (BPR) [12] is a hugely popular ranking-oriented model that measures the error between item pairs in order to learn relative relationships of items, e.g., user u prefers item i to j. BPR is an expert in learning from implicit feedback such as clicks and browses, but for the case of explicit feedback, it may lead to poor performance when absolute ratings are converted in a wrong way. To address this problem, transfer to rank (ToR) [11] exploits explicit ratings through a two-staged framework where ratings are firstly considered as examination behaviors in a global view to generate a coarse list of items, and then as purchasing behaviors in a local view to refine the previous list. Another example that using both explicit and implicit feedback is MERR_SVD++ [4], an extended work of SVD++. The difference between these two methods is the modeling objective, where SVD++ focuses on rating prediction, but MERR_SVD++ is designed to target item ranking. Besides leveraging feedback appropriately, the loss function also plays an important role in improving the ranking performance. For example, CoFiRank [16] aims to maximize NDCG over all the users where the error is defined on different lists of items. FocusedRank [8] utilizes a listwise and a pairwise loss function in one single model to ensure a global accuracy and simultaneously capture the local preference among items in the same list. Similar combination of different loss functions can be seen in URM [14] which utilizes both pointwise and listwise functions in one framework. Apart from these traditional matrix factorization-based approaches, neural network-based models are flourishing nowadays and have already become integral to the field of item ranking. DMF [19], for example, adopts a multi-layer network to learn the non-linear representations of users and items, and incorporates explicit ratings into the logistic loss function specifically, which is a clear evidence of the significance of both explicit feedback and logistic loss for performance improvements. Furthermore, the utility of different loss functions in modeling users' preferences have also been studied in CDAE [18]. We put some representative works in Table 1. We can see that methods taking preference context into consideration are fewer especially in the branch of item ranking, which impressively motivates us to design a novel solution.

Table 1. A summary of some related and representative state-of-the-art methods.

	w/o preference context	w/ preference context
Rating prediction	ICF [5], PMF [7]	SVD++ [3] MF-MPC [10]
Item ranking	BPR [12], ToR [11]	**CCR** (proposed in this paper)

3   Our Solution

In this section, we describe our proposed context-aware collaborative ranking (CCR) model according to the arrow indication in Fig. 1. We begin with a detailed illustration of the main idea in our CCR. This is followed by a rigorous mathematical specification of our CCR. We then describe the optimizing procedure based on a stochastic gradient descent (SGD) algorithm.

3.1   Problem Definition

Given n users, m items and a set of observed rating records in the form of (u, i, r_{ui}) triple, where r_{ui} is an explicit rating of item i given by user u, we aim to recommend a personalized list of items for each user. Notice that items in candidate lists are unobserved for the target user and are sorted in a descending order according to the preference scores predicted by the model. Main notations in this paper are described in Table 2.

3.2   Context-Aware Collaborative Ranking

We present the core processes of our CCR in Fig. 1. We can clearly see from the overall illustration that the matrix containing users' historical explicit feedback is converted into two indicator matrices, one of which is to distinguish between positive and negative samples, and the other is to suggest the preference context. After that, two converted matrices are modeled through a logistic loss function

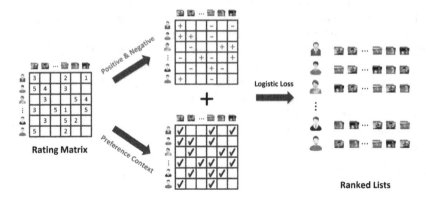

Fig. 1. An overview of our proposed model, i.e., context-aware collaborative ranking (CCR), for the item ranking problem. Notice that the original rating matrix is firstly transformed into a binary matrix and preference context, which are then combined to a logistic loss function to obtain the final ranked lists.

Table 2. Some notations and their explanations.

Notation	Description
n	number of users
m	number of items
u	user ID
i	item ID
r_{ui}	rating of user u to item i
$y_{ui} = \{+1, -1\}$	binary indicator derived from r_{ui}
d	number of latent dimensions
$\mathbb{M}$	rating range
$\mathcal{U} = \{u\}$	the whole set of users
$\mathcal{I} = \{i\}$	the whole set of items
$\mathcal{R} = \{(u, i, r_{ui})\}$	rating records in the training data
$S^P = \{(u, i, +1)\}$	the set of positive samples
$S^N = \{(u, i, -1)\}$	the set of negative samples
$\hat{r}_{ui}$	predicted preference of user u to item i
$U_{u\cdot} \in \mathbb{R}^{1 \times d}$	user-specific latent feature vector
$V_{i\cdot}, M_{i'\cdot}^r \in \mathbb{R}^{1 \times d}$	item-specific latent feature vector
$b_u \in \mathbb{R}$	user u's bias
$b_i \in \mathbb{R}$	item i's bias
$\mu \in \mathbb{R}$	global average rating value

to obtain the final ranked list for each user. Next, we spell out in detail how our CCR works.

Among the considerations important to devising an item ranking solution, the first and foremost is to convert the rating matrix to the binary matrix for sampling in the training process. One straightforward way used in most previous collaborative ranking models is comparing each score with a predefined threshold. Then all the ratings lower than the threshold are viewed as negative instances, otherwise, positive ones. This transformation is simple but may result in a problem that the threshold may not be suitable for all the users because some users tend to give lower ratings and some prefer scoring highly. Hence, we design a personalized method to overcome this problem, which is shown in the leftmost transformation of Fig. 1. To apply explicit records to the situation of ranking, we divide them into positive and negative sets by the following steps. For each user, we calculate the average value of all his/her ratings as a personalized threshold denoted by $\bar{r}_u$. We then transfer the original rating r_{ui} to the binary value y_{ui} using the following conversion rule,

$$y_{ui} = \begin{cases} +1, & r_{ui} \geq \bar{r}_u \\ -1, & r_{ui} < \bar{r}_u \end{cases}.$$ (1)

Finally, records with $y_{ui} = +1$ are positive samples and added to the set S^P (see entries marked by "+" in Fig. 1), otherwise, negative ones added to the set S^N (see entries marked by "−" in Fig. 1). For the balanced learning, besides these observed negative records, we randomly draw a portion of unobserved records to supplement the negative set where the number of sampled unobserved instances is ρ times that of observed samples, where ρ is a predefined integer number. Therefore, the set of negative samples S^N is composed of two parts, one of which is the observed records with $r_{ui} < \bar{r}_u$ and the other is sampled unobserved records. Notice that for the sampled unobserved pairs (u, i), $y_{ui} = -1$. When training our CCR, we randomly draw a triple (u, i, y_{ui}) from $S^P \cup S^N$ for each iteration.

The second one is the incorporation of preference context. Traditional MF-based models predict the score of a (u, i) pair as the dot product only between u's and i's latent vectors,

$$\hat{r}_{ui} = U_{u.} V_{i.}^T + b_u + b_i + \mu,$$ (2)

where $U_{u.}$ and $V_{i.}$ are latent factors, b_u and b_i are biases, and μ is the global average rating. But in most cases, users make decisions based on the previously purchasing experience rather than considering the target item only. In other words, the opinion on historical items also influences users' future choices. Consequently, we follow MF-MPC [10] and incorporate the preference context into the original prediction rule,

$$\hat{r}_{ui} = (U_{u.} + \bar{U}_{u.}^{\text{MPC}}) V_{i.}^T + b_u + b_i + \mu,$$ (3)

where $\bar{U}_{u\cdot}^{\mathrm{MPC}}$ is the representation of user u's inherent preference context defined as follows [10],

$$\bar{U}_{u\cdot}^{\mathrm{MPC}} = \sum_{r\in\mathbb{M}} \frac{1}{\sqrt{|\mathcal{I}_u^r\backslash\{i\}|}} \sum_{i'\in\mathcal{I}_u^r\backslash\{i\}} M_{i'\cdot}^r, \tag{4}$$

where $M_{i'\cdot}^r$ is the latent vector of item i' with $r_{ui'} = r$.

As we can see from the definition of $\bar{U}_{u\cdot}^{\mathrm{MPC}}$, all contextual items are classified into $|\mathbb{M}|$ groups based on their scores. Compared with calculating the arithmetic mean on those items without classification, the weighted average that grouping items by specific scores used here reduces the bias coming from high frequency values, since the summation of vectors in each group is divided by the group size. That's why the context term is beneficial to modeling users' habit of scoring. Equation(3) can thus be translated as the predicted rating of item i given by user u in the context of $\bar{U}_{u\cdot}^{\mathrm{MPC}}$.

Another issue in designing our CCR is the loss function. For the task of item ranking, we adopt the logistic loss combined with knowledge from both binary records and preference context to minimize the error between the real value and the predictive value, which is formulated as follows,

$$\ell(\hat{r}_{ui}, r_{ui}) = -\log\sigma(y_{ui}\hat{r}_{ui}), \tag{5}$$

where $y_{ui} = 1$ if (u, i, r_{ui}) is a positive instance, otherwise $y_{ui} = -1$.

Finally, the objective function of CCR is as follows,

$$\arg\min_{\Theta} \frac{1}{n} \sum_{u=1}^{n} \sum_{i=1}^{m} \ell(\hat{r}_{ui}, r_{ui}) + reg(u, i), \tag{6}$$

where $reg(u, i) = \frac{\lambda}{2}(\|U_{u\cdot}\|^2 + \|V_{i\cdot}\|^2 + \|b_u\|^2 + \|b_i\|^2 + \sum_{r\in\mathbb{M}}\sum_{i'\in\mathcal{I}_u^r\backslash\{i\}}\|M_{i'\cdot}^r\|^2)$ is the regularization term used to avoid overfitting, and $\Theta = \{U_{u\cdot}, V_{i\cdot}, b_u, b_i, \mu, M_{i'\cdot}^r\}$ are model parameters to be learned, where $u \in \{1,\ldots,n\}$, $i \in \{1,\ldots m\}$ and $r \in \mathbb{M}$.

We apply stochastic gradient descent (SGD) to learn the model and calculate the gradients of the model parameters for a randomly sampled triple of (u, i, y_{ui}). The detailed learning procedure is illustrated in Algorithm 1, which primarily consists of three parts, i.e., initializing the parameters (line 1), converting the ratings (lines 5–11) and training the model (lines 12–20). In particular, we initialize the latent feature vectors and the biases with random numbers for each user and item. Due to the space limitation, we omit equations of the detailed gradient calculation.

The computational complexity of our CCR is quantified as follows. The most time-consuming part is training the model. The time complexity of one iteration is $O(d|\mathbb{M}||S^P \cup S^N|)$ where S^P and S^N are the sets of positive and negative training samples. Since $d|\mathbb{M}|$ is a constant and is much smaller than $|S^P \cup S^N|$, the computation complexity of our CCR increases linearly in the size of $S^P\cup S^N$.

After sufficient training, at the prediction stage, our CCR estimates the preference scores of unobserved items for each user according to Eq.(3) and generates the final candidate list of items with the most highest scores.

Algorithm 1. The algorithm of context-aware collaborative ranking (CCR).

Input: The rating records $\mathcal{R}$.
Output: The learned model parameters Θ.
1: Initialization of all parameters.
2: **for** $u = 1, 2, .., n$ **do**
3:     Calculate the average rating $\bar{r}_u$.
4: **end for**
5: **for** each $(u, i, r_{ui}) \in \mathcal{R}$ **do**
6:     **if** $r_{ui} \geq \bar{r}_u$ **then**
7:         Add $(u, i, +1)$ to S^P.
8:     **else**
9:         Add $(u, i, -1)$ to S^N.
10:     **end if**
11: **end for**
12: **for** $t = 1, 2, .., T$ **do**
13:     Randomly sample $\rho|\mathcal{R}|$ unobserved instances with replacement and add them to S^N.
14:     **for** $t_2 = 1, 2, .., |S^P \cup S^N|$ **do**
15:         Randomly sample a (u, i, y_{ui}) triple.
16:         Calculate $\bar{U}_{u\cdot}^{\mathrm{MPC}}$ via Eq.(4).
17:         Calculate $\hat{r}_{ui}$ via Eq.(3).
18:         Calculate the gradients of b_u, b_i, μ, $U_{u\cdot}$, $V_{i\cdot}$ and $M_{i',\cdot}^r$, $r \in \mathbb{M}$ and update the model parameters accordingly.
19:     **end for**
20: **end for**

---

4   Experiments

4.1   Datasets

We conduct extensive empirical studies on four real-world datasets, i.e., MovieLens 100K (ML100K), MovieLens 1M (ML1M), MovieLens 10M (ML10M) and Neflix, to verify the effectiveness of our CCR, especially of the preference context and the logistic loss function. Ratings of ML10M range in $\mathbb{M} = \{0.5, 1, \ldots, 5\}$, while others are in the scale of $\mathbb{M} = \{1, 2, \ldots, 5\}$. For the Netflix dataset, we randomly draw 50,000 users and use their rating records as our experimental dataset, which is denoted as NF50KU. We do preliminary processing for each dataset as follows. First of all, we divide it into five parts of equal size. Then, we take three of them as the training data and the remaining two as test and validation data, respectively. We repeat these two steps for five times to form five copies of each dataset so that we can report average performance of all the methods. Finally, for each copy, we only keep records with rating 5 in test and validation data. Datasets and code (including all baseline models and our CCR) used in our empirical studies are made publicly available[1].

4.2   Evaluation Metrics

Five widely used metrics are adopted in our experiments to evaluate the ranking performance, including precision, recall, F1, normalized discounted cumulative gain (NDCG) and 1-call. Because a final recommendation list usually contains a small number of items, we report the results of all the methods on these metrics with top-5 items, denoted as Prec@5, Rec@5, F1@5, NDCG@5 and 1-call@5. In particular, NDCG measures the position of items in a candidate list, which means that the higher the relevant items are ranked, the larger NDCG is. So, when comparing ranking algorithms, we mainly focus on NDCG@5.

4.3   Baselines and Parameter Configurations

We implement the following baselines to show that the utilization of preference context and logistic function in our CCR results in remarkable improvements: (i) PMF [7] is a basic matrix factorization based method without the preference context, which is optimized via a square loss function. We use it as the most basic method to verify the effectiveness of both the logistic loss function and the preference context in item ranking. (ii) MF-MPC [10] extends PMF via incorporation of the preference context for rating prediction. We use it to verify that even with the preference context, a method targeting on rating prediction may not address the ranking problem well. (iii) PMF-R replaces the square loss in PMF via a ranking-oriented logistic loss function and adopts the same sampling strategy in our CCR for fair comparison. We use it to verify whether the preference context is helpful in item ranking.

We also compare our CCR with some closely related state-of-the-art item ranking methods, i.e., BPR and ToR, which will be introduced later. Notice that we do not include MERR_SVD++ [4] because it is built on SVD++ which is worse than MF-MPC in the previous work [10].

We utilize SGD to learn the model parameters for both our CCR and the compared baseline methods. We fix the learning parameter $\gamma = 0.01$, the dimension of latent vectors $d = 20$, the sampling size $\rho = 3$ for both our CCR and PMF-R, and select the tradeoff parameter of the regularization term $\lambda \in \{0.001, 0.01, 0, 1\}$, the number of iteration $T \in \{100, 500, 1000\}$ on the validation data of the first copy w.r.t. the NDCG@5 performance. Then, we test the models with the optimal parameters on the corresponding test data with five copies and report the average performance.

4.4   Comparison with Closely Related Methods

We put the main experimental results in Table 3, from which we can have following observations: (i) Overall the results show that our CCR achieves a significant

---

[1]   http://csse.szu.edu.cn/staff/panwk/publications/CCR/.

Table 3. Recommendation performance of our CCR and three closely related methods, i.e., PMF, MF-MPC and PMF-R, on four real-world datasets. The significantly best results are marked in bold.

Dataset	Method	Prec@5	Rec@5	F1@5	NDCG@5	1-call@5
ML100K	PMF	0.0002±0.0002	0.0003±0.0003	0.0002±0.0002	0.0003±0.0002	0.0010±0.0011
	MF-MPC	0.0063±0.0012	0.0043±0.0015	0.0043±0.0010	0.0086±0.0022	0.0258±0.0057
	PMF-R	0.0813±0.0050	0.0904±0.0112	0.0716±0.0057	0.1105±0.0104	0.3204±0.0220
	CCR	**0.1201**±0.0029	**0.1514**±0.0050	**0.1109**±0.0027	**0.1691**±0.0056	**0.4444**±0.0063
ML1M	PMF	0.0001±0.0000	0.0000±0.0000	0.0000±0.0000	0.0001±0.0001	0.0003±0.0002
	MF-MPC	0.0455±0.0039	0.0293±0.0020	0.0294±0.0024	0.0551±0.0047	0.1712±0.0140
	PMF-R	0.0914±0.0019	0.0715±0.0019	0.0652±0.0014·	0.1071±0.0021	0.3409±0.0050
	CCR	**0.1570**±0.0014	**0.1362**±0.0030	**0.1201**±0.0009	**0.1939**±0.0015	**0.5279**±0.0030
ML10M	PMF	0.0220±0.0008	0.0187±0.0007	0.0164±0.0006	0.0297±0.0011	0.0883±0.0028
	MF-MPC	0.0196±0.0006	0.0193±0.0006	0.0158±0.0004	0.0269±0.0007	0.0792±0.0023
	PMF-R	0.0895±0.0006	0.1121±0.0010	0.0821±0.0006	0.1222±0.0006	0.3380±0.0022
	CCR	**0.1335**±0.0008	**0.1817**±0.0007	**0.1280**±0.0007	**0.1909**±0.0006	**0.4809**±0.0015
NF50KU	PMF	0.0369±0.0029	0.0155±0.0012	0.0181±0.0014	0.0421±0.0038	0.1311±0.0080
	MF-MPC	0.0372±0.0028	0.0188±0.0016	0.0201±0.0017	0.0425±0.0033	0.1324±0.0093
	PMF-R	0.0910±0.0005	0.0515±0.0008	0.0519±0.0004	0.1021±0.0006	0.3194±0.0008
	CCR	**0.1389**±0.0009	**0.0968**±0.0008	**0.0887**±0.0006	**0.1640**±0.0008	**0.4566**±0.0022

improvement consistently on ML100K, ML1M, ML10M and NF50KU, which shows the effectiveness of our CCR in addressing the problem of item ranking. (ii) By comparing rating-oriented and ranking-oriented methods, i.e., PMF and PMF-R, MF-MPC and our CCR, the latter uniformly outperforms the former, from which we can draw a conclusion that the square loss can not be directly applied to the ranking scenario and the logistic loss is more suitable. (iii) Methods with preference context, i.e., MF-MPC and our CCR, generally have better performance than models without preference context, i.e., PMF and PMF-R, which suggests that either in rating prediction or item ranking, the preference context contributes to the lifts in recommendation performance.

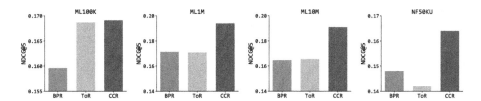

Fig. 2. Recommendation performance of our CCR and two state-of-the-art item ranking methods, i.e., BPR and ToR, on four real-world datasets.

4.5   Comparison with Advanced Ranking-Oriented Methods

In this subsection, we focus on the comparison between our CCR and two very competitive methods, i.e., Bayesian personalized ranking (BPR) [12] and transfer to rank (ToR) [11]. BPR is a factorization-based method with a logistic loss but without preference context. Since BPR only uses records with $r_{ui} = 5$ for training, for fair comparison, we keep the candidate items to be recommended the same as the set of unrated items in ToR and our CCR. ToR is a two-staged transfer learning framework which generates a candidate list by BPR firstly and then refines it by PMF.

We report the results in Fig. 2. We can see that our CCR achieves better performance than both BPR and ToR, which clearly shows the advantage of our CCR in item ranking, in particular of its joint learning of the knowledge from the numerical ratings and the inherent preference context.

5   Conclusions and Future Work

In this paper, we design a novel recommendation model called context-aware collaborative ranking (CCR) for item ranking with explicit feedback. Our CCR adopts a logistic loss function and considers users' interacted items as the inherent preference context in users' behavior modeling. In addition, we design a simple but effective sampling strategy to learn positive and negative knowledge from the explicit feedback. From the empirical studies with the closely related and advanced ranking-oriented recommendation methods on four real-world datasets, we find that our CCR is capable of capturing users' preferences more accurately.

In the future, we plan to explore several exciting directions. Firstly, we are interested in refining the way of utilizing the inherent preference context in our CCR so as to further improve the performance. Secondly, we attempt to study the effectiveness of different loss functions in dealing with the item ranking problem, expecting to provide guidance on choosing a proper loss function in a real application. Finally, we plan to extend our CCR to the paradigms of federated learning [20], deep learning [2] and listwise preference learning [17].

Acknowledgement. We thank the support of National Natural Science Foundation of China Nos. 61872249, 61836005 and 61672358.

References

1. Balakrishnan, S., Chopra, S.: Collaborative ranking. In: Proceedings of the 5th ACM International Conference on Web Search and Data Mining, pp. 143–152 (2012)
2. He, X., Liao, L., Zhang, H., Nie, L., Hu, X., Chua, T.S.: Neural collaborative filtering. In: Proceedings of the 26th International Conference on World Wide Web, pp. 173–182 (2017)
3. Koren, Y.: Factor in the neighbors: scalable and accurate collaborative filtering. ACM Trans. Knowl. Discov. Data **4**(1), 1:1–1:24 (2010)
4. Li, G., Chen, Q.: Exploiting explicit and implicit feedback for personalized ranking. Math. Prob. Eng. **2016** (2016)

5. Linden, G., Smith, B., York, J.: Amazon.com recommendations: item-to-item collaborative filtering. IEEE Internet Comput. **7**(1), 76–80 (2003)
6. Liu, N.N., Yang, Q.: EigenRank: a ranking-oriented approach to collaborative filtering. In: Proceedings of the 31st Annual International ACM SIGIR Conference on Research and Development in Information Retrieval, pp. 83–90 (2008)
7. Mnih, A., Salakhutdinov, R.R.: Probabilistic matrix factorization. In: Proceedings of the 21st International Conference on Neural Information Processing Systems, pp. 1257–1264 (2007)
8. Niu, S., Guo, J., Lan, Y., Cheng, X.: Top-k learning to rank: labeling, ranking and evaluation. In: Proceedings of the 35th International ACM SIGIR Conference on Research and Development in Information Retrieval, pp. 751–760 (2012)
9. Ouyang, Y., Liu, W., Rong, W., Xiong, Z.: Autoencoder-based collaborative filtering. In: Proceedings of the 21st International Conference on Neural Information Processing, pp. 284–291 (2014)
10. Pan, W., Ming, Z.: Collaborative recommendation with multiclass preference context. IEEE Intell. Syst. **32**(2), 45–51 (2017)
11. Pan, W., Yang, Q., Duan, Y., Tan, B., Ming, Z.: Transfer learning for behavior ranking. ACM Trans. Intell. Syst. Technol. **8**(5), 65:1–65:23 (2017)
12. Rendle, S., Freudenthaler, C., Gantner, Z., Schmidt-Thieme, L.: BPR: Bayesian personalized ranking from implicit feedback. In: Proceedings of the 25th Conference on Uncertainty in Artificial Intelligence, pp. 452–461 (2009)
13. Sedhain, S., Menon, A.K., Sanner, S., Xie, L.: AutoRec: autoencoders meet collaborative filtering. In: Proceedings of the 24th International Conference on World Wide Web, pp. 111–112 (2015)
14. Shi, Y., Larson, M., Hanjalic, A.: Unifying rating-oriented and ranking-oriented collaborative filtering for improved recommendation. Inf. Sci. **229**, 29–39 (2013)
15. Wang, S., Sun, J., Gao, B.J., Ma, J.: VSRank: a novel framework for ranking-based collaborative filtering. ACM Trans. Intell. Syst. Technol. **5**(3), 51:1–51:24 (2014)
16. Weimer, M., Karatzoglou, A., Le, Q.V., Smola, A.J.: COFI RANK - maximum margin matrix factorization for collaborative ranking. In: Proceedings of the 21st International Conference on Neural Information Processing Systems, pp. 1593–1600 (2007)
17. Wu, L., Hsieh, C., Sharpnack, J.: SQL-rank: a listwise approach to collaborative ranking. In: Proceedings of the 35th International Conference on Machine Learning, pp. 5311–5320 (2018)
18. Wu, Y., DuBois, C., Zheng, A.X., Ester, M.: Collaborative denoising auto-encoders for top-n recommender systems. In: Proceedings of the 9th ACM International Conference on Web Search and Data Mining, pp. 153–162 (2016)
19. Xue, H.J., Dai, X.Y., Zhang, J., Huang, S., Chen, J.: Deep matrix factorization models for recommender systems. In: Proceedings of the 26th International Joint Conference on Artificial Intelligence, pp. 3203–3209 (2017)
20. Yang, Q., Liu, Y., Chen, T., Tong, Y.: Federated machine learning: concept and applications. ACM Trans. Intell. Syst. Technol. **10**(2), 12:1–12:19 (2019)
21. Zhang, Z., Liu, Y., Zhang, Z., Shen, B.: Fused matrix factorization with multi-tag, social and geographical influences for poi recommendation. World Wide Web **22**(3), 1135–1150 (2019)

Context-Aware Helpfulness Prediction
for Online Product Reviews

Iyiola E. Olatunji[✉], Xin Li, and Wai Lam

Department of Systems Engineering and Engineering Management,
The Chinese University of Hong Kong, Shatin, Hong Kong
{olatunji,lixin,wlam}@se.cuhk.edu.hk

Abstract. Modeling and prediction of review helpfulness has become
more predominant due to proliferation of e-commerce websites and online
shops. Since the functionality of a product cannot be tested before buy-
ing, people often rely on different kinds of user reviews to decide whether
or not to buy a product. However, quality reviews might be buried deep in
the heap of a large amount of reviews. Therefore, recommending reviews
to customers based on the review quality is of the essence. Since there
is no direct indication of review quality, most reviews use the information that "X out of Y" users found the review helpful for obtaining the
review quality. However, this approach undermines helpfulness prediction
because not all reviews have statistically abundant votes. In this paper,
we propose a neural deep learning model that predicts the helpfulness
score of a review. This model is based on convolutional neural network
(CNN) and a context-aware encoding mechanism which can directly capture relationships between words irrespective of their distance in a long
sequence. We validated our model on human annotated dataset and the
result shows that our model significantly outperforms existing models for
helpfulness prediction.

Keywords: Helpfulness prediction · Context-aware · Product review

1 Introduction

Reviews have become an integral part of user's experience when shopping online.
This trend makes product reviews an invaluable asset because they help customers make purchasing decision, consequently, driving sales [7]. Due to the
enormous amount of reviews, it is important to analyze review quality and
to present useful reviews to potential customers. The quality of a review can
vary from a well-detailed opinion and argument, to excessive appraisal, to spam.
Therefore, predicting the helpfulness of a review involves automatic detection of
the influence the review will have on a customer for making purchasing decision.
Such reviews should be informative and self-contained [6].

The work described in this paper is substantially supported by a grant from the
Research Grant Council of the Hong Kong Special Administrative Region, China
(Project Code: 14204418).

F. L. Wang et al. (Eds.): AIRS 2019, LNCS 12004, pp. 56–65, 2020.
https://doi.org/10.1007/978-3-030-42835-8_6

Votes: [1, 8]
HS: 0.13
HAS: 0.85

I received an updated charger as well as the updated replacement power supply due to the recall. It looks as if this has solved all of the problems. I have been using this charger for some time now with no problems. No more heat issues and battery charging is quick and accurate. I can now recommend this charger with no problem. I use this charger several times a week and much prefer it over the standard wall type chargers. I primarily use Enelope batteries with this charger.

Fig. 1. Example of a review text with helpfulness score. **HS** = helpfulness score based on "X of Y approach" while **HAS** = human annotated helpfulness score.

Review helpfulness prediction have been studied using arguments [12], aspects (ASP) [25], structural (STR) and unigram (UGR) features [26]. Also, semantic features such as linguistic inquiry and word count (LIWC), general inquirer (INQ) [26], and Geneva affect label coder (GALC) [14] have been used to determine review helpfulness. However, using handcrafted features is laborious and expensive due to manual feature engineering and data annotation. Recently, convolutional neural networks (CNNs) [10], more specifically, the character-based CNN [5] has been applied to review helpfulness prediction and has shown to out-perform handcrafted features. However, it does not fully capture the semantic representation of the review since different reviewers have different perspective, writing style and the reviewer's language may affect the meaning of the review. That is, the choice of word of an experienced reviewer differs from that of a new reviewer. Therefore, modelling dependency between words is important.

Recent works on helpfulness prediction use the "X of Y approach" i.e. if X out of Y users votes that a review is helpful, then the helpfulness score of the review is X/Y. However, such simple method is not effective as shown in Fig. 1. The helpfulness score (HS = 0.13) implies that the review is unhelpful. However, this is not the case as the review text entails user experience and provides necessary information to draw a reasonable conclusion (self-contained). Hence, it is clear that the review is of high quality (helpful) as pointed out by human annotators (HAS = 0.85). This observation demonstrates that "X of Y" helpfulness score may not strongly correlate to review quality [26] which undermines the effectiveness of the prediction output.

Similarly, prior methods assume that reviews are coherent [5,26]. However, this is not the case in most reviews because of certain content divergence features such as sentiment divergence (opinion polarity of products compared to that of review) embedded in reviews. To address these issues, we propose a model that predicts the helpfulness score of a review by considering the context in which words are used in relation to the entire review. We aim to understand the internal structure of the review text.

In order to learn the internal structure of review text, we learn dependencies between words by taking into account the positional encoding of each word and employing the self-attention mechanism to cater for the length of longer sequences. We further encode our learned representation into CNN to produce an output sequence representation.

In our experiment, our framework outperforms existing state-of-the-art methods for helpfulness prediction on the Amazon review dataset. We conducted detailed experiments to quantitatively evaluate the effectiveness of each designed component of our model. We validated our model on the human annotated data. The code is available (https://github.com/iyempissy/PositionalCNN-for-helpfulness-prediction).

2   Related Works

Previous works on helpfulness prediction can be categorized broadly into three categories (a) score regression (prediction a helpfulness score between 0 and 1) (b) classification (classifying a review as either helpful or not helpful) (c) ranking (ordering reviews based on their helpfulness score). In this paper we define the problem of helpfulness prediction as a regression task. Most studies tend to focus on extracting specific features (handcrafted features) from review text.

Semantic features such as LIWC (linguistic inquiry and word count), general inquirer (INQ) [26], and GALC (Geneva affect label coder) [14] were used to extract meaning from the text to determine the helpfulness of the review. Extracting argument features from review text has shown to outperform semantic features [12] since it provides a more detailed information about the product. Structural (STR) and unigram (UGR) features [26] have also been exploited.

Content-based features such as review text and star rating and context-based features such as reviewer/user information are used for helpfulness prediction task. Content-based features are features that can be obtained from the reviews. They include length of review, review readability, number of words in review text, word-category features and content divergence features. Context-based features are features that can be derived outside the review. This includes reviewer features (profile) and features to capture similarities between users and reviews (user-reviewer Idiosyncrasy). Other metadata such as the probability of a review and its sentences being subjective have been successfully used as features [8,9,17,19,20,22]. Since review text are mostly subjective, it is a more complicated task to model all contributing features for helpfulness prediction. Thus, using handcrafted features has limited capabilities and laborious due to manual data annotation.

Several methods have been applied to helpfulness prediction task including support vector regression [9,26,29], probabilistic matrix factorization [23], linear regression [13], extended tensor factorization models [16], HMM-LDA based model [18] and multi-layer neural networks [11]. These methods allows the integration of robust constraints into the learning process and this in turn has improved prediction result. Recently, convolutional neural network (CNN) has shown significant improvement over existing methods by achieving the state-of-the-art performance [10,28]. CNNs automatically extract deep feature from raw text. This capability can alleviate manual selection of features. Furthermore, adding more levels of abstraction as in character-level representations has further improved prediction results over vanilla CNN. Embedding-gated CNN [3] and multi-domain gated CNN [4] are recent methods for predicting helpfulness prediction.

Moreover, attention mechanism has also been employed to CNN such as the ABCNN for modelling sentence pair [27]. Several tasks including textual entailment, sentence representation, machine translation, and abstractive summarization have applied self-attention mechanism and has shown significant result [1]. However, employing self-attention for developing context-aware encoding mechanism has not been applied to helpfulness prediction. Using self-attention mechanism on review text is quite intuitive because even the same word can have different meaning based on the context in which it is being used.

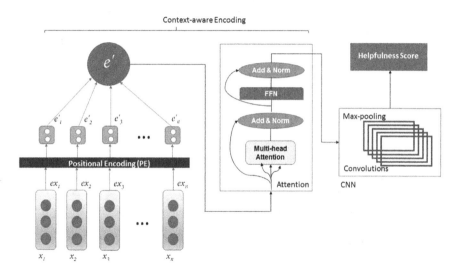

Fig. 2. Proposed context-aware helpfulness prediction model

3   Model

We model the problem of predicting the helpfulness score of a review as a regression problem. Precisely, given a sequence of review, we predict the helpfulness score based on the review text. As shown in Fig. 2, the sequence of words in the review are embedded and concatenated with their respective positional encoding to form the input features. These input features are processed by a self-attention block for generating context-aware representations for all tokens. Then such representation will be fed into a convolutional neural network (CNN) which computes a vector representation of the entire sequence (i.e the dependency between the token and the entire sequence) and then we use a regression layer for predicting the helpfulness score.

3.1 Context-Aware Encoding

The context-aware component of our model consists of positional encoding and self-attention mechanism. We augment the word embedding with positional encoding vectors to learn text representation while taking the absolute position of words into consideration.

Let $X = (x_1, x_2, ..., x_n)$ be a review consisting of a sequence of words. We map each word x_i in a review X to a l-dimensional (word embedding) word vector e_{x_i} stored in an embedding matrix $\mathbf{E} \in \mathbb{R}^{V \times l}$ where V is the vocabulary size. We initialize $\mathbf{E}$ with pre-trained vectors from GloVe [21] and set the embedding dimension l to 100. A review is therefore represented as $Y = (e_{x_1}, e_{x_2}, ..., e_{x_n})$. Since the above representation learns only the meaning of each word, we need the position of each word for understanding the context of each word. Let $S = (s_1, s_2, ..., s_n)$ be the position of each word in a sentence. Inspired by Vaswani et al. [24], the positional encoding, denoted as $PE \in \mathbb{R}^{n \times l}$, is a 2D constant matrix with position specific values calculated by the sine and cosine functions below:

$$PE\left(s_k, 2i\right) = sin\left(s_k/j^{2i/l}\right)$$
$$PE\left(s_k, 2i+1\right) = cos\left(s_k/j^{2i/l}\right) \tag{1}$$

where i is the position along the embedding vector e and j is a constant representing the distance between successive peaks (or successive troughs) of cosine and sine function. This constant is between 2π and 10000. Based on a tuning process, we set j to 1000. The sequence $\overline{P} = (\overline{P_1}, \overline{P_2}, ..., \overline{P_n})$, where $\overline{P_s} = PE(S)$ defined as the row vector corresponding to S in the matrix PE as in Eq. 1.

The final representation e' is obtained by adding the word embedding to the relative position values of each word in the sequence. Therefore, $e' = (e'_1, e'_2, ..., e'_n)$ where $e'_j = (\overline{P_j} + e_{x_j})$.

Self-attention is employed in our model. Given an input e', self-attention involves applying the attention mechanism on each e'_i using e'_i query vector and key-value vector for all other positions. The reason for using the self-attention mechanism is to capture the internal structure of the sentence by learning dependencies between words. The scaled dot-product attention is used which allows faster computation instead of the standard additive attention mechanism [2]. It computes the attention scores by:

$$Attention(Q, K, V) = softmax(\frac{(Q)(K)^T}{\sqrt{l}})V \tag{2}$$

where Q, K and V are the query, key and value matrices respectively. The above equation implies that we divide the dot product of queries with all keys by the key vector dimension to obtain the weight on the values.

We used multi-head attention similar to [24]. The multi-head attention mechanism maps the input vector e' to queries, keys and values matrices by using different linear projections. This strategy allows the self-attention mechanism to be applied h times. Then all the vectors produced by different heads are concatenated together to form a single vector.

Concisely, our model captures context for a sequence as follows: We obtain the relative position of the tokens in the sequence from Eq. 1. The self attention block, learns the context by relating or mapping different positions $s_1, s_2, ..., s_n$ of $\overline{P}$ via Eq. 1 so as to compute a single encoding representation of the sequence. By employing the multi-head attention, our model can attend to words from different encoding representation at different positions. We set heads h to 2. The query, key and value used in the self-attention block are obtained from the output of the previous layer of the context-aware encoding block. This design allows every position in the context-aware encoding block to attend over all positions of the input sequence. To consider positional information in longer sentences not observed in training, we apply the sinusoidal position encoding to the input embedding.

3.2 Convolutional Neural Network (CNN)

The output of the context-aware encoding representation e' is fed into the CNN to obtain new feature representations for making predictions. We employ multiple filters $f \in [1, 2, 3]$. This method is similar to learning uni-gram, bi-gram and tri-gram representations respectively. Specifically, for each filter, we obtain an hidden representation $r = Pool(Conv(e', filterSize(f, l, c)))$ where c is the channel size, $Pool$ is the pooling operation and $Conv(.)$ is the convolution operation. In our experiment, we use max pooling and average pooling. The final representation h is obtained by concatenating all hidden representation. i.e., $h = [r_1, r_2, r_3]$. These features are then passed to the regression layer to produce the helpfulness scores.

4 Dataset

We used two datasets for our experiments. The first dataset called D1 is constructed from the Amazon product review dataset [15]. This dataset consists of over 142 million reviews from Amazon between 1996 to 2014. We used a subset of 21,776,678 reviews from 5 categories, namely; health, electronics, home, outdoor and phone. We selected reviews with over 5 votes as done in [5,26]. The statistics of the dataset used are shown in Table 1. We removed reviews having less than 7 words for experimenting with different filter sizes. Note that this is the largest dataset used for helpfulness prediction task.

The second dataset called D2 is the human annotated dataset from Yang *et al.* [26]. This dataset consists of 400 reviews with 100 reviews selected randomly from four product categories (outdoor, electronics, home and books). The reason for using the human annotated dataset is to verify that our model truly learns deep semantics features of review text. Therefore, our model was not trained on the human annotated dataset but only used for evaluating the effectiveness of our model. We used only three categories for our experiment and performed cross-domain experiment on categories not in D2.

Table 1. Data statistic of Amazon reviews from 5 different categories. We used Health instead of Watches as done by Chen *et al.* [5] because it is excluded from newly published Amazon dataset.

Product category	# of reviews with 5+ votes	Total # of reviews
Phone	261,370	3,447,249
Outdoor	491,008	3,268,695
Health	550,297	2,982,326
Home	749,564	4,253,926
Electronics	1,310,513	7,824,482

5   Experimental Setup

Following the previous works [5, 25, 26], all experiments were evaluated using correlation coefficients between the predicted helpfulness scores and the ground truth scores. We split the dataset D1 into Train/Test/Validation (80, 20, 10). We used the same baselines as state-of-the-art convolutional model for helpfulness prediction [5] i.e. STR, UGR, LIWC, INQ [26], ASP [25]. CNN is the CNN model by [10] and C_CNN is the state-of-the-art character-based CNN from [5]. We added two additional variants (S_Attn and S_Avg) to test different components of our model. S_Attn involves using only self-attention without CNN while S_Avg is self-attention with CNN using average pooling and finally our model uses max pooling with context-aware encoding. We re-implemented all baselines as well as C_CNN as described by [5] but excluded the transfer learning part of their model since it is for tackling insufficient data problem. We used RELU for non-linearity and set dropout rate to 0.5 (for regularization). We used Adaptive moment estimation (Adam) as our optimizer. The learning rate was set to 0.001 and l to 100. We experimented with different filter sizes and found that $f \in [1, 2, 3]$ produces the best result. Also we tried using Recurrent Neural Network (RNN) such as LSTM and BiLSTM but they performed worse than CNN.

6   Results

As shown in Table 2, our context-aware encoding based model using max pooling outperforms all handcrafted features and CNN-based models including C_CNN with a large margin on D1. This is because by applying attention at different positions of the word embedding, different information about word dependencies are

Table 2. Experimental result for the dataset D1

	Phone	Outdoor	Health	Home	Electronics
STR	0.136	0.210	0.295	0.210	0.288
UGR	0.210	0.299	0.301	0.278	0.310
LIWC	0.163	0.287	0.268	0.285	0.350
INQ	0.182	0.324	0.310	0.291	0.358
ASP	0.185	0.281	0.342	0.233	0.366
CNN	0.221	0.392	0.331	0.347	0.411
C_CNN	0.270	0.407	0.371	0.366	0.442
S_Attn	0.219	0.371	0.349	0.358	0.436
S_Avg	0.194	0.236	0.336	0.318	0.382
Ours	**0.373**	**0.461**	**0.428**	**0.402**	**0.475**

Table 3. Experimental result for the dataset D2. (Fusion_all = STR + UGR + LIWC + INQ)

	Outdoor	Home	Electronics
Fusion_all	0.417	0.596	0.461
CNN	0.433	0.521	0.410
C_CNN	0.605	0.592	0.479
Ours	**0.748**	**0.758**	**0.699**

Table 4. Cross-domain comparison

D2	C_CNN	Ours	D1
Home	0.389	**0.586**	Phone
Electronics	0.436	**0.654**	Health

extracted which in turn handles context variation around the same word. However, using self-attention alone (S_Attn) (Table 2) performs poorly than CNN
as learning word dependencies alone is not sufficient for our task. We further
need to understand the internal structure of the review text. Since self-attention
can handle longer sequence length than CNN when modelling dependencies,
we resolve to capturing the dependencies using self-attention and then encode
the dependencies into a vector representation using CNN to further extract the
positional invariant features. Two variants are presented using average pooling
(S_Avg) and max pooling. S_Avg performs comparable to handcrafted features
probably due to its tendency of selecting tokens having low attention scores. Our
proposed model with max-pooling produces the best result on D1 (Table 2) and
significantly on D2 (Table 3) since it selects the best representation with most
attention. It implies that our model can capture the dependency between tokens

and the entire sequence. Likewise, our model understands the internal structure of review and has a high correlation to human score.

Since D2 does not include the cellphone and health category, we tested model trained on the cellphone and electronics category from D1 on the home and health category respectively on D2 and the result is quite surprising (Table 4). This shows that our model can effectively learn cross domain features and is robust to "out-of-vocabulary" (OOV) problem by predicting reasonable helpfulness score.

7   Conclusions

Predicting review helpfulness can substantially save a potential customer's time by presenting the most useful review. In this paper, we propose a context-aware encoding based method that learns dependencies between words for understanding the internal structure of the review.Experimental results on the human annotated data shows that our model is a good estimator for predicting the helpfulness of reviews and robust to the "out-of-vocabulary" (OOV) problem. In the future, we aim to explore some learning to rank models to effectively rank helpfulness score while incorporating some other factors that may affect helpfulness prediction including the types of products.

References

1. Ambartsoumian, A., Popowich, F.: Self-attention: a better building block for sentiment analysis neural network classifiers. In: Proceedings of the 9th Workshop on Computational Approaches to Subjectivity, Sentiment and Social Media Analysis, pp. 130–139 (2018)
2. Bahdanau, D., Cho, K., Bengio, Y.: Neural machine translation by jointly learning to align and translate. In: Proceedings of ICLR, pp. 1–15 (2015)
3. Chen, C., et al.: Review Helpfulness Prediction with Embedding-Gated CNN. arXiv (2018)
4. Chen, C., et al.: Multi-domain gated CNN for review helpfulness prediction. In: Proceedings of WWW, pp. 2630–2636 (2019)
5. Chen, C., Yang, Y., Zhou, J., Li, X., Bao, F.S.: Cross-domain review helpfulness prediction based on convolutional neural networks with auxiliary domain discriminators. In: Proceedings of NAACL-HLT, pp. 602–607 (2018)
6. Diaz, G.O., Ng, V.: Modeling and prediction of online product review helpfulness: a survey. In: Proceedings of ACL, pp. 698–708 (2018)
7. Duan, W., Gu, B., Whinston, A.B.: The dynamics of online word-of-mouth and product sales - an empirical investigation of the movie industry. J. Retail. **84**, 233–242 (2008)
8. Ghose, A., Ipeirotis, P.G.: Estimating the helpfulness and economic impact of product reviews: mining text and reviewer characteristics. IEEE Trans. Knowl. Data Eng. **23**(10), 1498–1512 (2011)
9. Kim, S.M., Pantel, P., Chklovski, T., Pennacchiotti, M.: Automatically assessing review helpfulness. In: Proceedings of EMNLP, pp. 423–430 (2006)

10. Kim, Y.: Convolutional neural networks for sentence classification. In: Proceedings of EMNLP, pp. 1746–1751 (2014)
11. Lee, S., Choeh, J.Y.: Predicting the helpfulness of online reviews using multilayer perceptron neural networks. Expert Syst. Appl. **41**(6), 3041–3046 (2014)
12. Liu, H., et al.: Using argument-based features to predict and analyse review helpfulness. In: Proceedings of EMNLP, pp. 1358–1363 (2017)
13. Lu, Y., Tsaparas, P., Ntoulas, A., Polanyi, L.: Exploiting social context for review quality prediction. In: Proceedings of WWW, pp. 691–700 (2010)
14. Martin, L., Pu, P.: Prediction of helpful reviews using emotions extraction. In: Proceedings of AAAI, pp. 1551–1557 (2014)
15. Mcauley, J., Targett, C., Hengel, A.V.D.: Image-based recommendations on styles and substitutes. In: Proceedings of SIGIR (2015)
16. Moghaddam, S., Jamali, M., Ester, M.: ETF: extended tensor factorization model for personalizing prediction of review helpfulness. In: Proceedings of the Fifth ACM International Conference on Web Search and Data Mining, pp. 163–172 (2012)
17. Mudambi, S.M., Schuff, D.: Research note: what makes a helpful online review? A study of customer reviews on Amazon.com. MIS Quart. **34**(1), 185–200 (2010)
18. Mukherjee, S., Popat, K., Weikum, G.: Exploring latent semantic factors to find useful product reviews. In: Proceedings of the 2017 SIAM International Conference on Data Mining, pp. 480–488 (2017)
19. Otterbacher, J.: 'Helpfulness' in online communities: a measure of message quality. In: Proceedings of the SIGCHI Conference on Human Factors in Computing Systems, pp. 955–964 (2009)
20. Pan, Y., Zhang, J.Q.: Born unequal: a study of the helpfulness of user-generated product reviews. J. Retail. **87**(4), 598–612 (2011)
21. Pennington, J., Socher, R., Manning, C.D.: GloVe: global vectors for word representation. In: Proceedings of EMNLP, pp. 1532–1543 (2014)
22. Salehan, M., Kim, D.J.: Predicting the performance of online consumer reviews: a sentiment mining approach to big data analytics. Decis. Support Syst. **81**, 30–40 (2016)
23. Tang, J., Gao, H., Hu, X., Liu, H.: Context-aware review helpfulness rating prediction. In: Proceedings of the 7th ACM Conference on Recommender Systems (2013)
24. Vaswani, A., et al.: Attention is all you need. In: Proceedings of NIPS (2017)
25. Yang, Y., Chen, C., Bao, F.S.: Aspect-based helpfulness prediction for online product reviews. In: Proceedings of International Conference on Tools with Artificial Intelligence (ICTAI), pp. 836–843 (2016). https://doi.org/10.1109/ICTAI. 2016.0130
26. Yang, Y., Yan, Y., Qiu, M., Bao, F.S.: Semantic analysis and helpfulness prediction of text for online product reviews. In: Proceedings of ACL-IJCNLP, pp. 38–44 (2015)
27. Yin, W., Schutze, H., Xiang, B., Zhou, B.: ABCNN: attention-based convolutional neural network for modeling sentence pairs. Trans. Assoc. Comput. Linguist. **4**, 259–272 (2016)
28. Zhang, X., Zhao, J., LeCun, Y.: Character-level convolutional networks for text classification. In: Proceedings of NIPS, pp. 649–657 (2015)
29. Zhang, Z., Varadarajan, B.: Utility scoring of product reviews. In: Proceedings of the 15th ACM International Conference on Information and Knowledge Management, pp. 51–57 (2006)

LGLMF: Local Geographical Based Logistic Matrix Factorization Model for POI Recommendation

Hossein A. Rahmani[1]([✉]), Mohammad Aliannejadi[2], Sajad Ahmadian[3], Mitra Baratchi[4], Mohsen Afsharchi[1], and Fabio Crestani[2]

[1] University of Zanjan, Zanjan, Iran
{srahmani,afsharchi}@znu.ac.ir
[2] Università della Svizzera Italiana, Lugano, Switzerland
{mohammad.alian.nejadi,fabio.crestani}@usi.ch
[3] Kermanshah University of Technology, Kermanshah, Iran
s.ahmadian@znu.ac.ir
[4] Leiden University, Leiden, The Netherlands
m.baratchi@liacs.leidenuniv.nl

Abstract. With the rapid growth of Location-Based Social Networks, personalized Points of Interest (POIs) recommendation has become a critical task to help users explore their surroundings. Due to the scarcity of check-in data, the availability of geographical information offers an opportunity to improve the accuracy of POI recommendation. Moreover, matrix factorization methods provide effective models which can be used in POI recommendation. However, there are two main challenges which should be addressed to improve the performance of POI recommendation methods. First, leveraging geographical information to capture both the user's personal, geographic profile and a location's geographic popularity. Second, incorporating the geographical model into the matrix factorization approaches. To address these problems, a POI recommendation method is proposed in this paper based on a Local Geographical Model, which considers both users' and locations' points of view. To this end, an effective geographical model is proposed by considering the user's main region of activity and the relevance of each location within that region. Then, the proposed local geographical model is fused into the Logistic Matrix Factorization to improve the accuracy of POI recommendation. Experimental results on two well-known datasets demonstrate that the proposed approach outperforms other state-of-the-art POI recommendation methods.

Keywords: Point-of-Interest · Contextual information · Recommender systems · Location-Based Social Networks

1 Introduction

With the spread of smartphones and other mobile devices, Location-Based Social Networks (LBSNs) have become very popular. Therefore, LBSNs are receiving

© Springer Nature Switzerland AG 2020
F. L. Wang et al. (Eds.): AIRS 2019, LNCS 12004, pp. 66–78, 2020.
https://doi.org/10.1007/978-3-030-42835-8_7

considerable attention not only for users but also from academia and industry. In LBSNs, users can share their experiences via check-ins to Points of Interests (POIs) about locations[1] where they have visited, such as restaurants, tourists spots and stores. Generally, the main task of POI recommendation is to recommend new and interesting POIs to users leading to improve the users' experience.

Much research has addressed POI recommendation by employing traditional recommendation methods such as Matrix Factorization (MF). MF obtains users' and POIs' latent factors based on the user-location frequency matrix, which shows the number of check-ins of users to POIs [8,13]. Due to the lack of check-in data, the MF-based POI recommendation methods suffer from data sparsity problem [1,2,14,19]. This problem refers to the sparsity of the user-POI matrix because the users mainly provide a few check-ins in their history. To address this problem and improve the accuracy of POI recommendation, other contextual information such as geographical, temporal, and categorical have been incorporated in the recommendation process [3,8,16]. The analysis of users' behavior indicates that geographical information has a higher impact on users' preference than other contextual information [6,18,22]. As a consequence, several POI recommendation methods have been proposed considering the geographical context [8,11,12,21]. However, the past work has considered geographical context only from the user's point of view, that is, the geographical influence is based on the distance between the user's location and POIs [8,11,12,21].

In this paper, we propose a new POI recommendation method which takes the geographical context from both users' and locations' perspectives to provide an effective geographical model. To this end, the user's high activity region is considered as the user's point of view for the proposed model. Furthermore, to model the location's point of view, we assume that the more check-ins around an unvisited POI, the less relevant this POI should be for recommendation. Moreover, the proposed geographical model is fused as a novel matrix factorization framework to improve the accuracy of recommendations. For this purpose, the proposed model is added to the logistic matrix factorization approach to propose a novel geographical-based POI recommendation. Experimental results on two real-world datasets demonstrate that considering the proposed geographical model into the matrix factorization approach achieves higher performance compared to other POI recommendation methods. This paper's contributions can be summarized as follows:

- A new geographical model is proposed that considers both of the users' and the locations' perspectives.
- A novel POI recommendation approach is proposed by fusing the geographical model into the logistic matrix factorization approach.
- The sparsity problem is addressed in the proposed method by modeling the geographical influence as an important contextual information.
- Several experiments are conducted on two well-known datasets demonstrating the improvement of the proposed method in the accuracy of POI recommendation compared to other state-of-the-art approaches.

---

[1] In this paper, we use the terms location and POI interchangeably with locations.

The remainder of the paper is organized as follows. The next section introduces relevant prior work on POI recommendation and contextual information. Section 3 gives a detailed introduction about modeling geographical information based on users' and locations' points of view. We conduct experiments and the results are presented in Sect. 4. Finally, we conclude the paper in Sect. 5.

2   Related Work

POI recommendation approaches mainly applies two types of techniques, including memory-based and model-based collaborative filtering into recommendation process. Memory-based approaches use users' check-in data in POI recommendation to predict users' preferences. One of the most important problems of these methods is data sparsity when a large number of elements in check-in data are empty (i.e. they do not provide any information) [14,16]. On the other hand, several previous research is based on model-based approaches such as matrix factorization to improve the accuracy and scalability of POI recommendation [10]. However, since there are a lot of available locations and a single user can visit only a few of them, CF-based approaches often suffer from data sparsity. As a consequence, the user-item matrix of CF becomes very sparse, leading to poor performance in cases where there is no significant association between users and items. Many studies have tried to address the data sparsity problem of CF by incorporating additional information into the model [8,19].

Furthermore, check-in data often include several significant contextual information such as geographical, temporal, categorical, and textual and matrix factorization methods attempt to consider such information to improve the quality of recommendations [4,5,15,17]. Rahmani et al. [17] propose a POI embedding model, CATAPE, that take into account the characteristics of POI by POI categories. CATAPE consists of two modules, Check-in module and Category module, to incorporate the user's sequence behaviour and location's properties.

It has been shown that geographical context is an important factor which considers location changes of users between POIs [16]. Past research has addressed how to model this type of information in recommendation process [8,14,19]. Ye et al. [19], showed that POIs visited by the users follow the Power-law Distribution (PD) when the geographical information is considered. Moreover, they proposed a memory-based CF method which suffers from a scalability problem about large-scale data. Cheng et al. [8] proved that users' check-ins revolve around multiple centers which are captured using a Multi-center Gaussian Model (MGM). Li et al. [14] considered the task of POI recommendation as to the problem of pairwise ranking, where they exploited the geographical information using an extra factor matrix. Zhang et al. [21] proposed a method that considered the geographical influence on each user separately. To this end, a model is proposed based on Kernel Density Estimation (KDE) of the distance distributions between POIs checked-in by each user. Yuan et al. [20] addressed the data sparsity problem assuming that users tend to rank higher the POIs that are geographically closer to the one that they have already visited.

More recently, Aliannejadi et al. [7] propose a two-phase collaborative ranking algorithm for POI recommendation. They push POIs with single or multiple check-ins at the top of the recommendation list, taking into account the geographical influence of POIs in the same neighborhood. They show that both visited, and unvisited POIs in the learning alleviates the sparsity problem. Guo et al. [12] proposed a Location neighborhood-aware Weighted Matrix Factorization (L-WMF) model that incorporate the geographical relationships among POIs to exploit the geographical characteristics from a location perspective.

The previous approaches mainly explored the geographical information from a user's perspective. In comparison to the other POI recommendation models, the method proposed in this paper is based on combining the users' and locations' points of view into a better geographical information model. To this end, the distance between users and POIs (from the user's point of view) and the check-in frequency on neighboring POIs (from the location's point of view) are used in the proposed model. Moreover, we address data sparsity taking into account the influence of POIs' neighbors in the recommendation strategy of our model.

3 Proposed Method

This section presents the proposed POI recommendation method called Local Geographical based Logistic Matrix Factorization (LGLMF). LGLMF consists of two main steps. In the first step, a Local Geographical Model (LGM) is proposed based on both users' and locations' points of view. Then, in the second step, the LGM is fused into a Logistic Matrix Factorization (LMF) approach. The fused matrix factorization model is used to predict the users' preferences. The details of the main steps of the proposed method are provided in the following subsections.

3.1 Local Geographical Model

In this section, the proposed local geographical model is introduced. Let $U = \{u_1, u_2, u_3, ..., u_m\}$ be the set of users and $P = \{p_1, p_2, p_3, ..., p_n\}$ be the set of POIs in a typical LBSN. Then, let $C \in \mathbb{R}^{m \times n}$ be a user-POI check-in frequency matrix with m users and n POIs. The value $c_{up} \in C$ show the check-in frequency of user u to the POI p. Then, the task of personalized top-N POI recommendation problem is formally defined as follows:

Definition 1 (TOP-N POI RECOMMENDATION). *Given a user-POI check-in frequency matrix C and a set of POIs $P^u \subseteq P$ that have been visited by the user u, identify $X = \{p_1, p_2, ..., p_N\}$, a set of POIs ordered based on the probability of a user's visit in the future such that $|X| \leq N$ and $X \cap P^u = \varnothing$.*

The proposed geographical model captures the geographical influence of both users' and locations' points of view. From the user's point of view, the geographical information can be modeled by considering the user's activity region. On the other hand, from the location's point of view, the geographical information can

be modeled as the number of check-ins on the neighbors of a selected POI. Therefore, it can be indicated how agreeable a location is relative to its neighbors. The
pseudo code of the proposed LGM is presented in Algorithm 1. The algorithm is
composed of three inner loops to model the geographical information, the first
two loops model the user's region (lines 2–5) and the third loop calculates the
probability of a user preferring a POI within a neighborhood, considering the
visits to its neighboring POIs (lines 6–10). For modeling the user's region, we
need to find each user's high activity location (in the real world, this could be the
user's residence region). To this end, the user's most frequently checked-in POI
is taken to infer his/her high activity location (line 1). Then, we scan the list
of unvisited POIs to find those that fall in the same region (in-region) for that
user, that is laying within α kilometers from the user's high activity location (the
user's perspective) (line 5). Moreover, based on in-region POIs for each user, we
consider the impact of checked-in neighboring POIs, whose distance is less than
γ meters from the unvisited POIs (the location's perspective) (line 7–10). The
POI locality is defined as follows:

Definition 2 (POI LOCALITY). *Given a set of POIs $P = \{p_1, p_2, ..., p_n\}$, each
p_i ($p_i \in P$) has a POI Locality with respect to user u denoted as p_i^u (Eq. 1),
which is the user $u's$ preference on POI p_i relative to its neighbors.*

$$p_i^u = 1 - \frac{L_p^u}{|P^u|} \tag{1}$$

Here, L_p^u denotes the number of neighbors of p_i visited by user u. Also, $|P^u|$ is
the cardinality of the set of POIs that user u has visited.

3.2   Constructing the Matrix Factorization Model

Traditional recommender systems (RSs) mainly rely on explicit feedback data
as input. The explicit feedback data includes the preferences of users about the
existing items. For example, in Netflix, users can express their preferences about
movies by providing star ratings. Frequently, explicit feedback data does not
exist in LBSNs. Therefore, check-in data can be considered as implicit feedback
data for RSs, forming a different recommendation problem [13].

Johnson in [13] previously proposed a Logistic Matrix Factorization (LMF)
model, achieving a significant result with the implicit feedback dataset of Spotify
music. The LMF takes a probabilistic approach that models the probability of a
user's preference on an item by a logistic function. However, LMF fails to consider contextual information into the recommendation process. In this section,
a novel matrix factorization method is proposed based on LMF by considering the proposed LGM as additional contextual information. Generally, the aim
of MF-based recommendation is to find two low-rank matrices including the
user-factors matrix $V \in \mathbb{R}^{m \times k}$ and item-factors matrix $L \in \mathbb{R}^{m \times k}$ where k is
the number of latent factors such that the inner product of these two matrices
approximate matrix $\hat{C}$, i.e. $\hat{C} = V \times L^T$. Each row of V ($v_u \in V$) represents a

---

Algorithm 1. The Proposed Local Geographical Model

    Input : U, P, α, γ
    Output: user-POI preference matrix $\hat{M}$
    `/* `$\hat{M}$` is a `$U \times P$` matrix, and all elements are intialized by 0.`   `*/`
 1 HAL $\leftarrow$ Find each user's high activity location
    `/* User's most frequently checked-in POI is taken as HAL`   `*/`
 2 **foreach** $u \in U$ **do**
 3   **foreach** $p \in P$ **do**
 4   **if** $p \notin P^u$ **then**
 5   **if** $distance(p, HAL_u) < \alpha$ **then**
 6   **foreach** $p^u \in P^u$ **do**
 7   **if** $distance(p, p^u) < \gamma$ **then**
 8 | $L_p^u \leftarrow L_p^u + 1$
 9   **end**
10                 $\hat{M}[u,p] \leftarrow 1 - \frac{L_p^u}{|P^u|}$ (Eq. 1)
11   **end**
12   **end**
13   **end**
14 **end**
15 **end**
16 **return** $\hat{M}$

---

user's vector of user's behaviour and each row of L ($l_p \in L$) represents the act of item's properties.

Suppose $e_{u,p}$ denotes the number of check-ins by user u on POI p (user u prefers POI p), and the parameters V and L are two latent factors for users and POIs, respectively. Also, consider β_u and β_p as user bias and POI bias. The probability $P(e_{up}|v_u, l_p, \beta_u, \beta_p)$ is defined to represent the preference of user u on POI p as follows:

$$P(e_{up}|v_u, l_p, \beta_u, \beta_p) = \frac{exp(v_u l_p^T + \beta_u + \beta_p)}{1 + exp(v_u l_p^T + \beta_u + \beta_p)} \tag{2}$$

Moreover, the parameters V, L, and β can be learned by solving the following optimization problems:

$$arg\ max_{V,L,\beta}\ logP(V, L, \beta|C) \tag{3}$$

where $logP(V, L, \beta|C)$ is defined as follows:

$$\sum_{u,p} \alpha c_{up}(v_u l_p^T + \beta_u + \beta_p) - (1 + \alpha c_{up})log(1 +$$
$$exp(v_u l_p^T + \beta_u + \beta_p)) - \frac{\lambda}{2}||v_u||^2 - \frac{\lambda}{2}||l_p||^2 \tag{4}$$

Finally, we fuse the proposed LGM (i.e., Algorithm 1) into the matrix factorization method. Therefore, the probability of a user u visiting a POI p can be calculated as follows:

$$Preference_{up} = P(e_{up}|v_u, l_p, \beta_u, \beta_p) \times \hat{M}(u, p) \tag{5}$$

where $P(e_{up}|v_u, l_p, \beta_u, \beta_p)$ is calculated by Eq. 2 and $\hat{M}(u, p)$ is calculated by Algorithm 1. A list of POI recommendations can be provided for each user by using the proposed probability function (i.e. Eq. 5). It should be noted that, differently from the LMF method, the proposed LGLMF model considers the contextual information into the recommendation process by fusing the proposed LGM.

4 Experiments

In this section, several experiments are conducted to compare the performance of LGLMF with the other POI recommendation methods. The details of the experiments are discussed in the following subsections.

4.1 Experimental Settings

Datasets. We evaluated the algorithms using two real-world check-in datasets[2] collected from Gowalla and Foursquare [16]. Gowalla includes check-ins from February 2009 to October 2010, while Foursquare includes check-in data from April 2012 to September 2013. Each check-in contains a user, a POI (latitude and longitude), and the check-in timestamp. Users with less than 15 check-in POIs and POIs with less than ten visitors have been removed from Gowalla. On the other hand, users with less than ten check-in POIs and also POIs with less than ten visitors have been removed from Foursquare. The statistical details of the datasets are presented in Table 1.

Table 1. Statistics of the evaluation datasets

Datasets	#Users	#POIs	#Check-ins	Sparsity
Gowalla	5,628	31,803	620,683	99.78%
Foursquare	7,642	28,483	512,523	99.87%

Evaluation Metrics. Three ranking-based evaluation metrics including Pre@N (Precision at N), Rec@N (Recall at N), and nDCG@N with $N \in \{10, 20\}$ are used to evaluate the performance of the recommendation methods. *Pre@N* refers to the ratio of recovered POIs to the N recommended POIs and *rec@N* refers to the ratio of recovered POIs to the number of POIs predicted by

---

[2] http://spatialkeyword.sce.ntu.edu.sg/eval-vldb17/.

the recommendation model. Moreover, $nDCG@N$ is a measure to indicate the ranking quality of the recommendation models. We partition each dataset into training data, validation data, and test data. For each user, we use the earliest 70% check-ins as the training data, the most recent 20% check-ins as the test data and the remaining 10% as the validation data. We determine the statistically significant differences using the two-tailed paired t-test at a 95% confidence interval ($p < 0.05$).

Comparison Methods. The proposed LGLMF model is compared with the POI recommendation approaches that consider geographical influence in the recommendation process. Moreover, the POI recommendation models which are based on the geographical information from the locations' points of view are considered in the experiments. The details of the compared methods are listed as follows:

- LMF [13]: A Logistic Matrix Factorization method that incorporates a logistic function.
- PFMMGM [8]: A method based on the observation that user's check-in around several centers, that applies Multi-center Gaussian Model (MGM) to study user's behavior.
- LRT [9]: A model that incorporates temporal information in a latent ranking model and learns the user's preferences to locations at each time slot.
- PFMPD: A method using the Power-law Distribution [19] that model people tend to visit nearby POIs. We integrate this model with the Probabilistic Factor Model (PFM).
- LMFT [18]: A method that considers a user's recent activities as more important than their past activities and multiple visits to a location, as indicates of a stronger preference for that location.
- iGLSR[3] [21]: A method that personalizes social and geographical influence on location recommendation using a Kernel Density Estimation (KDE) approach.
- L-WMF [12]: A location neighborhood-aware weighted probabilistic matrix factorization (L-WMF) model that incorporates the geographical relationships among POIs into the WMF as regularization to exploit the geographical characteristics from a location perspective.
- LGLMF[4]: Our proposed method that fused LMF with the proposed local geographical model.

Parameter Settings. For the baseline methods, the parameters are initialized as reported in the corresponding papers. We set the latent factors parameter as $k = 30$ for LMF, PFM, L-WMF. For PFGMGM, we set the distance threshold d to 15 and the frequency control parameter α to 0.2 based on the original paper.

---

[3] We evaluate iGLSR only on Gowalla as we do not have access to the social data of the Foursquare dataset.

[4] https://github.com/rahmanidashti/LGLMF.

Table 2. Performance comparison with baselines in terms of Pre@k, Rec@k, and nDCG@k for $k \in \{10, 20\}$ on Gowalla and Foursquare. The superscript † denotes significant improvements compared to baselines ($p < 0.05$).

Dataset	Method	Metrics					
		Pre@10	Pre@20	Rec@10	Rec@20	nDCG@10	nDCG@20
Gowalla	LMF	0.0328	0.0272	0.0325	0.0534	0.0167	0.0159
	PFMMGM	0.0240	0.0207	0.0258	0.0442	0.0140	0.01440
	LRT	0.0249	0.0182	0.0220	0.0321	0.0105	0.0093
	PFMPD	0.0217	0.0184	0.0223	0.0373	0.0099	0.0101
	LMFT	0.0315	0.0269	0.0303	0.0515	0.0157	0.0150
	iGLSR	0.0297	0.0242	0.0283	0.0441	0.0153	0.0145
	L-WMF	0.0341	0.0296	0.0351	0.0582	0.0183	0.0178
	LGLMF	**0.0373**†	**0.0317**†	**0.0383**†	**0.0629**†	**0.0212**†	**0.0208**†
Foursquare	LMF	0.0228	0.0189	0.0342	0.0565	0.0136	0.0148
	PFMMGM	0.0170	0.0150	0.0283	0.0505	0.0109	0.0126
	LRT	0.0199	0.0155	0.0265	0.0425	0.0117	0.0124
	PFMPD	0.0214	0.0155	0.0290	0.0426	0.0124	0.0128
	LMFT	0.0241	0.0194	0.0359	0.0568	0.0150	0.0161
	L-WMF	0.0248	0.0197	0.0387	0.0591	0.0162	0.0174
	LGLMF	**0.0266**	**0.0213**†	**0.0424**†	**0.0678**†	**0.0175**	**0.0192**†

For LRT, we set T as temporal states to 24 and the α and β as regularization parameters to 2.0. We tune the LGLMF parameters based on the validation data. We find the optimal values for the parameters using the validation data and use them in the test data.

4.2   Performance Comparison

Table 2 shows the results of experiments based on the Gowalla and Foursquare datasets. As you can see from these results, LGLMF obtains higher accuracy than the other POI recommendation methods based on both of the datasets. Therefore, it can be concluded that incorporating the contextual information into the matrix factorization leads to improve the quality of POI recommendation. In comparison to PFMPD, PFMMGM, and iGLSR as the three basic approaches in modeling the geographical influence, LGLMF achieves better results for both datasets based on all metrics. Among these baselines, iGLSR performs better. This is because iGLSR models geographical influence based on each user's behavior. It should be noted that previous models only consider the user's point of view for the geographical influence. Also, our proposed model outperforms the L-WMF that is state-of-the-art model that uses location's prospective geographical information. Compared to the state-of-the-art method, L-WMF, the improvements in terms Rec@20 and nDCG@20 on Gowalla are 8% and 15%, respectively. Therefore, the results confirm the effectiveness of our LGM model,

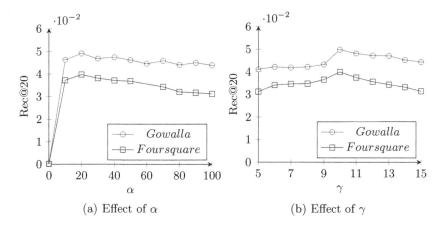

(a) Effect of α (b) Effect of γ

Fig. 1. Effect of different model parameters on the performance of LGLMF

which considers both of the users' and the locations' points of view in modeling the geographical influence.

Impact of Number of Visited POIs. Table 3 shows Rec@20 and nDCG@20 of all models based on different percentages of POIs that each user has visited in the training data. These results indicate that LGLMF achieves the highest accuracy in comparison to the other recommendation models for different number of POIs. Therefore, it is shown that LGLMF can address the sparsity problem where the training data is not enough to provide reliable recommendations. Also, we observe a more robust behavior of LGLMF compared to the baselines. Thus, the proposed local geographical model enables LGLMF to deal with noise and data sparsity effectively. This is clearer when LGLMF outperforms other methods with a larger margin in terms of Rec@20.

Impact of α and γ. Figure 1 shows the performance of LGLMF based on different values of α and γ. In Fig. 1a, the effect of different α values on the performance of LGLMF is reported based on Rec@20 metric. As you can see from these results, the optimal value of α for both Gowalla and Foursquare datasets is 20. Figure 1b shows the effect of different γ values on the performance of LGLMF based on Gowalla and Foursquare. It can be seen that the optimal value of γ for both datasets is 10. These results show that users tend to visit near locations and they make a region from their high activity location.

Model Flexibility. Our proposed geographical model can be easily fused to other POI recommendation models to improve their prediction quality. As shown in Table 4, the proposed local geographical model is added to other models to show its impact on accuracy improvement. To this end, the proposed model is added to the LRT and PFM methods, and their performances are compared

Table 3. Effect on Rec@20 and nDCG@20 of different number of POIs that users visited as training data on Gowalla and Foursquare. The superscript † denotes significant improvements compared to all baselines ($p < 0.05$).

Dataset	Method	Rec@20			nDCG@20		
		40%	60%	80%	40%	60%	80%
Gowalla	LMF	0.0205	0.0333	0.0455	0.0058	0.0095	0.0129
	PFMMGM	0.0350	0.0376	0.0414	0.0094	0.0107	0.0120
	LRT	0.0014	0.0318	0.0300	0.0003	0.0098	0.0083
	PFMPD	0.0235	0.0323	0.0346	0.0064	0.0093	0.0088
	LMFT	0.0205	0.0321	0.0426	0.0057	0.0088	0.0119
	iGLSR	0.0317	0.0357	0.0405	0.0097	0.0105	0.0128
	L-WMF	0.0382	0.0435	0.0471	0.0099	0.0110	0.0142
	LGLMF	**0.0479**†	**0.0533**†	**0.0580**†	**0.0137**†	**0.0158**†	**0.0187**†
Foursquare	LMF	0.0180	0.0266	0.0442	0.0048	0.0073	0.0122
	PFMMGM	0.0451	0.0466	0.0491	0.0097	0.0107	0.0120
	LRT	0.0402	0.0434	0.0438	0.0118	0.0125	0.0125
	PFMPD	0.0371	0.0389	0.0412	0.0117	0.0119	0.0124
	LMFT	0.0180	0.0288	0.0418	0.0049	0.0077	0.0112
	L-WMF	0.0473	0.0492	0.0537	0.0119	0.0131	0.0142
	LGLMF	**0.0500**†	**0.0578**†	**0.0660**†	**0.0126**	**0.0154**†	**0.0189**†

Table 4. Comparison of model flexibility with the related baselines in terms of Pre@20, Rec@20, and nDCG@20 on Gowalla and Foursquare. The superscript † denotes significant improvements compared to related baselines ($p < 0.05$).

Method	Gowalla			Foursquare		
	Pre@20	Rec@20	nDCG@20	Pre@20	Rec@20	nDCG@20
PFMPD	0.0184	0.0373	0.0101	0.0155	0.0426	0.0128
PFMMGM	0.0207	0.0442	0.0144	0.0150	0.0505	0.0126
PFMLGM	**0.0309**†	**0.0588**†	**0.0197**	**0.0198**†	**0.0639**†	**0.0193**
LRT	0.0182	0.0321	0.0093	0.0155	0.0425	0.0124
LRTLGM	**0.0330**†	**0.0616**†	**0.0224**†	**0.0230**†	**0.0717**†	**0.0234**†

with the original models. Table 4 indicates that our geographical model has a positive impact on the performance of other POI recommendation models.

5   Conclusions

In this paper, we proposed a novel Local Geographical model for POI recommendation to consider both users' and locations' point of view of geographical information. We incorporated the user's preference by Logistic Matrix Factorization and proposed a fused matrix factorization method to include the geographical information captured by our proposed Local Geographical model. Experimental results on two well-known datasets showed that the proposed method outperforms other state-of-the-art approaches through leveraging more conditions in the geographical information than competitive models. Also, in Sect. 4.2, we showed that LGM can be joint to other model and improve their recommendation process. Our future work will investigate how to incorporate other contextual information to our model like for example social and temporal information.

References

1. Ahmadian, S., Afsharchi, M., Meghdadi, M.: A novel approach based on multi-view reliability measures to alleviate data sparsity in recommender systems. Multimedia Tools Appl. **78**, 1–36 (2019)
2. Ahmadian, S., Meghdadi, M., Afsharchi, M.: A social recommendation method based on an adaptive neighbor selection mechanism. Inf. Process. Manag. **54**(4), 707–725 (2018)
3. Aliannejadi, M., Crestani, F.: Venue appropriateness prediction for personalized context-aware venue suggestion. In: Proceedings of the 40th International ACM SIGIR Conference on Research and Development in Information Retrieval, pp. 1177–1180. ACM (2017)
4. Aliannejadi, M., Crestani, F.: Personalized context-aware point of interest recommendation. ACM Trans. Inf. Syst. **36**(4), 45 (2018)
5. Aliannejadi, M., Mele, I., Crestani, F.: User model enrichment for venue recommendation. In: Ma, S., et al. (eds.) AIRS 2016. LNCS, vol. 9994, pp. 212–223. Springer, Cham (2016). https://doi.org/10.1007/978-3-319-48051-0_16
6. Aliannejadi, M., Rafailidis, D., Crestani, F.: A collaborative ranking model with multiple location-based similarities for venue suggestion. In: Proceedings of the 2018 ACM SIGIR International Conference on Theory of Information Retrieval, pp. 19–26. ACM (2018)
7. Aliannejadi, M., Rafailidis, D., Crestani, F.: A joint two-phase time-sensitive regularized collaborative ranking model for point of interest recommendation. IEEE Trans. Knowl. Data Eng. (2019)
8. Cheng, C., Yang, H., King, I., Lyu, M.R.: Fused matrix factorization with geographical and social influence in location-based social networks. In: Twenty-Sixth AAAI Conference on Artificial Intelligence (2012)
9. Gao, H., Tang, J., Hu, X., Liu, H.: Exploring temporal effects for location recommendation on location-based social networks. In: Proceedings of the 7th ACM Conference on Recommender Systems, pp. 93–100. ACM (2013)
10. Griesner, J.B., Abdessalem, T., Naacke, H.: POI recommendation: towards fused matrix factorization with geographical and temporal influences. In: Proceedings of the 9th ACM Conference on Recommender Systems, pp. 301–304. ACM (2015)
11. Guo, L., Jiang, H., Wang, X.: Location regularization-based poi recommendation in location-based social networks. Information **9**(4), 85–95 (2018)
12. Guo, L., Wen, Y., Liu, F.: Location perspective-based neighborhood-aware poi recommendation in location-based social networks. Soft. Comput. **23**, 1–11 (2019)
13. Johnson, C.C.: Logistic matrix factorization for implicit feedback data. In: Advances in Neural Information Processing Systems, vol. 27 (2014)

14. Li, X., Cong, G., Li, X.L., Pham, T.A.N., Krishnaswamy, S.: Rank-GeoFM: a ranking based geographical factorization method for point of interest recommendation. In: Proceedings of the 38th International ACM SIGIR Conference on Research and Development in Information Retrieval, pp. 433–442. ACM (2015)
15. Liu, X., Liu, Y., Aberer, K., Miao, C.: Personalized point-of-interest recommendation by mining users' preference transition. In: Proceedings of the 22nd ACM International Conference on Information and Knowledge Management, pp. 733–738. ACM (2013)
16. Liu, Y., Pham, T.A.N., Cong, G., Yuan, Q.: An experimental evaluation of point-of-interest recommendation in location-based social networks. Proc. VLDB Endow. **10**(10), 1010–1021 (2017)
17. Rahmani, H.A., Aliannejadi, M., Zadeh, R.M., Baratchi, M., Afsharchi, M., Crestani, F.: Category-aware location embedding for point-of-interest recommendation. In: International Conference on the Theory of Information Retrieval. ACM (2019)
18. Stepan, T., Morawski, J.M., Dick, S., Miller, J.: Incorporating spatial, temporal, and social context in recommendations for location-based social networks. IEEE Trans. Comput. Soc. Syst. **3**(4), 164–175 (2016)
19. Ye, M., Yin, P., Lee, W.C., Lee, D.L.: Exploiting geographical influence for collaborative point-of-interest recommendation. In: Proceedings of the 34th International ACM SIGIR Conference on Research and Development in Information Retrieval, pp. 325–334. ACM (2011)
20. Yuan, F., Jose, J.M., Guo, G., Chen, L., Yu, H., Alkhawaldeh, R.S.: Joint geo-spatial preference and pairwise ranking for point-of-interest recommendation. In: Proceedings of 28th International Conference on Tools with Artificial Intelligence, pp. 46–53. IEEE (2016)
21. Zhang, J.D., Chow, C.Y.: iGSLR: personalized geo-social location recommendation: a kernel density estimation approach. In: Proceedings of the 21st ACM SIGSPATIAL International Conference on Advances in Geographic Information Systems, pp. 334–343. ACM (2013)
22. Zhang, J.D., Chow, C.Y.: GeoSoCa: exploiting geographical, social and categorical correlations for point-of-interest recommendations. In: Proceedings of the 38th International ACM SIGIR Conference on Research and Development in Information Retrieval, pp. 443–452. ACM (2015)

IR Models

On the Pluses and Minuses of Risk

Rodger Benham[1]([⊠])[iD], Alistair Moffat[2][iD], and J. Shane Culpepper[1][iD]

[1] RMIT University, Melbourne, Australia
rodger.benham@rmit.edu.au
[2] The University of Melbourne, Melbourne, Australia

Abstract. Evaluating the effectiveness of retrieval models has been a mainstay in the IR community since its inception. Generally speaking, the goal is to provide a rigorous framework to compare the quality of two or more models, and determine which of them is the "better". However, defining "better" or "best" in this context is not a simple task. Computing the average effectiveness over many queries is the most common approach used in Cranfield-style evaluations. But averages can hide subtle trade-offs in retrieval models – a percentage of the queries may well perform worse than a previous iteration of the model as a result of an optimization to improve some other subset. A growing body of work referred to as *risk-sensitive evaluation*, seeks to incorporate these effects. We scrutinize current approaches to risk-sensitive evaluation, and consider how risk and reward might be recast to better account for human expectations of result quality on a query by query basis.

1 Introduction

Risk measures have emerged in IR in response to the goal of improving a system without negatively impacting the user's experience of the system's overall effectiveness. This is an issue because measured effectiveness is usually volatile across both systems and topics. That is, selecting one system over another because it has a higher mean effectiveness could be *risky*, as the mean may well disguise substantial variability of the system effectiveness across the range of queries. Several approaches have been proposed to quantitatively measure the tension between risk and reward: URisk [6,24], TRisk [10], ZRisk and GeoRisk [9].

Common to all of these is that they measure risk-reward trade-offs piecewise, with effectiveness decreases penalized by a linear factor, and hence with the "loss" rate for small erosions in effectiveness the same as for the rate for wholesale decreases. Previous studies have demonstrated that users are unable to discern small changes in effectiveness scores, so an interesting question is whether small losses should count as much as large losses. For example, Allan et al. [2] observe that bpref effectiveness and recall follow an S-shaped pattern, where there is a "large intermediary region in which the utility difference is not significant". Similar effects have been observed in the field of economics, and the application of an S-shaped weighting function for modeling the psychological value of monetary gains and losses has been proposed by Tversky and Kahneman [20], with losses

F. L. Wang et al. (Eds.): AIRS 2019, LNCS 12004, pp. 81–93, 2020.
https://doi.org/10.1007/978-3-030-42835-8_8

perceived as being twice as costly in a negative sense as similar-sized gains are in a positive sense. In IR-related experimentation, Turpin and Scholer [19] found that the only reliable signal of whether retrieval effectiveness scores impacted task performance was precision at depth one.

Here we explore whether an S-shaped risk function that strongly weights outliers produces different system orderings than the linear risk function that is embedded in all current proposals. If that were the case, running a user study to ascertain the shape of the applicable trade-off function for the IR domain would be an important next step in improving risk measures. We also take a broader view of the meaning of "risk", and in doing so, conclude that current terminology is potentially ambiguous and can be improved. In response, we propose changes to how practitioners discuss risk-based trade-offs, and further suggest reversing the sign of risk-inclusive evaluation results when they are reported.

2   Background

In an investment portfolio, risk (sometimes known as "beta") is compared against expected gain (referred to as "alpha") to distinguish between investment options that are safe and reliable but low return, and more speculative options that are potentially high-return, but also have a higher probability of leading to losses. Risk can be spread in this context, with a portfolio as a whole being acceptable if it makes the expected level of return, even if some components within it perform poorly. In IR, however, a user may abandon a search service that returns rankings of variable quality [22], even if its overall "mean" behavior is better than that of its competitors. Collins-Thompson [8] first demonstrated the utility of incorporating risk measures used by economists in IR evaluation, borrowing from the practice of forming risk-reward curves. In experiments in which the risk function counted the number of relevant documents lost due to query expansion failure, Collins-Thompson showed that two systems with the same mean effectiveness might possess "very different risk profiles."

Wang and Zhuhan [23] used a mean-variance approach to perform risk-sensitive retrieval, by modifying the language modeling formula to accept a parameter b to indicate the risk preference of the user, with the document selection problem modeled similarly to the investment selection technique of portfolio theory. The key idea is that if the documents at the head of the SERP are similar, and one is not relevant, then they all might be poor choices. Risk is then spread by diversifying the elements at the head of the result list. Although Wang and Zhuhan did not define a measure that could be used to instrument risk-reward profiles, their approach is an example of how lessons learned in economics might be applied in a retrieval model to accomplish a similar goal.

Wang et al. [24] proposed an approach for quantitatively measuring risk based on the differences in scores. The approach was later used in the TREC 2013 and 2014 Web Tracks under the alias URisk [6,7], which was adopted more readily than the original name, T_α. To calculate URisk, an experimental system is compared against a baseline system using the formula:

$$URisk_\alpha = (1/c) \cdot \left[\sum Wins - (1 + \alpha) \cdot \sum Losses \right], \qquad (1)$$

where a "win" is a case where the difference in score is positive for the experimental system, and a "loss" is the reverse, and where c is the number of paired comparisons. The parameter α is user-selected, and linearly scales the relative impact of losses, so that the computed value is an adjusted mean difference. Positive URisk values indicate that the experimental system comes out ahead on balance, conversely, negative values are indicative of risk. The URisk formula can be used as a cost function in learning-to-rank [24].

The TREC evaluation exercises demonstrated the practical applicability of using the URisk measure, which led to several alternative formulations of risk-sensitivity. An issue with URisk values was that although it was clear when an experimental system survived the risk threshold, it was unclear whether it was statistically significant. Dinçer et al. [10] proposed TRisk to solve this problem, which is a studentized version of URisk that can be used to perform an inferential risk and reward analysis between two systems, defined as:

$$TRisk_\alpha = URisk_\alpha / SE(URisk_\alpha), \qquad (2)$$

where SE is the standard error of the URisk sampling distribution. Like URisk, TRisk compares an experimental system against a baseline system, but computes a t-value which incorporates both mean and variance. When $t < -2.0$ (two standard errors), changing to the experimental system would give rise to significant risk, and when $t > 2.0$, a change to the experimental system would allow a significant reward.

Rather than a pair of systems, empirical studies often compare multiple systems. For example, Zhang et al. [28] propose a graphical evaluation approach to assess the bias-variance relationship of various query expansion models. Dinçer et al. [11] argue that unless the experimental method seeks to directly improve the reference model, it may not be reasonable to use just one baseline, especially if the baseline itself has a volatile effectiveness profile. Zhang et al. [27] apply the methods of Zhang et al. [28] to graphically evaluate the risk profiles of multiple TREC systems, and show that this can be done in an unbiased way. Dinçer et al. [9] propose an analytical method ZRisk to accommodate comparisons in terms of the risk and reward of a system against multiple baselines. A matrix of system and topic scores is used:

$$ZRisk(s_i, \alpha) = \sum_{q \in Q^+} \frac{x_{ij} - e_{ij}}{s_{ij}} + (1 + \alpha) \cdot \sum_{q \in Q^-} \frac{x_{ij} - e_{ij}}{s_{ij}}, \qquad (3)$$

as a form of weighted standardization [25] in which both wins and losses are scaled, with the expected values of cells based on both systems *and* topics. To normalize all of the scores to produce a fair comparison, the mean effectiveness and ZRisk are combined to produce the final result:

$$GeoRisk(s_i, \alpha) = \sqrt{Effectiveness(s_i) \cdot \Phi(ZRisk_\alpha / c)}. \qquad (4)$$

Here Φ is the cumulative distribution function of the standard normal distribution, which is used to ensure that ZRisk scores are in $[0, 1]$. That is, GeoRisk values combine information about mean, variance, and shape with respect to many baselines.

3   Broad Issues with Trade-Off Measures

The previous section discussed several quantitative risk measures. We now discuss a number of factors that are common to all of these approaches: the-user defined α parameter; the $(\alpha + 1)$ scalar component; and their naming.

The α Trade-Off Parameter. The α parameter scales the impact of losses relative to the baseline, with a range of different values employed in experimentation. Table 1 lists the α parameters used in a sample of ten papers that employed risk measures as part of their experimental regime. As risk evaluation goals to date have been driven more by experimental care (and caution) than by the measured experience of a cohort of users, it is unsurprising that a spread of α parameters has emerged, with no single value identified as the "reference" setting. Nevertheless, the use of different parameters makes comparing mechanisms a challenge across papers. A plausible solution for α selection, in line with the human experience of risk and reward, is to look to behavioral economics. Tversky and Kahneman [20] argue that to "break-even" in terms of perceived monetary gains and losses, individuals must earn twice as much from a "win" as they lose in a "loss", suggesting that $\alpha = 1$ be regarded as being a useful reference point. The obvious caveat here is that financial investments are quite different to IR effectiveness. User studies would need to be run to verify how closely related the user perception is of retrieval effectiveness loss to monetary loss. Similar prospect theory experiments have been carried out that explore whether gains and losses of time are perceptually similar to gains and losses of money [1,12].

The "Plus One" Loss Scalar. If, as conjectured, a loss should count twice as much as a gain, one might conclude that $\alpha = 2$ should be chosen, in accordance with the way that scalar coefficients are employed in a range of other ways in

Table 1. Differing sets of α employed for risk evaluation.

α	Citations
1, 5, 10	Collins-Thompson et al. [6], Dinçer et al. [11], Sousa et al. [18], Benham and Culpepper [3]
5	Collins-Thompson et al. [7], McCreadie et al. [17]
2	Gallagher et al. [13], Benham et al. [4]
1, 5, 10, 20	Dinçer et al. [9]
1, 2, 3, 4	Hashemi and Kamps [14]

IR evaluation. In fact, the definitions that have evolved employ $\alpha = 2$ to mean that losses incur a *three*-fold penalty, and that $\alpha = 1$ is the correct value to use when losses have twice the cost of a similar-magnitude gain. Similar, the use of $\alpha = 0.5$ does *not* imply that losses have half the weight of gains. Given the challenge of explaining in prose how the losses are being scaled (often in the experimental sections of research papers where space is a perennial issue), users of these measures are likely to make mistakes, as are their readers. Liu et al. [16] comment on the risks associated with such "off by one" errors.

Naming. If the output of (for example) URisk is positive, the sum of the rewards is greater than the sum of the α-scaled losses. That is, numerically "high" risk scores are desirable, but in English expression, have connotations that are oppo-site to that. Similarly, it is equally confusing (and hence "risky" in a commu-nications sense) to have numerically low (or negative) risk score values be an indication that a new system is yielding volatile scores and needs to be treated with caution.

Suggested Changes. We propose that URisk be renamed to URisk$^-$ (or U$^-$), and (compare with Eq. 1) be computed as

$$URisk^- = -(1/c) \cdot \left[\sum Wins - \hat{\alpha} \cdot \sum Losses \right].$$ (5)

Additionally, we suggest that TRisk be replaced by TRisk$^-$ (or T$^-$):

$$TRisk^- = URisk^- / SE(URisk^-),$$ (6)

and that ZRisk be subsumed by ZRisk$^-$ (or Z$^-$):

$$ZRisk^-(s_i, \hat{\alpha}) = -1 \cdot \left[\sum_{q \in Q^+} \frac{x_{ij} - e_{ij}}{s_{ij}} + \hat{\alpha} \cdot \sum_{q \in Q^-} \frac{x_{ij} - e_{ij}}{s_{ij}} \right].$$ (7)

Finally, GeoRisk becomes GeoRisk$^-$ (or Geo$^-$), calculated as:

$$GeoRisk^-(s_i, \hat{\alpha}) = \sqrt{Effectiveness(s_i) \cdot \Phi(ZRisk^-/c)}.$$ (8)

In these revised definitions the signs have been reversed, and the $(\alpha + 1)$ compo-nent has been replaced by a more conventional scalar, denoted as $\hat{\alpha}$ to distinguish it from α, with $\hat{\alpha} = 1 + \alpha$. We plan to use these revised definitions in our own future work, and encourage others to also adopt them.

4   Smooth Value Functions

This section explores a different question – whether, if differences in effectiveness are weighted greater for outliers, meaningful changes are detected in system rankings compared to the current linearly weighted risk-sensitive models.

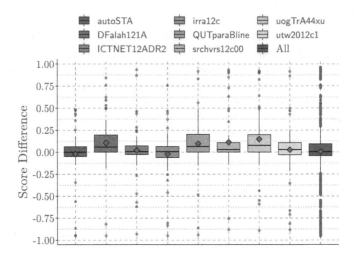

Fig. 1. Differences in ERR@20 for eight systems relative to the indriCASP baseline, for the TREC 2012 Web Track corpus. The "All" boxplot contains the score differences against all submitted runs to the track. Diamonds indicates the arithmetic means.

We follow Dinçer et al. [9] and past risk-sensitive evaluations, and use the run indriCASP as a baseline [6] to compute ERR@20 on the 2013 TREC Web Track corpus, where the systems evaluated against are the 48 runs submitted to the 2012 TREC Web Track. Also adopted from the methodology of Dinçer et al. [9] is the tabulation of risk comparisons against the most effective submitted run per research group, a total set of eight runs. The ERR@20 score of indriCASP is 0.195, and the median ERR@20 score of the 9 systems (top-eight runs combined with the indriCASP baseline) is 0.220 (the ERR@20 score of utw2012c1), so indriCASP is competitive among this set of champion systems.

Figure 1 shows the distribution of scores differences for each of these top-performing systems compared to indriCASP, as well as the score differences associated with all 48 systems submitted to the track. From this figure we observe that many values exceed the $1.5 \times IQR$ boundaries in the "All" boxplot, where score differences below -0.241 and above 0.292 are considered outliers.

Function Definitions. The linear piecewise function that moderates the impact of the sum of wins, minus the sum of losses, in the URisk$^-$ family of measures has the form:

$$l(x) = \begin{cases} x & x \geq 0 \\ \hat{\alpha} \cdot x & x \leq 0, \end{cases} \tag{9}$$

where $-1 \leq x \leq 1$ is the difference in effectiveness between baseline(s) and a run. For $\hat{\alpha} = 2$, the extrema of the domain gives the coordinates $(-1, -2)$ and $(1, 1)$. We take these two points, plus the origin, to develop an alternative continuously differentiable *smooth* weighting function. Since a user is less likely to notice small score differences [2,19], we sought to make extreme differences

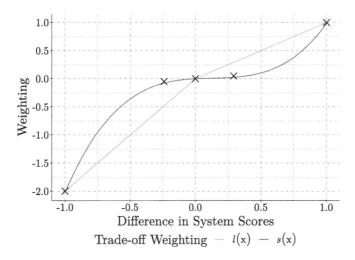

Fig. 2. The linear URisk⁻ function $l(x)$ with the parameter $\hat{\alpha} = 2$, versus the proposed cubic regression variant, $s(x)$. Crosses mark the five points used to model the curve.

(in both directions) count for more. Two more points, $(-0.241, -0.05)$ and $(0.292, 0.05)$, corresponding to the fences of the All boxplot in Fig. 2, were taken to define a range in which the score delta was low enough to not be problematic. We then used the R lm function to compute a cubic regression across the five points of interest, removing the y-intercept term d from the resultant function to ensure that it intersected with the origin. Figure 2 includes the result: $s(x) = 1.38426x^3 - 0.51659x^2 + 0.11578x$.

Risk Before Standardization in ZRisk⁻. In order to replace $l(x)$ with $s(x)$ in ZRisk⁻, it is necessary to first establish that ZRisk⁻ produces the same result if the trade-off is computed before standardization. If that is the case, $s(x)$ can be computed without having to renormalize. As a reminder, ZRisk⁻ standardizes the scores before computing the trade-off. Here we describe the scenario where we compute the trade-off and then standardize, which we call RiskZ⁻.

Given the ZRisk⁻ equation:

$$ZRisk^- (i, \hat{\alpha}) = -1 \cdot [z_{i+} + \hat{\alpha} \cdot z_{i-}]$$

$$= -1 \cdot \left[\sum_{q \in Q^+} \frac{x_{ij} - e_{ij}}{s_{ij}} + \hat{\alpha} \cdot \sum_{q \in Q^-} \frac{x_{ij} - e_{ij}}{s_{ij}} \right] \qquad (10)$$

$$= -1 \cdot [Wins_z + Losses_z] ,$$

with $Wins_z$ and $Losses_z$ treated independently to show that RiskZ⁻ is equivalent. Based on this, we can define RiskZ⁻ as:

$$RiskZ^- (i, \hat{\alpha}) = -1 \cdot \left[\sum_{q \in Q_+} z \left(x_{ij} - e_{ij} \right) + \sum_{q \in Q_-} z \left(\hat{\alpha} \cdot \left(x_{ij} - e_{ij} \right) \right) \right] \tag{11}$$
$$= -1 \cdot \left[Wins_t + Losses_t \right].$$

Focusing on the $Wins_t$ part of RiskZ$^-$, we evaluate the standardized score from the standard normal distribution:

$$Wins_t = \sum_{q \in Q_+} \frac{(x_{ij} - e_{ij}) - E[x_{ij} - e_{ij}]}{s_{ij}}. \tag{12}$$

To evaluate the expected value $E[x_{ij} - e_{ij}]$, observe that the expectation operator $E[\cdot]$ is linear. Hence, $E[x_{ij} - e_{ij}] = E[x_{ij}] - E[e_{ij}] = 0$, and therefore, $Wins_t = \sum_{q \in Q_+} \frac{x_{ij} - e_{ij}}{s_{ij}} = Wins_z$. In addition, $E[cX] = c \cdot E[X]$, meaning that a similar argument allows

$$Losses_t = \hat{\alpha} \cdot \sum_{q \in Q_-} \frac{x_{ij} - e_{ij}}{s_{ij}} = Losses_z. \tag{13}$$

That is, $RiskZ^- (i, \hat{\alpha}) = ZRisk^- (i, \hat{\alpha})$.

Finally, since calculating risk before normalizing gives the same result as ZRisk$^-$, $s(x_{ij} - e_{ij})$ can be used in place of the existing linear scaling applied in ZRisk$^-$:

$$RiskZ^-_{s(x)} (i, \hat{\alpha}) = -1 \cdot \left[\sum_{q \in Q_+} z \left(s(x_{ij} - e_{ij}) \right) + \sum_{q \in Q_-} z \left(s(x_{ij} - e_{ij}) \right) \right], \tag{14}$$
$$= - \sum_{q \in Q} z \left(s(x_{ij} - e_{ij}) \right).$$

Smooth Cost Functions. Wang et al. [24] proved that URisk using $l(x)$ has the property of being consistent. This is an important property for our formula, if it is to be used as a cost function in a learning-to-rank (LtR) scenario. Although we do not explicitly run any LtR experiments using the $s(x)$ cost function, we show that at least one case exists where a smooth value function can easily be used in a cost function.

The derivative of $s(x)$ is $s'(x) = 4.15278x^2 - 1.03318x + 0.11578$. Since the discriminant of $s'(x)$ is $= -0.005$, it has no real solutions, meaning $s(x)$ must be one-to-one. Moreover, since $4.15278 > 0$, it is clear that $s'(x)$ only returns positive values. With that in mind, combined with the knowledge that $s(x)$ is one-to-one, we have that $s(x)$ is strictly monotonically increasing; and hence no cases possible in which d_i and d_j could be swapped inconsistently, provided that the evaluation metric also has the property of being consistent.

Since $s(x)$ is consistent, URisk with $s(x)$ can be used as a cost function with learning-to-rank retrieval models such as LambdaMART [5].

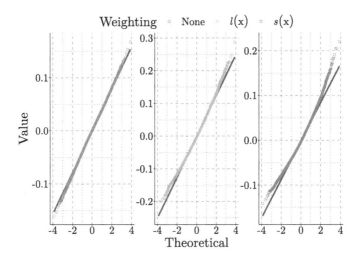

Fig. 3. The Q-Q plot of ICTNET12ADR3 bootstraped replicates of the mean URisk⁻ values against the indriCASP reference system, using no risk weighting, the standard linear risk function $l(x)$ with $\hat{\alpha} = 2$, and our smooth weighting function $s(x)$.

5   Experiments

Distribution Properties. Since TRisk⁻ is a parametric inference test, it is important to verify that the score distributions of the risk functions are amenable to statistical tests that assume normality. Hesterberg et al. [15] note that:

> *The shape of the bootstrap distribution approximates the shape of the sampling distribution, so we can use the bootstrap distribution to check the normality of the sampling distribution.*

Figure 3 shows a Q-Q plot of 10,000 bootstrapped replicates of the mean URisk⁻ values generated with both approaches against the median scoring ERR@20 run ICTNET12ADR3, as well as a standard differences in means comparison labeled *None*, with the code to generate bootstrap replicates adapted from Urbano et al. [21]. There is evidence that the $s(x)$ score distribution has a moderate right-tail, and we flag this as a possible issue for t-test inferences since it violates the normality assumption. That could be because large differences in scores correspond to a larger mapping of the "risk" of changing to the ICTNET12ADR3 system. Despite this, the values from the $l(x)$ and no risk functions fall along their respective reference lines, providing support for the inferences made by TRisk⁻ using these functions on the 2012 TREC Web Track dataset.

Results. Table 2 shows the difference in weighting functions across the top-eight systems from the 2012 Web Track.

No values fall outside the $-2.0 < t < 2.0$ "non-statistical" region when TRisk⁻ is used with a smooth value function. As can be seen from the table, the linear value function appears to have strong agreement with the smooth one when

Table 2. Risk values of the top-eight runs submitted to the 2012 TREC Web Track measured using ERR@20, comparing the $l(x)$ and $s(x)$ weighting functions. URisk⁻ and TRisk⁻ are measured for all runs against the indriCASP baseline. ZRisk⁻ and GeoRisk⁻ are measured using all submitted systems to the track, along with the indri-CASP baseline. Shaded cells indicate the system in that row that has the least risk according to the column's measure. As the standard deviation is different for each TRisk⁻ computation, and no t-values fall outside of the statistical region, no TRisk⁻ cells are shaded. All risk measures use $\hat{\alpha} = 2$.

System	$l(x)$ U⁻	$s(x)$ U⁻	$l(x)$ T⁻	$s(x)$ T⁻	$l(x)$ Z⁻	$s(x)$ Z⁻	$l(x)$ Geo⁻	$s(x)$ Geo⁻
autoSTA	0.12	0.10	1.63	1.85	8.14	0.91	−0.31	−0.30
DFalah121A	−0.05	0.02	−0.85	0.52	7.02	0.61	−0.41	−0.39
ICTNET12ADR2	0.05	0.03	0.78	0.75	6.80	0.17	−0.35	−0.33
irra12c	0.12	0.08	1.70	1.72	5.86	0.27	−0.31	−0.29
QUTparaBline	−0.04	0.03	−0.57	0.62	6.51	0.97	−0.40	−0.38
srchvrs12c00	−0.07	−0.02	−1.08	−0.50	8.53	1.42	−0.42	−0.40
uogTrA44xu	−0.09	−0.03	−1.29	−0.63	5.29	0.70	−0.43	−0.41
utw2012c1	0.06	0.05	0.79	1.15	6.33	0.37	−0.35	−0.33

comparing risk values, suggesting that they do not generate different outcomes. And while the rankings of ZRisk⁻ are different between the two functions, when combined as GeoRisk⁻, the rankings are identical.

System Risk Ordering. Table 2, carried out on the 2012 TREC Web Track dataset, indicates that a well-behaved smooth loss-weighting function rarely changes the risk-aware system comparisons. Note, however, that only one collection and one metric were employed, and that further work is required to ascertain whether non-linear penalties provide an alternative to current piecewise-linear approaches to risk-reward analysis and LtR optimization.

To further check to see if $s(x)$ and $l(x)$ are meaningfully different loss functions, we empirically compare the similarity of the rankings generated by the URisk⁻, ZRisk⁻, and GeoRisk⁻ versions of each. Ranking TRisk⁻ t-values by different system outputs is not possible, as these values are expressed in units of U⁻ per standard error of U⁻, where the standard error relates to two systems only. Like Table 2, we evaluate risk values using all 48 submitted systems, where URisk⁻ is evaluated against the indriCASP baseline [6]. For differences in orderings between $s(x)$ and $l(x)$ to have practical value, there would ideally be disagreement in the systems deemed to have the least risk. To measure the similarities of their orderings, we modulate the growth of their respective set sizes between 1 and the 49 systems (48 for URisk⁻ excluding indriCASP) in steps of 5, and compute their similarities. As the sets produced might be non-conjoint, we cannot use popular similarity measures such as Kendall's τ or Spearman's ρ, and instead employ the Rank-Biased Overlap measure proposed by Webber et al. [26], since it meets our non-conjointness requirements and it can produce top-heavy similarity scores. We fix the persistence parameter $\phi = 0.9$ for all

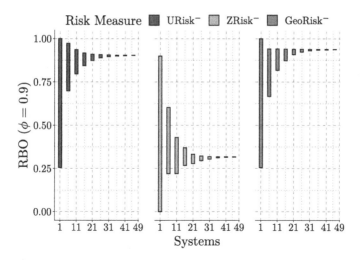

Fig. 4. RBO ($\phi = 0.9$), measured between $l(x)$ and $s(x)$ loss penalties, and computed over systems sets of increasing size, with the systems ordered by increasing risk scores. indriCASP is the baseline used for URisk$^-$ scores, and all systems (including indriCASP) are the baseline for ZRisk$^-$ and GeoRisk$^-$. All risk measures use $\hat{\alpha} = 2$.

experimentation; an RBO value of 1.0 indicates complete agreement, and an RBO value of 0.0 indicates that the two lists are disjoint.

Figure 4 shows the resultant RBO ($\phi = 0.9$) values. The lower boundary of each bar corresponds to the minimum RBO value for that set size, and the top-value is the maximum possible value, and is the lower value plus the RBO residual (the extent of the possible uncertainty as a result of the rankings being finite and not fully specified). As RBO ($\phi = 0.9$) gives an expected viewing depth of 10, we expect to see a degree of convergence of the boundaries of the RBO range as the set size increases past this point.

When all systems are considered in the RBO ($\phi = 0.9$) calculation, ZRisk$^-$ is the only measure that appears to be ranking systems very differently with the smooth value function, with a score of 0.316. But when combined with information about the mean effectiveness of the systems using GeoRisk$^-$, RBO ($\phi = 0.9$) gives a very strong similarity of 0.937 with a negligible residual. URisk$^-$ has a marginally smaller similarity score of 0.903.

6   Conclusion

We have explored a non-linear weighting function for IR risk evaluation measures. That function weights large differences greater than small differences in scores, on the assumption that a user is more likely to observe such changes if they occur in search results. Additionally, we proposed changes to the naming and formulae used in common risk measures, to more naturally align linguistic conventions surrounding the terminology with mathematical interpretations of the results. In preliminary experiments with the ERR metric and TREC 2012 Web Track data, and several popular risk measures, we found no evidence to indicate that using a smooth risk function might lead to different evaluation outcomes when undertaking a risk-sensitive experimental comparison. Further work is clearly warranted, to gain a better understanding of the connection between human expectations and perception and changes in search quality, before the true value of risk-reward experimental analysis can be fully realized.

Acknowledgments. The first author was supported by an RMIT Vice Chancellor's PhD Scholarship. This work was also partially supported by the Australian Research Council's Discovery Projects Scheme (DP190101113).

References

1. Abdellaoui, M., Kemel, E.: Eliciting prospect theory when consequences are measured in time units: "time is not money". Manag. Sci. **60**(7), 1844–1859 (2013)
2. Allan, J., Carterette, B., Lewis, J.: When will information retrieval be good enough? In: Proceedings of SIGIR, pp. 433–440 (2005)
3. Benham, R., Culpepper, J.S.: Risk-reward trade-offs in rank fusion. In: Proceedings of ADCS, pp. 1:1–1:8 (2017)
4. Benham, R., Culpepper, J.S., Gallagher, L., Lu, X., Mackenzie, J.: Towards efficient and effective query variant generation. In: Proceedings of DESIRES (2018)
5. Burges, C.: From RankNet to LambdaRank to LambdaMART: an overview. Learning **11**(23–581), 81 (2010)
6. Collins-Thompson, K., Macdonald, C., Bennett, P., Diaz, F., Voorhees, E.M.: TREC 2013 web track overview. In: Proceedings of TREC (2014)
7. Collins-Thompson, K., Macdonald, C., Bennett, P., Diaz, F., Voorhees, E.M.: TREC 2014 web track overview. In: Proceedings of TREC (2015)
8. Collins-Thompson, K.: Accounting for stability of retrieval algorithms using risk-reward curves. In: Proceedings of SIGIR, pp. 27–28 (2009)
9. Dinçer, B.T., Macdonald, C., Ounis, I.: Risk-sensitive evaluation and learning to rank using multiple baselines. In: Proceedings of SIGIR, pp. 483–492 (2016)
10. Dinçer, B.T., Macdonald, C., Ounis, I.: Hypothesis testing for the risk-sensitive evaluation of retrieval systems. In: Proceedings of SIGIR, pp. 23–32 (2014)
11. Dinçer, B.T., Ounis, I., Macdonald, C.: Tackling biased baselines in the risk-sensitive evaluation of retrieval systems. In: de Rijke, M., et al. (eds.) ECIR 2014. LNCS, vol. 8416, pp. 26–38. Springer, Cham (2014). https://doi.org/10.1007/978-3-319-06028-6_3
12. Festjens, A., Bruyneel, S., Diecidue, E., Dewitte, S.: Time-based versus money-based decision making under risk: an experimental investigation. J. Econ. Psychol. **50**, 52–72 (2015)
13. Gallagher, L., Mackenzie, J., Culpepper, J.S.: Revisiting spam filtering in web search. In: Proceedings of ADCS, p. 5 (2018)
14. Hashemi, S.H., Kamps, J.: University of Amsterdam at TREC 2014: contextual suggestion and web tracks. In: Proceedings of TREC (2014)
15. Hesterberg, T., Moore, D.S., Monaghan, S., Clipson, A., Epstein, R.: Bootstrap Methods and Permutation Tests, vol. 5. W. H. Freeman and Company, New York (2005)

16. Liu, C., Yan, X., Han, J.: Mining control flow abnormality for logic error isolation. In: Proceedings of SDM, pp. 106–117 (2006)
17. McCreadie, R., et al.: University of Glasgow at TREC 2014: experiments with terrier in contextual suggestion, temporal summarisation and web tracks. In: Proceedings of TREC (2014)
18. Sousa, D.X.D., Canuto, S.D., Rosa, T.C., Martins, W.S., Gonçalves, M.A.: Incorporating risk-sensitiveness into feature selection for learning to rank. In: Proceedings of CIKM, pp. 257–266 (2016)
19. Turpin, A., Scholer, F.: User performance versus precision measures for simple search tasks. In: Proceedings of SIGIR, pp. 11–18 (2006)
20. Tversky, A., Kahneman, D.: Advances in prospect theory: cumulative representation of uncertainty. J. Risk Uncertain. **5**(4), 297–323 (1992)
21. Urbano, J., Lima, H., Hanjalic, A.: Statistical significance testing in information retrieval: an empirical analysis of type I, type II and type III errors. In: Proceeding of SIGIR, pp. 505–514 (2019)
22. Voorhees, E.M.: Overview of TREC 2003. In: Proceeding of TREC, pp. 1–13 (2003)
23. Wang, J., Zhuhan, J.: Portfolio theory of information retrieval. In: Proceeding of SIGIR, pp. 115–122 (2009)
24. Wang, L., Bennett, P.N., Collins-Thompson, K.: Robust ranking models via risk-sensitive optimization. In: Proceeding of SIGIR, pp. 761–770 (2012)
25. Webber, W., Moffat, A., Zobel, J.: Score standardization for inter-collection comparison of retrieval systems. In: Proceeding of SIGIR, pp. 51–58 (2008)
26. Webber, W., Moffat, A., Zobel, J.: A similarity measure for indefinite rankings. ACM Trans. Inf. Sys. **28**(4), 20:1–20:38 (2010)
27. Zhang, P., Hao, L., Song, D., Wang, J., Hou, Y., Hu, B.: Generalized bias-variance evaluation of TREC participated systems. In: Proceedings of CIKM, pp. 1911–1914 (2014)
28. Zhang, P., Song, D., Wang, J., Hou, Y.: Bias-variance decomposition of IR evaluation. In: Proceedings of SIGIR, pp. 1021–1024 (2013)

Randomised vs. Prioritised Pools for Relevance Assessments: Sample Size Considerations

Tetsuya Sakai[(⊠)] and Peng Xiao

Waseda University, Tokyo, Japan
tetsuyasakai@acm.org

Abstract. The present study concerns depth-k pooling for building IR test collections. At TREC, pooled documents are traditionally presented in random order to the assessors to avoid judgement bias. In contrast, an approach that has been used widely at NTCIR is to prioritise the pooled documents based on "pseudorelevance," in the hope of letting assessors quickly form an idea as to what constitutes a relevant document and thereby judge more efficiently and reliably. While the recent TREC 2017 Common Core Track went beyond depth-k pooling and adopted a method for selecting documents to judge dynamically, even this task let the assessors process the usual depth-10 pools first: the idea was to give the assessors a "burn-in" period, which actually appears to echo the view of the NTCIR approach. Our research questions are: (1) Which depth-k ordering strategy enables more efficient assessments? Randomisation, or prioritisation by pseudorelevance? (2) Similarly, which of the two strategies enables higher inter-assessor agreements? Our experiments based on two English web search test collections with multiple sets of graded relevance assessments suggest that randomisation outperforms prioritisation in both respects on average, although the results are statistically inconclusive. We then discuss a plan for a much larger experiment with sufficient statistical power to obtain the final verdict.

Keywords: Evaluation · Graded relevance · Pooling · Relevance assessments · Web search

1 Introduction

Depth-k pooling, i.e., the approach of taking top k documents from each submitted run to form a pool for relevance assessments, is simple and still a widely-used approach to building information retrieval test collections. Generally speaking, however, the pooled documents are ordered for the assessors differently at TREC[1] and NTCIR[2]. In a paper given at CLEF 2001, Voorhees explained the TREC approach [20, p. 357]: "*Each pool is sorted by document identifier so*

---

[1] http://trec.nist.gov/.

[2] http://research.nii.ac.jp/ntcir/index-en.html.

© Springer Nature Switzerland AG 2020
F. L. Wang et al. (Eds.): AIRS 2019, LNCS 12004, pp. 94–105, 2020.
https://doi.org/10.1007/978-3-030-42835-8_9

assessors cannot tell if a document was highly ranked by some system or how many systems (or which systems) retrieved the document." An almost identical comment by Harman can be found in the TREC book published in 2005 [8, p. 33]. The philosophy there is to *randomise* the document judging order to avoid judgement biases[3]: for example, if the assessor knows that a document was retrieved by many participating systems at top ranks, then this knowledge might make her overestimate its relevance.

It is interesting that many pooling-based IR tasks of NTCIR do not follow the above advice. In fact, they do the exact opposite. At CLEF 2003, Kando explained [10, p. 38]: "*Pooled document lists to be judged are sorted in descending order of likelihood of being relevant (not the order of the document IDs)*" and remarks that the NTCIR's decision was "*based on comparative tests and interviews with assessors.*" In 2008, Sakai *et al.* [19] introduced a specific implementation of NTCIR's ordering approach, now widely used at NTCIR with the NTCIRPOOL tool[4]: the pooled documents are sorted by "pseudorelevance," where the first sort key is the number of runs containing the document at or above the pool depth k (the larger the better), and the second sort key is the sum of ranks of that document within those runs (the smaller the better). Thus, documents that were retrieved by many systems at high ranks are prioritised. This NTCIR approach aims to let the assessors go through the documents roughly in decreasing order of relevance so that they can quickly form an idea as to what constitutes a relevant document, and thereby enhance judgement efficiency and reliability.

While approaches to dynamically selecting documents to judge have been explored (as discussed in Sect. 2), depth-k pooling is still the mainstream approach to collecting relevance assessments. Hence, the present study addresses the following questions.

RQ1. Which depth-k ordering strategy enables more efficient assessments? Randomisation, or prioritisation by pseudorelevance?

RQ2. Similarly, which of the two strategies enables higher inter-assessor agreements?

Our experiments based on two English web search test collections with multiple sets of graded relevance assessments suggest that randomisation outperforms prioritisation in both respects on average, although the results are statistically inconclusive. By utilising our t-test results and existing power analysis tools [16], we then discuss a plan for a much larger experiment with sufficient statistical power to obtain the final verdict.

---

[3] The "sort by document number" advice from TREC should not be taken literally: if the publication date is embedded in the document identifier, then sorting by document ID would mean sorting by time, which is not what we want. Similarly, if the target document collection consists of multiple subcollections and the document IDs contain different prefixes accordingly, such a sort would actually cluster documents by source (See [5]), which again is not what we want. Throughout this study, we interpret the advice from TREC as "randomise".

[4] http://research.nii.ac.jp/ntcir/tools/ntcirpool-en.html.

The IR community, like many other research communities, tend to publish results that are statistically significant, while leaving statistically insignificant results in "file drawers" [15]. Instead of making such *dichotomous decisions* [7], scientists should examine an *effect* in question (e.g., what is the magnitude of the difference in judgement efficiency between randomised and prioritised document pool environments?), and redesign future experiments to ensure sufficient statistical power. The present study takes exactly this approach to pursue **RQ1** and **RQ2**.

2   Related Work

While the present study concerns the traditional depth-k pooling, several alternative approaches to pooling have been proposed. Early well-known methods are from SIGIR '98: Zobel [21] proposed to allocate more judging resources to more promising topics; Cormack *et al.* [4] proposed to allocate more judging resources to more promising runs. TREC did not adopt these methods for fear of introducing bias [20]. The TREC Million Query Track [1,3] used the *Minimal Test Collections* (MTC) and *statAP* methods: MTC iteratively orders documents to be judged according to how much information they provide about a difference in average precision; statAP samples documents to be judged based on a sampling distribution that tries to place higher weights on relevant documents.

The TREC Common Core Track, introduced in 2017 [2], started re-examining the problem of how best to go beyond depth-k pooling. They adopted a version of the *MaxMean* method of Losada, Parapar, and Barreiro [11], which dynamically selects which run to process based on the judgements so far; this is similar in spirit to the aforementioned method of Cormack *et al.* in that it tries to focus judging resources on those runs that continue to contribute relevant documents. The Common Core Track 2017 overview paper mentions *judgement bias*, i.e., the bias caused by presenting top-ranked documents to the assessors first, and *run bias*, i.e., underestimating runs that do not contribute many relevant documents early in their rankings. While the overview paper reports that there was no indication of run bias in their experiments, judgement bias was not tested.

Despite their merits, we also observe the following difficulties regarding dynamic document selection approaches in general:

1. They require that once a relevance assessment is made, that is final. In contrast, with depth-k pooling, assessors can correct their judgements at any time in any order, as long as the judgement interface allows.
2. They complicate logistics: the assessment cost is more difficult to anticipate, and the re-allocation of assessors to topics can be less flexible compared to depth-k pooling.

Moreover, even in the Common Core Track, organisers point out that it is important to give each assessor an initial *burn-in period*, in which the assessor learns about the topic and optionally make changes to their initial relevance assessments; hence they implemented a hybrid approach where the assessor initially processes a traditional depth-10 pool and then moves to the MaxMean-based dynamic judging phase. Therefore, our research questions regarding depth-k pools (See Sect. 1) may be relevant to this track as well. Note also that the aim of the burn-in period resembles that of NTCIR's document prioritisation based on pseudorelevance.

Document judging order was a concern even before TREC. For example, in 1988, Eisenberg and Barry [6] reported on a small-scale experiment where 15 document descriptions were presented (on paper) to each assessor in either increasing or decreasing order of relevance. Based on their results, they caution against judgement bias and recommend randomising the presentation order. The work of Huang and Wang from 2004 also recommends randomisation [9], but their experimental results actually suggest that the order does not matter if the number of documents to judge is 75 or greater. Note that, in modern large-scale depth-k pooling-based evaluations, the number of documents to judge per topic is typically several *hundreds* (See Sect. 3).

In 2018, Damessie *et al.* [5] compared three document ordering methods: the aforementioned NTCIRPOOL approach (hereafter referred to as PRI for "prioritised"), randomised ordering (hereafter referred to as RND), and their own method which presents document blocks, where each block contains likely non-relevant documents followed by a single pseudorelevant document. While the third method is beyond the scope of the present study as it has not yet been tested in actual evaluation forums, their results suggest that PRI achieves better inter-assessor agreement than RND. In terms of experimental scale, whereas their experiments involved only 240 topic-document pairs (eight topics, each with 30 pooled documents), our experiments involve a total of 38,841 topic-document pairs, with multiple independent judgements per pair, as described in Sect. 3. Moreover, we consider assessor efficiency in addition to agreement. Another difference between the work of Damessie *et al.* and ours lies in the judgement interface: ours has a document list panel, which allows the assessors to revisit previously judged documents for correcting the judgements, or to judge in an order different from the presented one. Our efficiency experiments show that assessors do indeed rejudge documents, and that they tend to rejudge more under the PRI condition, as we shall discuss in Sect. 4.

Also in 2018, Losada, Parapar, and Barreiro [12] reported on a study on when to stop judging documents to reduce the assessment cost, under the premise that pooled documents are ranked by a kind of pseudorelevance. They remark: *"Although there is still room for debate, we believe that a relevance-based ordering of assessments should not be an obstacle in practice,"* which also appears to support the PRI approach.

3 Data

This section describes how we collected multiple relevance assessment sets based on the RND and PRI document ordering approaches to address **RQ1** (efficiency) and **RQ2** (inter-assessor agreement). We use Dataset 1 (Sect. 3.1) to address **RQ1**, and Dataset 2 (Sect. 3.2) to address **RQ2**.

3.1 Dataset 1 for RQ1

Our experiment for addressing **RQ1** (efficiency) was unique in that it was embedded in the official relevance assessment process of a recent web search task, namely, the English subtask of the NTCIR-14 We Want Web (WWW-2) task [14]. This task used `clueweb12-B13`[5] as the target corpus; it had 80 test topics, and received 19 runs from five participating groups. A depth-50 pool was created for each topic, and a total of 27,627 topic-document pairs needed to be judged. The maximum number of pooled documents per topic was 504; the minimum was 209. Two assessors were assigned to each topic, giving us 55,254 judgements. Twenty international-course Computer Science students of Waseda University were hired as assessors, and each of them handled eight topics.

For each topic, we created both RND and PRI versions of the pooled document list. For 27 topics, we gave the PRI list to both assessors; for another 27, we gave the RND list to one assessor and the PRI list to the other; finally, for the remaining 26, we gave the RND list to both assessors. The assignment was randomised, and each assessor experienced both RND and PRI. To address **RQ1**, we compare several assessor activity statistics (to be described in Sect. 4) based on observations from the RND condition (79 topic-assesor pairs) and those based on observations from the PRI condition (81 topic-assessor pairs).

A web-browser-based relevance assessment interface [18] was provided to the assessors, with the topic (title and description) shown at the top, a document list panel on the left, and a document content panel on the right. The assessors were required to choose from:

Highly relevant. It is *likely* that the user with the information need shown will find this page relevant (Relevance grade: 2);

Relevant. It is *possible* that the user with the information need shown will find this page relevant (Relevance grade: 1);

Nonrelevant. It is *unlikely* that the user with the information need shown will find this page relevant (Relevance grade: 0);

Error. Due to some problem with the clueweb data, the content is not shown on the right panel (Relevance grade: 0).

We refer to the above dataset as Dataset 1. The reason for having the aforementioned three different combinations of document ordering strategies across different topics (PRI-PRI, RND-PRI, RND-RND) was to try to address both **RQ1** and **RQ2** with the same data. However, after a preliminary analysis, it became apparent that this dataset is not ideal for addressing **RQ2** (inter-assessor agreement), because comparing the above three conditions would confound the effect of document ordering and the choice of topics. Hence, we decided to construct a separate dataset for addressing **RQ2**.

---

[5] http://lemurproject.org/clueweb12/.

3.2   Dataset 2 for RQ2

Our dataset for addressing **RQ2** (inter-assessor agreement), which we call Dataset 2, was constructed by conducting our own relevance assessments on an existing English web search test collection, namely, the NTCIR-13 We Want Web (WWW-1) collection [13]. This collection also uses `clueweb12-B13` as the target corpus. While the official relevance assessments of WWW-1 were conducted by crowd workers called "lancers" [13], we do not use these assessments for addressing **RQ2**. This is because we want a controlled environment where all of our assessors are from the same population (international-course Computer Science students of Waseda University). While the original WWW-1 collection comes with 100 topics, we conducted our own relevance assessments for only 50 topics, whose topic IDs are odd numbers. Unlike Dataset 1, the WWW-1 collection used depth-30 pools, and this gave us a total of 11,214 topic-document pairs to judge. (Since we have 27,627 topic-document pairs in Dataset 1, the total number of pairs used in our experiments is 38,841, as we have mentioned in Sect. 2). The maximum number of pooled documents per topic was 282; the minimum was 158.

The judgement interface is the same as the one we used for Dataset 1. A total of 15 international-course Computer Science students were hired at Waseda University; they were assigned to topics at random; each student handled either 10 or 20 topics. Four students were assigned to each topic; two of them used a PRI list, while the other two used a RND list. Thus, we can compare the inter-assessor agreement in PRI and RND conditions, while freezing the set of topics.

4   Efficiency

To address **RQ1**, we consider the following topicwise judgement *efficiency* criteria, using the activity logs from our assessment interface:

TJ1D. Time to judge the first document;
TF1RH. Time to find the first Relevant or Highly relevant document;
TF1H. Time to find the first Highly relevant document;
ATBJ. Average time between judging two documents;
NREJ. Number of times the label of a judged document is corrected to another
   label.

For each criterion, we wanted to compare the mean over the 79 topic-assessor pairs for the RND case and the mean over the 81 pairs for the PRI case using a two-sample t-test. In practice, however, we removed observations that are longer than three minutes for the first three criteria, since we do not know from the user logs whether they actually represent the time spent on examining the documents or the time the users spent away from the interface. As such cases were rare, we managed to retain 70 or more topic-assessor pairs for RND and 74 or more for PRI, as we shall show later. As for **ATBJ**, we also removed observations (i.e., time between two judgements) longer than three minutes before averaging for each topic-assessor pair.

Table 1. Efficiency comparison of RND and PRI: for each criterion, Student's two-sample t-test was conducted. Glass's Δ is based on the sample standard deviation of RND. Sample sizes for RND and PRI are denoted by n_1 and n_2, respectively.

Criterion	RND mean (sample size)	PRI mean (sample size)	p-value	Δ	Achieved power (n required for 70% power)
TJ1D	38.5 s ($n_1 = 70$)	39.9 s ($n_2 = 75$)	0.832	0.035	–
TF1RH	26.7 s ($n_1 = 73$)	32.5 s ($n_2 = 75$)	0.305	0.172	17.6% ($n = 432$)
TF1H	21.4 s ($n_1 = 70$)	23.9 s ($n_2 = 74$)	0.606	0.080	–
ATBJ	14.6 s ($n_1 = 79$)	13.9 s ($n_2 = 81$)	0.567	0.090	–
NREJ	10.4 times ($n_1 = 79$)	13.3 times ($n_2 = 81$)	0.373	0.187	14.1% ($n = 621$)

Table 1 summarises the comparisons of our efficiency criteria based on two-sample t-tests. The effect sizes (Glass's Δ, which quantifies the magnitude of the difference in standard deviation units [17]) are based on the sample standard deviations of the RND data. It can be observed that none of the differences are statistically significant, but that the Δ's are not small for **TF1RH** and **NREJ** (0.172 and 0.187, respectively). That is, there is a weak indication that *in an* RND *environment, assessors can find the first relevant document more quickly, and makes fewer judgement corrections*[6]. Since **TF1RH** and **NREJ** may be worth investigating with larger sample sizes in a future experiment, Table 1 also shows the actual statistical powers as well as future sample sizes for achieving 70% statistical power for these two criteria. Sakai's power analysis script `future.sample.unpairedt` [16] was used for this. It can be observed that our achieved statistical powers are 14.1–17.6%, which is not adequate for addressing the questions regarding **TF1RH** and **NREJ** above; instead of having around $n = 80$ topic-assessor pairs per sample, we need at least $n = 621$ pairs per sample if we want to ensure at least 70% statistical power for both cases. We will utilise this result and the sample size consideration from our agreement experiment (Sect. 5) to discuss the design of a future experiment in Sect. 6.

5   Agreement

We address **RQ2** primarily by comparing inter-assessor agreements in the RND environment ("RND-RND agreements") and those in the PRI environment ("PRI-PRI agreements") at the level of relevance grades (0, 1, 2) using quadratic weighted κ, as discussed in Sect. 5.1. While there never are true gold document relevance assessments in an ad hoc IR task and therefore it is difficult to directly discuss which relevance assessment sets are more reliable[7], we view inter-assessor

---

[6] Although it is debatable whether making fewer judgement corrections is *better*, it does imply higher efficiency.

[7] We refrain from treating the official assessments as the gold data: we argue that they are also just one version of qrels.

Table 2. Overall inter-assessor agreement in terms of quadratic weighted κ's with 95%CIs ($n = 11,214$).

	RND2	PRI1	PRI2
RND1	0.36 [0.34, 0.38]	0.31 [0.29, 0.33]	0.38 [0.36, 0.40]
RND2	–	0.30 [0.29, 0.32]	0.44 [0.43, 0.46]
PRI1	–	–	0.30 [0.28, 0.31]

Table 3. Mean per-topic quadratic weighted κ's (over 50 topics).

	RND2	PRI1	PRI2
RND1	0.285	0.259	0.285
RND2	–	0.272	0.341
PRI1	–	–	0.247

agreement as an important indicator of reliability. In addition, in Sect. 5.2, we also compare the agreement between system rankings after evaluating the official NTCIR-13 WWW-1 systems using four versions of relevance assessments: two based on the RND pools, and two based on the PRI pools. This provides an alternative way to compare the RND-RND agreements with the PRI-PRI agreements, although only 13 runs were submitted to the WWW-1 task and hence the results should be considered preliminary.

5.1   Relevance Label Agreement

Since we have two independent RND-based assessments and two independent PRI-based assessments per topic, we refer to them as RND1, RND2, PRI1, PRF2 qrels for convenience hereafter. Note that each of these qrels files does not represent a single assessor: different assessors handled different topics in each qrels file.

Table 2 compares all combinations of the four qrels files in terms of overall quadratic weighted κ: that is, all 11,214 topic-document pairs are treated as one batch of observations. It can be observed that the agreement between RND1 and RND2 (0.36 95%CI[0.34, 0.38]) is substantially higher than that between PRI1 and PRI2 (0.30 95%CI[0.28, 0.31]). However, this result should be interpreted with caution, since the agreement between RND1 and PRI2 (0.38) and that between RND2 and PRI2 (0.44) are even higher: the table actually suggests that PRI1 is substantially different from the other three, rather than that inter-assessor agreements are higher when RND pools are used.

The above overall κ's rely heavily on topics that have more pooled documents. Alternatively, we can compute a κ for each topic and then average them across topics, to let each topic contribute to the final score equally. Table 3 shows the mean per-topic κ's computed thus. The trend is the same as Table 2, in that PRI1 disagrees with the other three qrels files more, and that the agreement between

Table 4. Comparison of mean κ's of RND1-RND2 and PRI1-PRI2 with the paired t-test ($n = 50$ topics). Glass's Δ is based on the sample standard deviation of RND1-RND-1. Power analysis results are also shown.

p-value	Δ	Achieved power	n required for 70% power
0.134	0.223	32.1%	$n = 135$

Table 5. System rankings ($n = 13$ systems) with four versions of relevance assessments, compared by Kendall's τ with 95%CIs.

(a) MSnDCG@10	RND2	PRI1	PRI2
RND1	0.821 [0.622, 0.920]	0.641 [0.317, 0.831]	0.692 [0.397, 0.857]
RND2	–	0.718 [0.440, 0.871]	0.667 [0.357, 0.845]
PRI1	–	–	0.846 [0.670, 0.932]
(b) Q@10	RND2	PRI1	PRI2
RND1	0.846 [0.670, 0.932]	0.667 [0.357, 0.845]	0.846 [0.670, 0.932]
RND2	–	0.769 [0.527, 0.896]	0.846 [0.670, 0.932]
PRI1	–	–	0.769 [0.527, 0.896]
(c) nERR@10	RND2	PRI1	PRI2
RND1	0.718 [0.440, 0.871]	0.487 [0.100, 0.746]	0.692 [0.397, 0.857]
RND2	–	0.769 [0.527, 0.896]	0.769 [0.527, 0.896]
PRI1	–	–	0.641 [0.317, 0.831]

RND1 and RND2 (0.285) outperforms that between PRI1 and PRF2 (0.247) on average.

Since we are primarily interested in the difference between the above two mean κ scores, we conducted a paired t-test on the data, and a power analysis using Sakai's `future.sample.pairedt` tool [16]. The results are shown in Table 4. It can be observed that the difference is not statistically significant; Glass's Δ (based on the sample standard deviation of the per-topic κ between RND1 and RND2) is 0.223; the achieved power is about 32%, and we should use $n = 135$ topics instead of $n = 50$ if we want 70% statistical power. We shall utilise this result to design a future experiment in Sect. 6.

5.2   System Ranking Agreement

Using the four versions of qrels (RND1, RND2, PRI1, PRI2), we evaluated the 13 runs submitted to the NTCIR-13 WWW-1 English subtask in terms of the three official measures (MSnDCG@10, Q@10, and nERR@10)[8], we compared the system rankings in terms of Kendall's τ. As was mentioned earlier, the results

---

[8] Microsoft version of normalised discounted cumulative gain, cutoff-version of Q-measure, and normalised expected reciprocal rank, respectively [13].

reported in this section should be considered preliminary due to the small number of runs.

Table 5 compares the system rankings according to our different qrels versions and the three official evaluation measures in terms of Kendall's τ. The wide 95%CIs indicate that the results are quite inconclusive: for example, with Q@10, while the τ for RND1-RND2 is 0.846 and that for PRI1-PRI2 is 0.769, the CIs are [0.670, 0.932] and [0.527, 0.896], respectively, and hence we do not have sufficient data to conclude that the RND environment leads to more consistent system rankings than the PRI environment. Moreover, note that, in terms of MSnDCG@10, the τ for RND1-RND2 is slightly *lower* than that for PRI1-PRI2 (0.821 vs. 0.846). We need more runs if we want more reliable system ranking consistency results, although this is difficult for task organisers to control.

6   Designing a Future Experiment

In our efficiency experiment with Dataset 1 (based on depth-50 pools, 19 runs, and about 80 topic-assessor pairs per sample), two efficiency criteria TF1RH and NREJ have effect sizes that may be worth investigating further (Table 1). As was discussed in Sect. 4, the sample size (i.e., number of topic-assessor pairs) per group should be at least 621 in order to achieve 70% power for both criteria. On the other hand, from our agreement experiment with Dataset 2 (based on depth-30 pools, 13 runs, and 50 topics), we should prepare about 135 topics in order to achive 70% power for the comparison of the mean κ (i.e., per-topic inter-assessor agreement) for the RND environment and that for the PRI environment (Table 4).

Based on the above requirements, a possible future experiment to further pursue **RQ1** and **RQ2** would be to construct a set containing 160 topics (which is more than enough for the agreement experiment), and eight independent qrels: four based on RND and another four based on **PRI**. Thus, for both RND and **PRI**, the sample size would be $160 * 4 = 640$, which should be enough for the efficiency experiment.

For both Datasets 1 and 2, the average number of pooled documents per topic is about 230. While we may not be able to control the number of runs submitted, we can control the pool depth to ensure that we have no more than 230 documents per topic on average. If we have 160 topics, this would give us $160 * 230 = 36,800$ documents to judge on average; with eight independent assessments per topic, the total number of judgements amounts to $8 * 36,800 = 294,400$. While this would be an expensive experiment, we argue that conducting this single experiment is better than conducting multiple seriously underpowered experiments that only give us inconclusive results.

7   Conclusions and Future Work

We addressed the following questions. **RQ1**: Which depth-k ordering strategy enables more efficient assessments? Randomisation (RND), or prioritisation by pseudorelevance (PRI)? **RQ2**: Similarly, which of the two strategies enables higher inter-assessor agreements? Our experiments based on two English web search test collections with multiple sets of graded relevance assessments suggest that randomisation outperforms prioritisation in both respects, although the results are statistically inconclusive. Our main findings are:

- In our efficiency experiments, RND outperformed PRI on average in terms of **TF1RH** (time to find the first relevant or highly relevant document) with Glass's $\Delta = 0.172$; however, the achived power is as low as 17.6%, and we need $n = 432$ topic-assessor pairs per group in order to achieve 70% power;
- In our efficiency experiments, RND outperformed PRI on average in terms of **NREJ** (number of corrected judgements, assuming fewer is better) with $\Delta = 0.187$; however, the achieved power is as low as 14.5%, and we need $n = 621$ topic-assessor pairs per group in order to achieve 70% power;
- In our agreement experiments, RND outperformed PRI on average in terms of per-topic quadratic weighted κ with $\Delta = 0.223$; however, the achieved power is as low as 32.1%, and we need $n = 135$ topics in order to achieve 70% power.
- Based on the above sample size considerations, we plan to conduct a large scale relevance assessment experiment with 160 topics, each with about 230 documents to judge and eight independent assessments. Thus a total of about 294,400 assessments will be collected to further pursue **RQ1** and **RQ2**.

As we have argued in Sect. 6, conducting a sufficiently powered experiment once to obtain concrete conclusions is preferrable to repeating seriously underpowered experiments[9]. We plan to report on the outcomes of our future experiment elsewhere.

Acknowledgements. This work was partially supported by JSPS KAKENHI Grant Number 16H01756.

References

1. Allan, J., Carterette, B., Aslam, J.A., Pavlu, V., Dachev, B., Kanoulas, E.: Million query track 2007 overview (2008)
2. Allan, J., Harman, D., Kanoulas, E., Li, D., Van Gysel, C., Voorhees, E.: TREC common core track overview. In: Proceedings of TREC 2017 (2018)
3. Carterette, B., Pavlu, V., Fang, H., Kanoulas, E.: Million query track 2009 overview. In: Proceedings of TREC 2009 (2010)
4. Cormack, G.V., Palmer, C.R., Clarke, C.L.: Efficient construction of large test collections. In: Proceedings of ACM SIGIR 1998, pp. 282–289 (1998)
5. Damessie, T.T., Culpepper, J.S., Kim, J., Scholer, F.: Presentation ordering effects on assessor agreement. In: Proceedings of ACM CIKM 2018, pp. 723–732 (2018)

---

[9] "It is astonishing how many papers report work in which a slight effect is investigated with a small number of trials. Given that such investigations would generally fail even if the hypothesis was correct, it seems likely that many interesting research questions are unnecessarily discarded." [22, p. 225].

6. Eisenberg, M., Barry, C.: Order effects: a study of the possible influence of presentation order on user judgments of document relevance. J. Am. Soc. Inf. Sci. **39**(5), 293–300 (1988)

7. Harlow, L.L., Mulaik, S.A., Steiger, J.H.: What If There Were No Significance Tests? (Classic Edition). Routledge, London (2016)

8. Harman, D.K.: The TREC test collections. In: Voorhees, E.M., Harman, D.K. (eds.) TREC: Experiment and Evaluation in Information Retrieval (Chapter 2). The MIT Press, Cambridge (2005)

9. Huang, M.H., Wang, H.Y.: The influence of document presentation order and number of documents judged on users' judgments of relevance. J. Am. Soc. Inf. Sci. **55**(11), 970–979 (2004)

10. Kando, N.: Evaluation of information access technologies at the NTCIR workshop. In: Peters, C., Gonzalo, J., Braschler, M., Kluck, M. (eds.) CLEF 2003. LNCS, vol. 3237, pp. 29–43. Springer, Heidelberg (2004). https://doi.org/10.1007/978-3-540-30222-3_4

11. Losada, D.E., Parapar, J., Barreiro, Á.: Multi-armed bandits for ordering judgements in pooling-based evaluation. Inf. Process. Manag. **53**(3), 1005–1025 (2017)

12. Losada, D.E., Parapar, J., Barreiro, Á.: When to stop making relevance judgments? A study of stopping methods for building information retrieval test collections. J. Assoc. Inf. Sci. Technol. **70**(1), 49–60 (2018)

13. Luo, C., Sakai, T., Liu, Y., Dou, Z., Xiong, C., Xu, J.: Overview of the NTCIR-13 we want web task. In: Proceedings of NTCIR-13, pp. 394–401 (2017)

14. Mao, J., Sakai, T., Luo, C., Xiao, P., Liu, Y., Dou, Z.: Overview of the NTCIR-14 we want web task. In: Proceedings of NTCIR-14 (2019)

15. Rosenthal, R.: The "file drawer problem" and tolerance for null results. Psychol. Bull. **86**(3), 638–641 (1979)

16. Sakai, T.: Statistical significance, power, and sample sizes: a systematic review of SIGIR and TOIS, 2006–2015. In: Proceedings of ACM SIGIR 2016, pp. 5–14 (2016)

17. Sakai, T.: Laboratory Experiments in Information Retrieval: Sample Sizes, Effect Sizes, and Statistical Power. TIRS, vol. 40. Springer, Singapore (2018). https://doi.org/10.1007/978-981-13-1199-4

18. Sakai, T.: How to run an evaluation task. Information Retrieval Evaluation in a Changing World. TIRS, vol. 41, pp. 71–102. Springer, Cham (2019). https://doi.org/10.1007/978-3-030-22948-1_3

19. Sakai, T., et al.: Overview of the NTCIR-7 ACLIA IR4QA task. In: Proceedings of NTCIR-7, pp. 77–114 (2008)

20. Voorhees, E.M.: The philosophy of information retrieval evaluation. In: Peters, C., Braschler, M., Gonzalo, J., Kluck, M. (eds.) CLEF 2001. LNCS, vol. 2406, pp. 355–370. Springer, Heidelberg (2002). https://doi.org/10.1007/3-540-45691-0_34

21. Zobel, J.: How reliable are the results of large-scale information retrieval experiments? In: Proceedings of ACM SIGIR 1998, pp. 307–314 (1998)

22. Zobel, J.: Writing for Computer Science, 3rd edn. Springer, London (2014). https://doi.org/10.1007/978-1-4471-6639-9

Cross-Level Matching Model
for Information Retrieval

Yifan Nie and Jian-Yun Nie[✉]

University of Montreal, Montreal H3T 1J4, Canada
yifan.nie@umontreal.ca, nie@iro.umontreal.ca

Abstract. Recently, many neural retrieval models have been proposed and shown competitive results. In particular, interaction-based models have shown superior performance to traditional models in a number of studies. However, the interactions used as the basic matching signals are between single terms or their embeddings. In reality, a term can often match a phrase or even longer segment of text. This paper proposes a Cross-Level Matching Model which enhances the basic matching signals by allowing terms to match hidden representation states within a sentence. A gating mechanism aggregates the learned matching patterns of different matching channels and outputs a global matching score. Our model provides a simple and effective way for word-phrase matching.

Keywords: Information retrieval · Neural network · Ranking

1 Introduction

Recently many neural models for information retrieval have been proposed and demonstrated their effectiveness [4,6,10,14]. Generally, a neural retrieval model learns either the representations of query and document or the interactions between them through a series of neural layers [3,4]. Those neural layers such as RNN or 1D-convolutions aggregate low-level representations/interactions to produce higher level features [8,14]. Afterwards, a matching function is applied on the representations or interaction patterns to produce a matching score.

It has been found [4] that interaction-based neural models usually perform better than representation-based models because the former can capture more precise matching signals between components (words) in the document and the query. However, in interaction-based models, the basic interaction signals from which patterns are extracted are matchings between single words. This may limit the ability of the models to match different, but semantically similar elements.

In reality, there exists the need to match a term with a phrase. For instance, for the query "what's the standard barrel length for an AR", it is helpful to match the query phrase "standard barrel length" with the terms "AK47", "Carbine" in relevant documents, since they are all related to guns. Similarly, for the query "what's the nickname for Nevada", it is also helpful to match the query term "Nevada" to the document phrase "Silver State", because they both refer to

© Springer Nature Switzerland AG 2020
F. L. Wang et al. (Eds.): AIRS 2019, LNCS 12004, pp. 106–117, 2020.
https://doi.org/10.1007/978-3-030-42835-8_10

the State of Nevada. Since the neural layers aggregates low-level terms into higher level representations, it is possible to map the terms inside a phrase into hidden representations and match them with terms, thereby providing additional matching signals to interaction-based models.

Inspired by the above observations, for a neural retrieval model, instead of matching the query and document at only one layer, a better strategy is to produce the matching signals between the query and document at every layer and across layers. To address this issue, in this study, we propose a Cross-level Matching Model for Information Retrieval (CLMM). Our contributions are two-fold: (1) We perform matching between query and document at every representation layer and across layers to produce different matching patterns. (2) We employ a gating mechanism to dynamically aggregate the matching patterns learned by each matching channel to produce a global matching score, thereby paying more attention to more important matching channels. Our experiments on public dataset confirms the effectiveness of cross-level matching over single level matching.

The remainder of this paper is organized as follow: In Sect. 2, we will present related work of neural retrieval models. In Sect. 3, we will illustrate our proposed CLMM model. In Sect. 4, we will present our experimental study. In Sect. 5, we will conclude this paper and point our possible future work.

2   Related Work

Given a query q and a document d, the core of a neural retrieval model is expected to produce matching score between them. Depending on how this matching score is obtained, the existing models could be roughly divided into representation- and interaction-based models [4].

Representation-based models first learn representations of query and document through a series of neural representation learning layers, and then match the final layers of query and document to produce a relevance score by a matching function. For example, in DSSM [6], the representations are learned by feed forward neural network and the matching is performed by a simple cosine similarity. In CDSSM [14], the representations are learned by convolutional network and the matching function is the cosine similarity. In SMN [16], the representations are learned by recurrent neural network and the matching is performed by 2D convolutions.

It has been shown that interaction-based models generally perform better than representation-based models [4]. In interaction-based models such as MatchPyramid [10,11], ARC-II [5] and DRMM [4], the relevance scores are calculated in a different way. First, query and document terms are represented by their embeddings $w(q)$ and $w(d)$. Afterwards, the term-to-term interactions between query and document are constructed through cosine similarity, dot product or histogram. Those interaction signals are then fed into feed forward or convolutional neural layers in order to learn the interaction patterns. However, the basic features $w(q)$ and $w(d)$ are usually the embeddings of single terms. A crucial problem in natural language is that the meaning of a term can often be expressed by a phrase or more complex construct. The basic term-level interactions may miss important matching signals between document and query. Therefore, in this paper, we explore the usefulness of matching terms against hidden states generated within a sentence. The latter can encode information about phrases. In this way, we can solve the problem of word-phrase matching. We call it cross-level matching.

The recent MACM [9] also considers multiple levels of interaction. However, our approach proposed in this paper is different from [9] in several aspects: First, instead of only employing term embeddings, we learn different layers of representations for the query and document and match the representations at different levels. Second, we match the query and document not only at the same level (i.e. $(h^{q,(i)}, h^{d,(i)})$), but also across layers (i.e. $(h^{q,(i)}, h^{d,(j)}), i \neq j$). Third, instead of obtaining only a scalar score at each level, we produce a vector representing the matching pattern of each matching channel $(h^{q,(i)}, h^{d,(j)})$ which is expected to be more informative than the scalar value.

This work is also different from [2] in several aspects: First, instead of kernel pooling, we employ 2D convolutions to analyze the matching patterns of each matching channel. Second, instead of concatenating the learned patterns from each matching channel, we employ a gating mechanism to attentively combine them, thereby paying more attention to important matching channels dynamically. To better investigate the effectiveness of cross-level matching, we propose our CLMM model, which will be presented in detail in the next section.

3   Cross-Level Matching Model

The architecture of our proposed Cross-level Matching Model is illustrated in Fig. 1. The model could be roughly divided into 3 parts: representation learning module, cross-level matching channels and gated aggregation module. The details of the components will be presented as follows.

Representation Learning Module: Given a query q and a document d, we first extract their term embeddings through an embedding lookup matrix and represent them as $q = [t_1^q, t_2^q, ..., t_n^q]$, $d = [t_1^d, t_2^d, ..., t_m^d]$, where t_i^q, t_j^d are the term embeddings for the ith query term and the jth document term. Once the term embeddings are extracted, we learn L layers of representations for the query and document by either Bi-LSTM or 1D-convolutions. For the BiLSTM encoder:

$$h_i^{q,(1)} = BiLSTM(t_i^q, h_{i-1}^{q,(1)}, h_{i+1}^{q,(1)}) \tag{1}$$

$$h_i^{q,(l)} = BiLSTM(h_i^{q,(l-1)}, h_{i-1}^{q,(l)}, h_{i+1}^{q,(l)}), \quad l = 2..L \tag{2}$$

$$h_i^{d,(1)} = BiLSTM(t_i^d, h_{i-1}^{d,(1)}, h_{i+1}^{d,(1)}) \tag{3}$$

$$h_i^{d,(l)} = BiLSTM(h_i^{d,(l-1)}, h_{i-1}^{d,(l)}, h_{i+1}^{d,(l)}), \quad l = 2..L \tag{4}$$

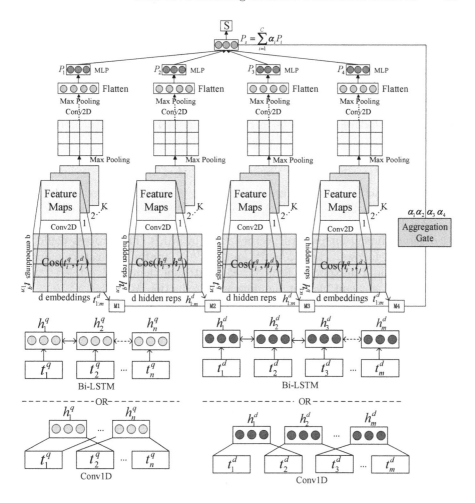

Fig. 1. Cross-level matching model

where $h_i^{q,(l)}$ and $h_i^{d,(l)}$ represent the hidden state of the ith query and document term at layer l. For the Conv1D encoder:

$$h_i^{q,(1)} = f(W_1^q * [t_{i-w(1)}^q; ..; t_{i+w(1)}^q] + b_1^q) \tag{5}$$

$$h_i^{q,(l)} = f(W_l^q * [h_{i-w(l)}^{q,(l-1)}; ...; h_{i+w(l)}^{q,(l-1)}] + b_l^q), \ l = 2, ..., L \tag{6}$$

$$h_i^{d,(1)} = f(W_1^d * [t_{i-w(1)}^d; ..; t_{i+w(1)}^d] + b_1^d) \tag{7}$$

$$h_i^{d,(l)} = f(W_l^d * [h_{i-w(l)}^{d,(l-1)}; ...; h_{i+w(l)}^{d,(l-1)}] + b_l^d), \ l = 2, ..., L \tag{8}$$

where $h_i^{q,(l)}$ and $h_i^{d,(l)}$ represent the hidden representations of the ith query and document term at layer l. $2w(l) + 1$ is the Conv1D window size at layer l. f is the $tanh$ activation function.

Cross-Level Matching Channels: Once the representations of each layer for the query $[h^{q,(0)}, .., h^{q,(L)}]$ and the document $[h^{d,(0)}, .., h^{d,(L)}]$ are learned, we perform cross-level matching for each of the combinations of the abstraction layers between query and document by calculating a cosine interaction matrix. As an example, Fig. 1 only illustrates the case with Layer 0 (embedding layer) and Layer 1, with total 4 cross matching channels. The process could be summarized as follows, where $I^{l,m}$ represents the interaction matrix for the lth and m^{th} representation layer of the query and the document.

$$I_{ij}^{l,m} = Cos(h_i^{q,(l)}, h_j^{d,(m)}), \ l = 0, .., L, m = 0, .., L \tag{9}$$

Once the interaction matrices are built, the interaction patterns are learned through a series of 2D-convolutions. Finally the interaction patterns of the last max-pooled layers are flattened into vectors $Q^{l,m}$ as in [11] and compressed into reduced dimension pattern vectors $P^{l,m}$ by MLP. The process could be summarized as follows, where $C^{k,(l,m)}$ and $M^{k,(l,m)}$ are the kth feature maps of the convolved and maxpooled layer for the matching channel (l, m). $W_{l,m}$ and $b_{l,m}$ are the weight and bias for the dimension reduction MLP.

$$C_1^{k,(l,m)} = Conv2D(I^{l,m}) \tag{10}$$

$$M_1^{k,(l,m)} = Maxpool(C_1^{k,(l,m)}) \tag{11}$$

$$C_2^{k,(l,m)} = Conv2D(M_1^{k,(l,m)}) \tag{12}$$

$$M_2^{k,(l,m)} = Maxpool(C_2^{k,(l,m)}) \tag{13}$$

$$Q^{l,m} = Flatten(M_2^{l,m}) \tag{14}$$

$$P^{l,m} = f(W_{l,m}Q^{l,m} + b_{l,m}) \tag{15}$$

Gated Aggregation: To aggregate the matching patterns $P^{l,m}$ learned from each matching channel, a better strategy is to attentively combine them rather than concatenating them together, since for each query-document pair, some matching channels might be more important than the others.

In order to achieve attentive combination of the matching patterns of all matching channels, akin to [9], we calculate a channel-importance score $M^{l,m}$ for each of the matching channels (l, m) from their interaction matrices $I^{l,m}$. We first take the maximum value $M_i^{l,m}$ of each row i of the interaction matrix $I^{l,m}$, which represents the strongest interaction between the ith query term/hidden representation and all document terms/hidden representations. Afterwards, we take the average of all these $M_i^{l,m}$ values across the rows to obtain the global maximum interaction of the whole query with respect to the entire document. The process could be summarized as follows.

$$M_i^{l,m} = \max_{j=1..v} I_{ij}^{l,m} \tag{16}$$

$$M^{l,m} = \frac{1}{u} \sum_{i=1..u} M_i^{l,m} \tag{17}$$

where u, v are the number of rows and columns for the interaction matrix $I^{l,m}$ of the matching channel (l, m). Intuitively, the higher the value $M^{l,m}$ is, the more we will rely on this matching channel.

Once the channel-importance scores $M^{l,m}$ are produced, we feed them into a softmax gate to get normalized weight for each matching channel.

$$\alpha_{l,m} = \frac{exp(\beta_{l,m}M^{l,m})}{\sum_{r,s} exp(\beta_{r,s}M^{r,s})} \tag{18}$$

where $\beta_{l,m}$ are learnable scalar parameters, and $M^{l,m}$ are the channel-importance scores for each matching channel. Finally the matching patterns $P^{l,m}$ learned by each matching channel are attentively aggregated with the channel-specific weights $\alpha_{l,m}$, and fed into a scoring MLP to produce a global matching score S.

$$P_s = \sum_{(l,m)} \alpha_{l,m}P^{l,m} \tag{19}$$

$$S = f(W_sP_s + b_s) \tag{20}$$

The training is done with a pair-wise loss: given a training example (Q, D_+, D_-), we hope that the score $S(Q, D_+)$ should be higher than the score $S(Q, D_-)$. The loss is defined in Eq. 21, where Θ includes all trainable parameters of the CLMM Model:

$$L(Q, D_+, D_-; \Theta) = max(0, 1 - (S(Q, D_+) - S(Q, D_-))) \tag{21}$$

Alternative Configurations: To investigate the best strategy to aggregate the learned matching patterns, we also build several alternative combination schemas:

CLMM-Concat: Once we obtain the flattened vector $Q^{l,m}$ of the last maxpooled layer from each matching channel, we don't compress them into dimension-reduction MLP, but directly concatenate them together, map it into P_s by MLP and feed them into the last scoring layer.

CLMM-MLP: After obtaining the flattened vector $Q^{l,m}$ of the last max-pooled layer from each matching channel, we compress them through dimension-reduction MLPs to produce $P^{l,m}$. Then, we concatenate the $P^{l,m}$ together and feed it into the last scoring layer.

CLMM-MLP-Maxpool: Same as CLMM-MLP, after obtaining the flattened vector $Q^{l,m}$, we first compress them through dimension-reduction MLPs to produce $P^{l,m}$. Then we perform dimension-wise maxpooling on $P^{l,m}$ across all matching channels to obtain P_s and feed it to the last scoring layer.

4   Experimental Study

4.1   Dataset and Setting

In this study, experiments are conducted on MSMARCO[1] dataset. For MSMARCO, since it is a competition and doesn't disclose the evaluation set's judgment, we evaluate the method on the development set, which is randomly split into validation and test sets with a ratio of 1:9. The statistics of the datasets are shown in Table 1.

Table 1. Statistics of datasets

	# train_q	# valid_q	# test_q	# train_triples	#avg_doc_len
MSMARCO	68,750	698	6282	39.8M	58

We employ pretrained GloVe.6B.300d embeddings[2], and fine-tune them during training. Due to memory limitations, we learn 1 layer of hidden representations for both the BiLSTM and Conv1D representation modules, and perform matching on 4 channels, namely $(H^{q,(0)}, H^{d,(0)})$, $(H^{q,(1)}, H^{d,(1)})$, $(H^{q,(0)}, H^{d,(1)})$, $(H^{q,(1)}, H^{d,(0)})$, where $H^{q,(0)}$, $H^{q,(1)}$ represent the embedding layer and first hidden layer for query and $H^{d,(0)}$, $H^{d,(1)}$ represent the embedding layer and first hidden layer for document. The hidden size for one direction of the BiLSTM is set to 128, so the bi-directional hidden representation's size is 256. The hidden size for Conv1D is set to 256 and the convolutional window size is set to 2.

We limit the max number of 2D convolution layers to 2 and fix the number of 2D feature maps to [32, 16] for the 2 convolution layers, set the max query length and document length to be $n = 20$, $m = 100$ due to memory limitations, and apply zero padding when needed as done in [10]. We fix the pooling size of all max pooling layers to be $(2, 2)$, and omit OOV document terms. All hidden sizes in the aggregation components are set to 256.

4.2   Baselines and Evaluation Metrics

In order to demonstrate the effectiveness of CLMM, we compare our CLMM with the following baselines:

BM25 [12], **LM** [17]: Traditional retrieval models.

MatchPyramid [10]: An interaction-based model which doesn't learn hidden representations for query and document and directly matches the query and document term embeddings through 2D-convolutions. This model is equivalent to CLMM with only one matching channel $(H^{q,(0)}, H^{d,(0)})$.

---

[1] http://www.msmarco.org/dataset.aspx.
[2] https://nlp.stanford.edu/projects/glove/.

SMN [16]: SMN first learns hidden representations of query and document through RNNs and matches the hidden states of query and document through 2D-convolutions. This model is equivalent to CLMM with only one matching channel $(H^{q,(1)}, H^{d,(1)})$.

DRMM [4]: DRMM represents the interactions between query and document by histograms instead of interaction matrices.

MACM [9]: A modified version of MatchPyramid which produces a matching score at every level of interaction. The matching scores of all layers are aggregated dynamically through a gating mechanism to produce a global matching score.

C-KNRM [2]: C-KNRM first builds bi-gram representations on top of query and document terms by 1D convolutions. Afterwards, the matching patterns of 4 matching channels between the uni-grams and bi-grams of query and document are learned through kernel pooling. The learned patterns are concatenated to produce a final matching score.

We employ MAP [13], nDCG [7] and MRR [1] as evaluation metrics.

4.3   Experimental Results

The main experimental results are summarized in Table 2. We perform paired t-test with Bonferroni correction on CLMM models with respect to BM25, LM, DRMM, MatchPyramid, SMN, MACM and C-KNRM baselines. The statistically significant results ($p < 0.05$) are marked with $*$. CLMM-BiLSTM represents the proposed CLMM model with BiLSTM as representation learning module, and CLMM-Conv represents CLMM model with 1D-convolutions as representation learning module. Conv(1, 1) is a model to be compared within the CLMM-Conv group. It employs 1 layer 1D-convolution to learn hidden representations of query and document and match the hidden representations of query and document through 2D-convolutions in a similar way to MatchPyramid.

From Table 2, we first observe that with the best aggregating strategy, CLMM-BiLSTM-Gate and CLMM-Conv-Gate outperform all the baselines on all evaluation metrics. This confirms the effectiveness of our proposed CLMM model.

Second, by comparing the results of MatchPyramid, SMN and CLMM-BiLSTM-Gate, we notice that CLMM-BiLSTM-Gate outperforms both Match-Pyramid and SMN. MatchPyramid doesn't learn hidden representations of the query and document and directly matches query and document term embeddings. It is equivalent to CLMM with one matching channel $(H^{q,(0)}, H^{d,(0)})$. SMN learns 1 layer of hidden representations of the query and document and matches the hidden representations of the query and document. It is equivalent to CLMM with one matching channel $(H^{q,(1)}, H^{d,(1)})$. From this comparison, we can observe that involving multiple matching channels is better than using

Table 2. Experimental results

MSMARCO	MAP	NDCG1	NDCG3	NDCG10	NDCG20	MRR
BM25	0.1847	0.1214	0.1959	0.2668	0.2942	0.1873
LM	0.1717	0.1095	0.1828	0.2476	0.2743	0.1739
DRMM	0.0967	0.0535	0.0955	0.1388	0.1582	0.0979
MatchPyramid	0.2053	0.1407	0.2203	0.2940	0.3221	0.2081
SMN	0.1941	0.1332	0.2096	0.2744	0.3028	0.1970
MACM	0.2091	0.1463	0.2297	0.2970	0.3236	0.2123
C-KNRM	0.1883	0.1303	0.2006	0.2657	0.2946	0.1909
CLMM-BiLSTM-MLP	0.1931*	0.1297*	0.2060*	0.2746*	0.3045*	0.1957*
CLMM-BiLSTM-concat	0.1657*	0.1046	0.1729	0.2369*	0.2658*	0.1686*
CLMM-BiLSTM-MLP-Maxpool	0.1769*	0.1191*	0.1860*	0.2493*	0.2791*	0.1801*
CLMM-BiLSTM-Gate	**0.2195***	**0.1571***	**0.2406***	**0.3080***	**0.3382***	**0.2223***
Conv(1, 1)	0.1370	0.0867	0.1398	0.1935	0.2199	0.1391
CLMM-Conv-MLP	0.2158*	0.1500*	0.2352*	0.3060*	0.3346*	0.2186*
CLMM-Conv-concat	0.1758*	0.1176	0.1848*	0.2485*	0.2785*	0.1782*
CLMM-Conv-MLP-Maxpool	0.2156*	0.1550*	0.2355*	0.3040*	0.3320*	0.2186*
CLMM-Conv-Gate	**0.2310***	**0.1653***	**0.2592***	**0.3244***	**0.3524***	**0.2343***

any of the single matching channels. The same holds true for the comparison between MatchPyramid, Conv(1, 1) and CLMM-Conv-Gate.

Third, among the different aggregation strategies, the gated aggregation works the best, for both the BiLSTM and Conv case. This confirms the advantage of using a gating mechanisms to attentively combine the learned interaction patterns from all matching channels over non-attention-based aggregations.

Finally, our proposed CLMM-Gate outperforms MACM and C-KNRM. The major difference between CLMM-Gate and MACM is that MACM only takes advantage of the matching signals between query and document on the same level, whereas CLMM-Gate has matching signals between terms and hidden representations of phrases. This result demonstrates the usefulness of those additional signals. Although C-KNRM also models the interactions between terms and phrases, it directly concatenates the learned patterns of different matching channels. Our CLMM-Gate employs an attentive gating mechanism to aggregate the learned patterns from different matching channels which could better aggregate the matching patterns across channels.

4.4 Discussions

In order to further understand the advantage of matching different representation layers of the query and document, we take a representative test query "what is the standard barrel length for an AR" (a type of gun), and a relevant passage to this query. We visualize the interaction matrices $I^{0,0}$, $I^{1,1}$ and $I^{1,0}$ of CLMM-BiLSTM-Gate for the matching channels $(H^{q,(0)}, H^{d,(0)})$, $(H^{q,(1)}, H^{d,(1)})$ and $(H^{q,(1)}, H^{d,(0)})$ respectively in Fig. 2.

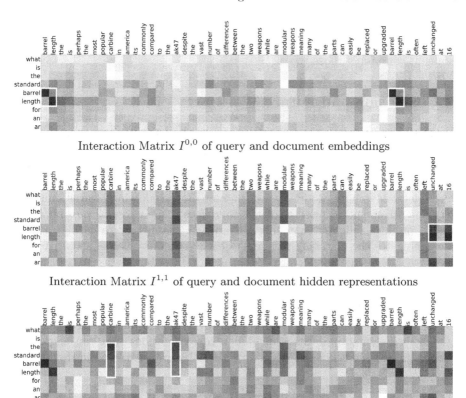

Interaction Matrix $I^{0,0}$ of query and document embeddings

Interaction Matrix $I^{1,1}$ of query and document hidden representations

Interaction Matrix $I^{1,0}$ of query hidden representation and document embeddings

Fig. 2. Visualization of matching matrices

From Fig. 2a, we can observe that the term embedding matching channel $I^{0,0}$ is responsible to identify the exact-matched terms. In this example, the terms "barrel length" which occur in both the query and document have very high matching intensities. This shows that the channel $I^{0,0}$ is very useful to fulfil the need for lexical matches.

From Fig. 2b, we notice that the hidden representation matching channel $I^{1,1}$ is responsible to match in the latent semantic space. In this case, query terms "barrel length" and relevant document terms "unchanged at 16" are mapped into hidden representations and matched with high intensities, which helps the model to successfully identify the answer to this query. This demonstrates that the channel $I^{1,1}$ is essential to generalizing query and document terms and performing matching in the latent semantic space.

Figure 2c shows that the cross-level matching channel $I^{1,0}$ (query hidden representation with document term embeddings) is also helpful. In this case, the model successfully associates the document terms such as "Carbine" and "AK47" with hidden representations of query phrase "standard barrel length".

Since the semantics of "barrel length" are related to guns, matching them with guns such as "Carbine" and "AK47" will help the model to find the relevant document containing those terms.

5   Conclusion and Future Work

Most of the existing neural retrieval models rely on either the representations or interactions of only one layer to perform matching. However, the relevant semantics of a term could also be expressed in phrases. Therefore there exists the need for term-phrase matching. To address this challenge, in this paper, we propose a Cross-level Matching Model for Information Retrieval, which learns multiple query and document representations and matches them across all possible layer pairs to produce different matching patterns. A channel-aware gating mechanism aggregates the matching patterns of each matching channel attentively to produce a global matching score. Experiments on public dataset confirm the advantage of employing multiple matching channels to enhance the basic term matching signals.

This work could be extended in several ways. First, other representation learning modules such as the Transformer [15] could be tested. Second, it is possible to create several layers of hidden representations that can aggregate even longer text segments or sentences. This will also be explored in the future.

References

1. Craswell, N.: Mean reciprocal rank. In: Liu, L., Özsu, M.T., et al. (eds.) Encyclopedia of Database Systems, 2nd edn. Springer, Boston (2018). https://doi.org/10.1007/978-0-387-39940-9_488
2. Dai, Z., Xiong, C., Callan, J., Liu, Z.: Convolutional neural networks for soft-matching n-grams in ad-hoc search. In: Proceedings of the Eleventh ACM International Conference on Web Search and Data Mining, WSDM 2018, Marina Del Rey, CA, USA, 5–9 February 2018, pp. 126–134 (2018)
3. Dehghani, M., Zamani, H., Severyn, A., Kamps, J., Croft, W.B.: Neural ranking models with weak supervision. In: SIGIR 2017, Shinjuku, Tokyo, Japan, 7–11 August 2017, pp. 65–74 (2017)
4. Guo, J., Fan, Y., Ai, Q., Croft, W.B.: A deep relevance matching model for ad-hoc retrieval. In: CIKM 2016, Indianapolis, IN, USA, 24–28 October 2016, pp. 55–64 (2016)
5. Hu, B., Lu, Z., Li, H., Chen, Q.: Convolutional neural network architectures for matching natural language sentences. In: NIPS 2014, 8–13 December 2014, Montreal, Quebec, Canada, pp. 2042–2050 (2014)
6. Huang, P., He, X., Gao, J., Deng, L., Acero, A., Heck, L.P.: Learning deep structured semantic models for web search using clickthrough data. In: CIKM 2013, San Francisco, CA, USA, 27 October–1 November 2013, pp. 2333–2338 (2013)
7. Järvelin, K., Kekäläinen, J.: Cumulated gain-based evaluation of IR techniques. ACM Trans. Inf. Syst. 20(4), 422–446 (2002)

8. Melamud, O., Goldberger, J., Dagan, I.: context2vec: learning generic context embedding with bidirectional LSTM. In: Proceedings of the 20th SIGNLL Conference on Computational Natural Language Learning, CoNLL 2016, Berlin, Germany, 11–12 August 2016, pp. 51–61 (2016)
9. Nie, Y., Sordoni, A., Nie, J.: Multi-level abstraction convolutional model with weak supervision for information retrieval. In: SIGIR 2018, Ann Arbor, MI, USA, 08–12 July 2018, pp. 985–988 (2018)
10. Pang, L., Lan, Y., Guo, J., Xu, J., Cheng, X.: A study of match pyramid models on ad-hoc retrieval. CoRR abs/1606.04648 (2016)
11. Pang, L., Lan, Y., Guo, J., Xu, J., Wan, S., Cheng, X.: Text matching as image recognition. In: Proceedings of the Thirtieth AAAI Conference on Artificial Intelligence, 12–17 February 2016, Phoenix, Arizona, USA, pp. 2793–2799 (2016)
12. Robertson, S.E., Zaragoza, H.: The probabilistic relevance framework: BM25 and beyond. Found. Trends Inf. Retr. **3**(4), 333–389 (2009)
13. Sakai, T., Kando, N.: On information retrieval metrics designed for evaluation with incomplete relevance assessments. Inf. Retr. **11**(5), 447–470 (2008)
14. Shen, Y., He, X., Gao, J., Deng, L., Mesnil, G.: Learning semantic representations using convolutional neural networks for web search. In: WWW 2014, Seoul, Republic of Korea, 7–11 April 2014, pp. 373–374 (2014)
15. Vaswani, A., et al.: Attention is all you need. In: Advances in Neural Information Processing Systems 30: Annual Conference on Neural Information Processing Systems 2017, 4–9 December 2017, Long Beach, CA, USA, pp. 6000–6010 (2017)
16. Wu, Y., Wu, W., Xing, C., Zhou, M., Li, Z.: Sequential matching network: a new architecture for multi-turn response selection in retrieval-based chatbots. In: ACL 2017, Vancouver, Canada, 30 July–4 August, vol. 1, pp. 496–505 (2017)
17. Zhai, C., Lafferty, J.D.: A study of smoothing methods for language models applied to ad hoc information retrieval. In: SIGIR 2001, New Orleans, Louisiana, USA, pp. 334–342 (2001)

Understanding and Improving Neural Ranking Models from a Term Dependence View

Yixing Fan[✉], Jiafeng Guo, Yanyan Lan, and Xueqi Cheng

CAS Key Lab of Network Data Science and Technology,
Institute of Computing Technology, Chinese Academy of Sciences,
Beijing 100190, China
{fanyixing,guojiafeng,lanyanyan,cxq}@ict.ac.cn

Abstract. Recently, neural information retrieval (NeuIR) has attracted a lot of interests, where a variety of neural models have been proposed for the core ranking problem. Beyond the continuous refresh of the state-of-the-art neural ranking performance, the community calls for more analysis and understanding of the emerging neural ranking models. In this paper, we attempt to analyze these new models from a traditional view, namely term dependence. Without loss of generality, most existing neural ranking models could be categorized into three categories with respect to their underlying assumption on query term dependence, i.e., independent models, dependent models, and hybrid models. We conduct rigorous empirical experiments over several representative models from these three categories on a benchmark dataset and a large click-through dataset. Interestingly, we find that no single type of model can achieve a consistent win over others on different search queries. An oracle model which can select the right model for each query can obtain significant performance improvement. Based on the analysis we introduce an adaptive strategy for neural ranking models. We hypothesize that the term dependence in a query could be measured through the divergence between its independent and dependent representations. We thus propose a dependence gate based on such divergence representation to softly select neural ranking models for each query accordingly. Experimental results verify the effectiveness of the adaptive strategy.

Keywords: Understanding · Term dependence · Query adaptation

1 Introduction

Recently, deep neural networks have led to exciting breakthroughs in speech recognition, computer vision, and natural language processing (NLP) tasks. This also inspires researchers to apply neural models for the core ranking problem in the information retrieval (IR) community. During the past few years, a large number of neural ranking models have been proposed, leading to a hot topic

© Springer Nature Switzerland AG 2020
F. L. Wang et al. (Eds.): AIRS 2019, LNCS 12004, pp. 118–130, 2020.
https://doi.org/10.1007/978-3-030-42835-8_11

named NeuIR. However, beyond continuous refresh of the state-of-the-art neural ranking performance, the community calls for more analysis and understanding of the emerging neural ranking models.

There have been a few studies making progress in understanding the architecture of neural ranking models. For example, in [5], the authors categorized existing neural ranking models into two types according to their model architecture, namely representation-focused models and interaction-focused models. Mitra et al. [15] also provided similar idea, but named the two categories as lexical matching models and semantic matching models. They show in general interaction-focused models work better than representation-focused models since ranking is more directly about interaction between the query and the document. In [3], the authors studied different granularity of IR tasks to analyze what information is important or extraneous at each level of a neural ranking model.

In this paper, we try to analyze neural ranking models from a different dimension. Unlike previous works [5,15] which categorize neural ranking models mainly based on model architecture, we take a traditional IR view, namely term dependence view, to look at these existing neural ranking models. Term dependence has been a long-studied problem in IR. It has been widely accepted that it is of great importance to model the term dependence in an effective retrieval model [2,13,24]. In [13], the authors have introduced three term independence assumptions, namely full independence, sequential dependence, and full dependence, under the framework of Markov random field.

When we look at existing neural ranking models from the term dependence view, we find that these models can be categorized into three groups, namely independent model, dependent model, and hybrid model. Although the existing neural ranking models do not mention term dependence in their model design, they actually take one of the three underlying assumptions on term dependence. We then conduct rigorous empirical comparisons to analyze the three categories of models based on both a benchmark LETOR4.0 data and a large scale click-through data collected from a commercial search engine. We find that there is no clear winner between the three types of models. Even the hybrid model does not show consistent advantages as one may expect. Moreover, beyond the average performance, we also look at the detailed performance on each query. We find that each category of models have their own advantages and perform better on a subset of queries. If there is an oracle that can select a right model for each query, we can significantly improve the ranking performance. This indicates that there is a large room for the design or optimization of neural ranking models.

Based on the above observations, we introduce an adaptive strategy for neural ranking models, which attempts to select neural models with different dependence assumption for each query accordingly. Specifically, we hypothesize that the term dependence in a query could be measured through certain divergence between its independent and dependent representations. We propose a term dependence gate based on such divergence, and use it to softly select between an independent and a dependent neural ranking model for each query. We evaluate the effectiveness of the proposed adaptive strategy using the same two datasets mentioned above. The experimental results demonstrate that by adapting to each query with respect to term dependence, one can obtain significant performance improvement.

2   Related Work

In this section, we briefly review the studies relevant to our work, including understanding on neural ranking models and term dependence in retrieval models.

2.1   Understanding on Neural Ranking Models

There have been a few efforts to understand the neural ranking models. For example, Guo et al. [5,7] has analyzed the architecture of the existing neural ranking models, and categorized these models into different groups. Cohen et al. [3] proposed a probe based methodology to evaluate what information is important or extraneous at each level of a network. Nie et al. [17] proposed to compare the representation-focused models and interaction-focused models under the same condition. They built a similar convolution networks to learn either representations and interaction patterns between query and document. Though several works have made their efforts in understanding the neural ranking models, to the best of our knowledge, there are no works trying to understand the neural ranking models from the term dependence view.

2.2   Term Dependence in Retrieval Models

Different dependence assumptions between query terms have been made in designing retrieval models. Note here term dependence, broadly speaking, is also known as *term co-occurrence*, *adjacency*, *lexical affinities*, and *proximity* in IR. Without loss of generality, existing models can be divided into three classes, namely independent model, dependent model, and hybrid model, according to the degree of the underlying dependence assumptions.

Firstly, the independent models assume each query term independent from others. In this way, to compute the relevance of a document, one can first estimate the matching between the document and each query term separately, and aggregate these matching signals to produce the final relevance score. A large number of models have been designed under this branch [22,25,28]. Although many independent models (e.g., BM25 and QL) are simple and effective on different queries, they are often considered insufficient by ignoring the term dependencies (such as *information* and *retrieval*) which may help filter out irrelevant document efficiently [13]. Obviously, it is insufficient to treat each term independently as the term dependence exists in queries everywhere. Secondly, the dependent models assume query terms be dependent on each other in some way [13]. In this way, the relevance score can no longer be decomposed to each query term, but rather be computed with respect to dependent units, such as phrases, n-grams or even the whole query [1,9,23,24]. For example, The bi-term language model [24] attempts to capture the term dependence between term pairs under the language model framework. Although the dependence assumption seems more powerful than the independence assumption, the performance of the dependent models is not consistently the best so far as we know. The possible reason is that there is very little hope of accurately modeling general term dependencies due to data sparsity, if at all [13]. Lastly, the hybrid models propose to combine both assumptions to improve the retrieval performance. There have been a number of retrieval models developed in this manner [12,13,20]. For example, in [13], Metzler et al. constructs a Markov random field on query terms which models multiple query term dependencies (i.e., single terms, ordered phases, and unordered phrases) simultaneously. Although hybrid models take into account multiple dependence assumptions, they actually pose a strong underlying assumption that some fixed combination of independence and dependence assumptions could fit all the queries.

3   Dependence View of Neural Ranking Models

In this section, we first introduce the dependence view of the neural ranking models. Then, we conduct experiments to analyze existing models with different dependence assumptions.

3.1   Dependence Categorization

There have been a few taxonomies proposed for existing neural ranking models. For example, in [5], the neural ranking models are categorized into representation-focused and interaction-focused model based on their architectures. Different from the architecture view, we look at existing neural ranking models from the dependence view, which have been mainly investigated over traditional retrieval methods [2,13]. Although existing neural ranking models do not mention the term dependence in their model design, they actually take a specific assumption on term dependence. Without loss of generality, existing neural ranking models can be categorized into three categories, namely independent models, dependent models, and hybrid models. The independent model, as its name suggested, assumes independence between terms. In this way, the relevance score could be decomposed with respect to each query term. Representative models include:

- **DRMM:** The DRMM [5] treats both query and document as bag of word embeddings. Each query term interacts with the document to produce the term level matching score.
- **K-NRM:** The K-NRM [27] is a neural ranking model built upon DRMM, which uses a kernel pooling layer to replace the matching histogram layer in DRMM.

The dependent model, assumes the terms are in some way dependent on each other. More specifically, according to the range of term dependence, there are two types of dependence, namely partially dependent and fully dependent. The partial dependent model assumes the terms are dependent on each other within a local contextual window. Representative models include:

- **ARCII:** The ARCII [8] utilizes a one-dimensional convolution neural network to enhance the term representation by a local context, where the window size determines the range of dependent scope.
- **MatchPyramid:** The MatchPyramid [18] constructs a matching matrix based on term-term interactions. Then, a two dimensional convolution neural network is applied on the matching matrix to capture the proximity between terms in pre-defined size windows.

The fully dependent model assumes all terms are dependent with each other. Representative models include:

- **ARCI:** The ARCI [8] firstly learns the global representation for both query and document. Then, the final score is obtained based on the interaction between these two representations.
- **DSSM:** The DSSM [9] also learned a global representation for each text, but employs a fully connected neural network on the tri-letters instead.

Other models like CDSSM [23] and MVLSTM [26] also belong to this category.

The hybrid model considers both assumptions simultaneously and combines models from different categories. Representative models include:

- **PACRR:** The PACRR [10] captures both the independent (i.e., unigram) term matching and the dependent (i.e., n-gram) term matching by convolution neural networks.
- **Duet:** The Duet [16] combines a local model with a distributed model for query-document matching. The local model captures the term level interaction independently and the distributed model learns global representation for both query and document in a fully dependent way.

Some other models such as Conv-KNRM [4], MatchTensor [11], and DeepRank [19] also fall into this category.

3.2   Experimental Setting

To better understand the characteristics of models with different dependence assumptions, we conduct empirical analysis over representative models on benchmark datasets.

Data Sets. To compare the results of different dependent models, we conduct experiments on LETOR4.0 dataset [21] and a large scale click-through dataset. We choose these two datasets since they contain sufficiently large collections of

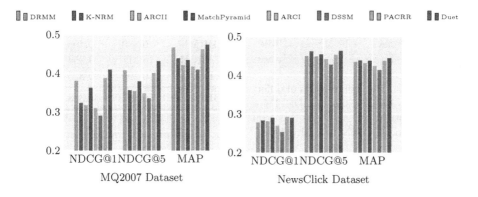

Fig. 1. Performance comparison of different dependent models on two datasets.

queries, which are desirable for training and comparing many data-hungry (i.e., neural) retrieval models. Specifically, in LETOR4.0, we leverage the MQ2007 dataset as the testbed since it contains much more queries than MQ2008. The click-through data, namely NewsClick, is collected from a commercial news search engine, where clicked documents are viewed to be relevant, and the others are viewed as irrelevant. We apply some typical data pre-processing techniques, such as word segmentation, stopping words and low frequency words (less than 100) removing. After these preprocessing, the final NewsClick dataset contains 223,783 queries and 6,292,911 documents.

Evaluation Methodology. For MQ2007, We follow the data partition in Letor4.0 [21], and 5-fold cross-validation is conducted to minimize overfitting as in [5]. Specifically, the parameters for each model are tuned on 4-of-5 folds. The last fold in each case is used for evaluation. For NewsClick, we partitioned the dataset into training/validation/testing sets according to the proportion 8:1:1. Here, we adopt normalized discounted cumulative gain (NDCG) and mean average precision (MAP) as the evaluation metrics.

Model Details. Here, we choose two representative models from different categories to conduct the experiments. Specifically, we choose DRMM and K-NRM as the independent model. For dependent model, we selected two representative models for both the partial dependent model and the fully dependent model, i.e., MatchPyramid and ARCII as the partial dependent model, and ARCI and DSSM as the fully dependent model. For the hybrid model, we choose the PACRR and Duet. The implementations of these models are based on the open-source toolkit MatchZoo [6]. To train these models for the MQ2007 dataset, we have utilized the pre-trained term vectors on the Wikipedia corpus[1] using the CBOW model [14]. All other trainable parameters are randomly initialized by uniform distribution within $[-0.2, 0.2]$.

---

[1] http://en.wikipedia.org/wiki/Wikipediadatabase.

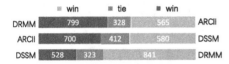

Fig. 2. The pairwise comparison of different models on MQ2007 dataset. DRMM is a independent model, ARCII is a partial dependent model, DSSM is a fully dependent model.

Model Name	NDCG@1	NDCG@5	MAP
DRMM	0.380	0.408	0.467
ARCII	0.317	0.354	0.449
DSSM	0.290	0.335	0.409
ORACLE	0.497	0.528	0.542

Fig. 3. Performance comparison of different retrieval models on MQ2007 dataset.

3.3 Empirical Analysis

The overall results are depicted in the Fig. 1. We have the following observations:

1. For the independent model, we found that the performance winner is not consistent between DRMM and K-NRM on different datasets. K-NRM can outperform DRMM on the larger dataset (i.e., NewsClick) when the word embeddings can be learned in an end-to-end way, but may not work well as DRMM when the dataset is relatively small (i.e., MQ2007).
2. For the dependent model, the partially dependent models are always better than the fully dependent models in terms of all evaluation metrics. This might be due to the fact that modeling full dependence is much more complicated than modeling partial dependence, since the sparsity problem becomes much more severe in the full dependence [13].
3. For the hybrid models, we found that Duet outperforms the PACRR on MQ2007 dataset in terms of all the three metrics. However, on NewsClick dataset, the PACRR performs better than Duet in terms of NDCG@1.
4. When comparing the four groups of models, the hybrid models (i.e., PACRR and Duet) in general can perform better than the independent models (i.e., DRMM and K-NRM) and the dependent models (i.e., MatchPyramid and ARCII). However, there are still some exceptions. For example, DRMM outperforms PACRR on MQ2007 in terms of NDCG@5 and MAP.

From the above results, we find that models with different dependence assumptions have their own advantages. There is no single model, with a fixed assumption, that can achieve the best performance over all the datasets. Here we further conduct some detailed comparisons between pairs of neural ranking models with different dependence assumptions on MQ2007. For each pair of models, we report the number of queries over which one model performs better (i.e., "win") or the same (i.e., "tie") as compared with the other. From the results in Fig. 2 we find that each model have their own advantages on a specific group of queries. For example, when compare DRMM with ARCII, there are about 799 queries which DRMM performs better than ARCII. However, there are also 565 queries where ARCII gets higher performance. Similarly, the conclusion can be drawn from the other two pairs.

It is not surprising to see that models with a specific dependence assumption can fit well on queries which share the same dependence assumption. In consequence, when a model only takes a specific assumption on the term dependence, it may inevitably fail on queries that do not fit that assumption. Therefore, an intuitive way is to select the right dependent model for each query. As shown in Fig. 3, if we have an oracle that can always select the best model among the three (e.g., in terms of MAP) for each query adaptively, the retrieval performance would be significantly boosted. Based on the above analysis, we argue that rather than using a pre-determined dependence assumption, a better ranking strategy is to adapt to each query with the right dependence assumption.

4   Dependence-Based Query Adaptation Strategy

In this section, we introduce an adaptive strategy for neural ranking models with respect to term dependence. The key idea is as follows. Since retrieval models under different dependence assumptions may fit different queries, we attempt to learn to measure the degree of term dependence in a query, and use this measure to select retrieval models with the right dependence assumption for each query.

In an abstract level, we consider two types of neural ranking models, i.e., independent models and dependent models, as the basic components. Then, a term dependence gate is employed to softly select between them adaptively. For the independent model, we choose a variant of the DRMM as the implementation. Specifically, we replace the matching histogram with a sorted top-k pooling layer [10], where the strongest signals are always placed at the top positions to keep the strength preserving property. In this way, the varied DRMM can be learned in an end-to-end way. For the dependent model, we choose two existing neural models, i.e., MatchPyramid [18] and ARCI [8] as the partially dependent model and fully dependent model respectively. In the following, we will describe the term dependence gate, which is the key component in our adaptive strategy.

4.1   Term Dependence Gate

The term dependence gate attempts to measure the dependence degree between query terms, and use this measure to softly select the above sub-models with different dependence assumptions adaptively. The key idea of the term dependence measure is as follows. If we assume no dependence between query terms, the meaning of a query is a union of its terms. In other words, we may obtain a query representation by some simple aggregation of its term representations. We name this representation of a query as its *fully-independent representation*. If we assume dependence between query terms, the meaning of a query then becomes a union of its dependent units. In an extreme case, i.e., the full dependence assumption, all query terms are dependent to each other in some way. In this case, the meaning of a query can no longer be decomposed into smaller units. We may obtain the query representation from its term representations through some complicated semantic interactions. We name this representation of a query as its *fully-dependent representation*. If we find that the fully-dependent representation of a query is very close to its fully-independent representation, it indicates that there might be very weak or even no dependence between query terms. On the contrary, if we find that the fully-dependent representation of a query is significantly different from its fully-independent representation, it indicates that there might exist strong dependence between query terms.

Based on the above ideas, we design the following term dependence gating network. Specifically, we firstly obtain the fully-independent representation $\mathbf{q}_{ind}$ using a simple sum over its term embeddings. To obtain its fully-dependent representation $\mathbf{q}_{dep}$, we employ a CNN over its term representations to capture the complicated semantic interactions. Given these two query representations, we take a simple but effective way by directly taking the difference $\mathbf{q}_{dep} - \mathbf{q}_{ind}$ as the input, and feed it into a feed forward neural network to form the gate. In this way, the final gating function is as follows:

$$g(\mathbf{Q}) = \sigma(\mathbf{W}_g[\mathbf{q}_{dep} - \mathbf{q}_{ind}]^T + \mathbf{b}_g), \tag{1}$$

where $\mathbf{W}_g$ and $\mathbf{b}_g$ are parameters to be learned, and σ is the sigmoid activation function to keep the value of gate among $[0, 1]$.

Finally, we use this term dependence gating network to softly select the two sub-models and obtain the relevance score by

$$f(\mathbf{Q}, \mathbf{D}) = g(\mathbf{Q}) \cdot f_i(\mathbf{Q}, \mathbf{D}) + (1 - g(\mathbf{Q})) \cdot f_d(\mathbf{Q}, \mathbf{D}). \tag{2}$$

where $f_i(\mathbf{Q}, \mathbf{D})$ and $f_d(\mathbf{Q}, \mathbf{D})$ denote the output score of the independent model and the dependent model, respectively.

4.2   Model Training

The introduced adaptive model can be learned in an end-to-end way. We utilize the pairwise hinge loss to train our model:

$$\mathcal{L}(\mathbf{Q}, \mathbf{D}^+, \mathbf{D}^-; \theta) = \max(0, 1 - f(\mathbf{Q}, \mathbf{D}^+) + f(\mathbf{Q}, \mathbf{D}^-))$$

where $f(\mathbf{Q}, \mathbf{D})$ denotes the relevance score and D^+ ranks higher than D^-. θ includes all the parameters to be learned.

5   Experiment

In this section, we conduct experiments to verify the effectiveness of the adaptive model based on the same MQ2007 and NewsClick datasets, which have been introduced in the previous section.

5.1   Experimental Settings

We refer to our proposed model as **ADNR** (i.e., Adaptive Neural Ranking). Since the dependent sub-module could be a partially dependent model or a fully dependent model, we refer to these two variants as $ADNR_{PD}$ and $ADNR_{FD}$, respectively. For the network configurations (e.g. number of layers and hidden nodes), we tuned the hyper-parameters via the validation set. Specifically, the embedding size is set to 50. In the independent model, the k in top-k pooling layer is set to 100 and 20 On MQ2007 and NewsClick as their document length differs significantly, and the multi-layer perceptron is set to 3 layers with the hidden size set to 10. In the dependent model, we have 64 kernels with size 3×3 in the convolution layer, set the max pooling size to 3×5, and use a 2-layer perceptron for output. We perform significant tests using the paired t-test. Differences are considered statistically significant when the p-value is lower than 0.01. All other trainable parameters are randomly initialized by uniform distribution within $[-0.2, 0.2]$.

In addition to the neural ranking models, we also include several traditional retrieval models as baselines: (1) BM25 [22] is a classic and highly effective independent model. (2) PDFR [20] is a partially dependent model, which assumes adjacent query terms are dependent. (3) SD [13] is a fully dependent model which utilize the Markov random field to model the sequential dependence. (4) WSD [2] is a hybrid model which combines a fully independent model, a sequentially dependent model, and a fully dependent model with handcrafted features.

5.2   Overall Comparison

In this section we compare the ADNR models against all the baselines on the two datasets. A summary of the main results is displayed in Table 1.

Firstly, for the independent models, we can see that DRMM is a strong baseline which performs better than traditional ranking model (i.e., BM25). K-NRM can obtain better performance when in larger dataset (i.e., NewsClick). Secondly, for the dependent models, we find that the traditional retrieval model, i.e., PDFR and SD, can outperform the neural dependent models on MQ2007 dataset, but become worst on NewsClick. It indicates that when there are sufficient data, the neural dependent models could better capture the term dependence patterns and achieve better performance than traditional dependent models. Thirdly, for the hybrid models, we can see that WSD performs significantly better than other traditional models such as BM25, PDFR, and SDM by taking into account both uni-gram matching and dependent term matching. However, it is still less effective than PACRR and Duet, which can capture more complex term dependence patterns through deep neural networks. Overall, we find Duet the best performing model among all the baseline methods by linearly combining a dependence sub-model and an independence sub-model. Finally, we observe that the two variants of ADNR can achieve better performances than all baseline methods. For example, on NewsClick, the relative improvement of $ADNR_{IP}$ over the best performing baseline (i.e., Duet) is about 8.1% in terms of MAP. For the two

Table 1. Comparison of different retrieval models over the MQ2007 and NewsClick datasets. Significant improvement or degradation with respect to ADNR$_{IP}$ is indicated $(+/-)$ (p-value ≤ 0.01).

Model name	MQ2007			NewsClick		
	NDCG@1	NDCG@5	MAP	NDCG@1	NDCG@5	MAP
BM25	0.358^-	0.384^-	0.450^-	0.207^-	0.385^-	0.378^-
DRMM	0.380^-	0.408^-	0.467^-	0.278^-	0.450^-	0.433^-
K-NRM	0.323^-	0.356^-	0.439^-	0.283^-	0.461^-	0.438^-
PDFR	0.345^-	0.371^-	0.442^-	0.223^-	0.415^-	0.393^-
MatchPyramid	0.362^-	0.379^-	0.434^-	0.290^-	0.454^-	0.437^-
ARCII	0.317^-	0.354^-	0.421^-	0.281^-	0.449^-	0.431^-
SD	0.383^-	0.395^-	0.455^-	0.248^-	0.421^-	0.408^-
ARCI	0.310^-	0.348^-	0.417^-	0.270^-	0.442^-	0.422^-
DSSM	0.290^-	0.335^-	0.409^-	0.253^-	0.427^-	0.413^-
WSD	0.385^-	0.399^-	0.457^-	0.249^-	0.423^-	0.410^-
PACRR	0.387^-	0.401^-	0.462^-	0.292^-	0.453^-	0.437^-
Duet	0.409	0.431	0.474^-	0.290^-	0.463^-	0.444^-
ADNR$_{IF}$	0.408	0.431	0.480	0.330^-	0.498	0.474
ADNR$_{IP}$	**0.413**	**0.439**	**0.487**	**0.337**	**0.500**	**0.480**

variants of ADNR, the ADNR$_{IP}$ could consistently outperform the ADNR$_{IF}$, this may due to the fact that the partial dependent model is more effective than the fully dependent model. Meanwhile, it is noteworthy that the ADNR is built upon an independent model (i.e., DRMM) and a dependent model (e.g., MatchPyramid and ARCI) with a term dependence gating network. When we compare ADNR with its sub-models, we can see that the performance can be significantly improved through adaptive combination, e.g., on NewsClick, the relative improvement of ADNR$_{IP}$ over DRMM and MatchPyramid is about 10.9% and 9.8% in terms of MAP, respectively. All these results demonstrate the effectiveness of the adaptive strategy.

6   Conclusions

In this paper, we try to understand the neural ranking models from the term dependence view. In this way, The neural ranking models are categorized into three classes according to the underlying assumption on the term dependence. Moreover, we conducted rigorous empirical comparisons over three categories of models, and find that on one category of models can achieve best performance for all queries. We proposed a novel term dependence gate which learns to measure the term dependence degree in the query. Experimental results on a benchmark dataset and a large click-through dataset demonstrate the effectiveness of the adaptive strategy. For future work, we will try to employ natural language processing methods, e.g., dependency grammar analysis and syntactic analysis, to measure the term dependence.

Acknowledgements. This work was funded by the National Natural Science Foundation of China (NSFC) under Grants No. 61902381, 61425016, 61722211, 61773362, and 61872338, the Youth Innovation Promotion Association CAS under Grants No. 20144310, and 2016102, the National Key R&D Program of China under Grants No. 2016QY02D0405, and the Foundation and Frontier Research Key Program of Chongqing Science and Technology Commission (No. cstc2017jcyjBX0059).

References

1. Bendersky, M., Kurland, O.: Utilizing passage-based language models for document retrieval. In: Macdonald, C., Ounis, I., Plachouras, V., Ruthven, I., White, R.W. (eds.) ECIR 2008. LNCS, vol. 4956, pp. 162–174. Springer, Heidelberg (2008). https://doi.org/10.1007/978-3-540-78646-7_17
2. Bendersky, M., Metzler, D., Croft, W.B.: Learning concept importance using a weighted dependence model. In: WSDM, pp. 31–40. ACM (2010)
3. Cohen, D., O'Connor, B., Croft, W.B.: Understanding the representational power of neural retrieval models using NLP tasks. In: SIGIR, pp. 67–74. ACM (2018)
4. Dai, Z., Xiong, C., Callan, J., Liu, Z.: Convolutional neural networks for soft-matching n-grams in ad-hoc search. In: WSDM, pp. 126–134. ACM (2018)
5. Guo, J., Fan, Y., Ai, Q., Croft, W.B.: A deep relevance matching model for ad-hoc retrieval. In: CIKM, pp. 55–64. ACM (2016)
6. Guo, J., Fan, Y., Ji, X., Cheng, X.: MatchZoo: a learning, practicing, and developing system for neural text matching. In: Proceedings of the 42Nd International ACM SIGIR Conference on Research and Development in Information Retrieval, SIGIR 2019, pp. 1297–1300. ACM, New York, NY, USA (2019)
7. Guo, J., et al.: A deep look into neural ranking models for information retrieval. arXiv preprint arXiv:1903.06902 (2019)
8. Hu, B., Lu, Z., Li, H., Chen, Q.: Convolutional neural network architectures for matching natural language sentences. In: NIPS, pp. 2042–2050 (2014)
9. Huang, P.-S., He, X., Gao, J., Deng, L., Acero, A., Heck, L.: Learning deep structured semantic models for web search using clickthrough data. In: CIKM, pp. 2333–2338. ACM (2013)
10. Hui, K., Yates, A., Berberich, K., de Melo, G.: A position-aware deep model for relevance matching in information retrieval. CoRR (2017)
11. Jaech, A., Kamisetty, H., Ringger, E., Clarke, C.: Match-tensor: a deep relevance model for search. arXiv preprint arXiv:1701.07795 (2017)
12. Lioma, C., Simonsen, J.G., Larsen, B., Hansen, N.D.: Non-compositional term dependence for information retrieval. In: SIGIR, pp. 595–604. ACM (2015)
13. Metzler, D., Croft, W.B.: A Markov random field model for term dependencies. In: SIGIR, pp. 472–479. ACM (2005)
14. Mikolov, T., Sutskever, I., Chen, K., Corrado, G.S., Dean, J.: Distributed representations of words and phrases and their compositionality. In: NIPS, pp. 3111–3119 (2013)
15. Mitra, B., Craswell, N.: Neural models for information retrieval. arXiv preprint arXiv:1705.01509 (2017)

16. Mitra, B., Diaz, F., Craswell, N.: Learning to match using local and distributed representations of text for web search. In: WWW, pp. 1291–1299. International World Wide Web Conferences Steering Committee (2017)
17. Nie, Y., Li, Y., Nie, J.-Y.: Empirical study of multi-level convolution models for IR based on representations and interactions. In: SIGIR, pp. 59–66. ACM (2018)
18. Pang, L., Lan, Y., Guo, J., Xu, J., Wan, S., Cheng, X.: Text matching as image recognition. In: AAAI, pp. 2793–2799 (2016)
19. Pang, L., Lan, Y., Guo, J., Xu, J., Xu, J., Cheng, X.: DeepRank: a new deep architecture for relevance ranking in information retrieval. In: CIKM, pp. 257–266. ACM (2017)
20. Peng, J., Macdonald, C., He, B., Plachouras, V., Ounis, I.: Incorporating term dependency in the DFR framework. In: SIGIR, pp. 843–844. ACM (2007)
21. Qin, T., Liu, T.-Y., Xu, J., Li, H.: LETOR: a benchmark collection for research on learning to rank for information retrieval. Inf. Retr. **13**(4), 346–374 (2010)
22. Robertson, S.E., Walker, S.: Some simple effective approximations to the 2-Poisson model for probabilistic weighted retrieval. In: Croft, B.W., van Rijsbergen, C.J. (eds.) SIGIR, pp. 232–241. Springer, London (1994). https://doi.org/10.1007/978-1-4471-2099-5_24
23. Shen, Y., He, X., Gao, J., Deng, L., Mesnil, G.: A latent semantic model with convolutional-pooling structure for information retrieval. In: CIKM, pp. 101–110. ACM (2014)
24. Srikanth, M., Srihari, R.: Biterm language models for document retrieval. In: SIGIR, pp. 425–426. ACM (2002)
25. Turtle, H., Croft, W.B.: Evaluation of an inference network-based retrieval model. TOIS **9**(3), 187–222 (1991)
26. Wan, S., Lan, Y., Guo, J., Xu, J., Pang, L., Cheng, X.: A deep architecture for semantic matching with multiple positional sentence representations. In: AAAI, vol. 16, pp. 2835–2841 (2016)
27. Xiong, C., Dai, Z., Callan, J., Liu, Z., Power, R.: End-to-end neural ad-hoc ranking with kernel pooling. In: SIGIR, pp. 55–64. ACM (2017)
28. Zhai, C., Lafferty, J.: A study of smoothing methods for language models applied to ad hoc information retrieval. In: ACM SIGIR Forum, vol. 51, pp. 268–276. ACM (2017)

Training

Generating Short Product Descriptors Based on Very Little Training Data

Peng Xiao[1], Joo-Young Lee[2], Sijie Tao[1], Young-Sook Hwang[2], and Tetsuya Sakai[1(✉)]

[1] Waseda University, Tokyo, Japan
xp1994@fuji.waseda.jp, tsjmailbox@ruri.waseda.jp, tetsuyasakai@acm.org
[2] WiderPlanet Co. Ltd., Seoul, South Korea
{jooyoung,yshwang}@widerplanet.com

Abstract. We propose a pipeline model for summarising a short textual product description for inclusion in an online advertisement banner. While a standard approach is to truncate the advertiser's original product description so that the text will fit the small banner, this simplistic approach often removes crucial information or attractive expressions from the original description. Our objective is to shorten the original description more intelligently, so that users' click through rate (CTR) will improve. One major difficulty in this task, however, is the lack of large training data: machine learning methods that rely on thousands of pairs of the original and shortened texts would not be practical. Hence, our proposed method first employs a semisupervised sequence tagging method called TagLM to convert the original description into a sequence of entities, and then a BiLSTM entity ranker which determines which entities should be preserved: the main idea is to tackle the data sparsity problem by leveraging sequences of entities rather than sequences of words. In our offline experiments with Korean data from travel and fashion domains, our sequence tagger outperforms an LSTM-CRF baseline, and our entity ranker outperforms LambdaMART and RandomForest baselines. More importantly, in our online A/B testing where the proposed method was compared to the simple truncation approach, the CTR improved by 34.1% in the desktop PC environment.

Keywords: Advertisement · Classification · Sequence tagging · Summarisation

1 Introduction

The present study concerns online advertising, which is a key driving force in internet businesses and therefore has a tremendous social and economical impact. Figure 1 shows some examples of online advertisement on Korean websites: the two on the left are from the fashion domain, and the two on the right are from the travel domain. It can be observed that each ad consists of an image, a textual

© Springer Nature Switzerland AG 2020
F. L. Wang et al. (Eds.): AIRS 2019, LNCS 12004, pp. 133–144, 2020.
https://doi.org/10.1007/978-3-030-42835-8_12

Fig. 1. Examples of online advertisement (LEFT: fashion; RIGHT: travel)

product description, a price, and a link (to view or purchase). (Some English translations of Korean product descriptions will be provided later in Sect. 4.4).

The textual product descriptions are provided by the advertisers, but they are generally too long to fit the ad banner; therefore, when generating an online ad, the descriptions are simply trunctated to a fixed length. That is, only the top K characters are actually shown to the users. This simplistic approach often removes crucial information or attractive expressions from the original description. Hence, our objective is to shorten the original description more intelligently, so that users' click through rate (CTR) will improve. One major difficulty in this task, however, is the lack of large training data. It is practically very difficult to obtain large training data for this task because (a) the target domains of our ads are season sensitive and manual annotation cannot catch up with the pace; and (b) while we are interested in popular products that get clicked within a short time window, such products constitute only a very small percentage of the entire product catalogue. Machine learning methods that rely on thousands of pairs of the original and shortened texts would not be practical in our task. We therefore first employ a semisupervised sequence tagging method called TagLM [11] to convert the original description into a sequence of entities, and then a BiL-STM [3][1] entity ranker which determines which entities should be preserved: the main idea is to tackle the data sparsity problem by leveraging sequences of entities rather than sequences of words. In our offline experiments with Korean data from travel and fashion domains, our sequence tagger outperforms an LSTM-CRF [5][2] baseline, and our entity ranker outperforms LambdaMART [2] and Random Forest [1] baselines. More importantly, in our online A/B testing where the proposed method was compared to the simple truncation approach, the CTR improved by 34.1% in the desktop PC environment.

---

[1] BiLSTM: Bidirectional Long Short-Term Memory.

[2] LSTM: Long Short-Term Memory.
  CRF: Conditional Random Fields.

2   Related Work

Our task is similar to what Sun *et al.* [13] refer to as *product title summarisation*. They tackled the problem of extracting key information from product titles for E-commerce sites. However, their method based on a multi-source pointer network requires a large training data: their experiments used over 400K instances. In contrast, our requirement is to shorten product descriptions effectively given only about 1,000 training instances. To handle the small training data problem, we tackle the above task in two steps: in the first step, we transform the input sequence of words into a sequence of domain-specific entities; in the second step, we rank the entities to determine which ones should be included in the final output given a length limit. Hence, below we discuss some prior art in sequence tagging.

Early work in sequence tagging utilised statistical models such as Hidden Markov Models, Conditional Random Fields models [7], and Maximum Entropy Markov Models [9]. Recently, given the rise of LSTM [4] and BiLSTM [3] networks, Huang et al. [5] proposed a variety of LSTM-based models for sequence tagging tasks, including LSTM, BiLSTM, LSTM-CRF, and BiLSTM-CRF networks. LSTM is an RNN[3] which is known to be effective in many NLP tasks that require context understanding. Furthermore, BiLSTM helps the network capture not only past context but also future context for the current prediction. In LSTM-CRF and BiLSTM-CRF, the CRF layer can utilise sentence-level tag information to correct unlikely tags predicted by LSTM or BiLSTM. Ma et al. [8] proposed a BiLSTM-CNNs-CRF network to utilize character-level features to improve the accuracy of BiLSTM-CRF[4].

TagLM is a state-of-the-art hierarchical neural sequential tagging model proposed by Peters *et al.* [11]. The main contribution of TagLM is the introduction of bidirectional LM (Language Model) embedding into the sequence tagging model, thereby improving the accuracy. For this reason, we adopt TagLM as our sequence tagging component, as we shall describe in Sect. 3.2.

3   Proposed Method

Our proposed method first employs TagLM [11] to convert the original description into a sequence of entities, and then a BiLSTM entity ranker which determines which entities should be preserved: as was discussed in Sect. 1, the main idea is to tackle the data sparsity problem by leveraging sequences of entities rather than sequences of words.

Our proposed method comprises five steps:

1. Pre-training LM and Word Embeddings from Unlabelled Data;
2. Sequence Tagging by TagLM;
3. Brand Name Tag Correction (for fashion only);

---

[3] RNN: Recurrent Neural Network.
[4] CNN: Convolutional Neural Network.

4. Entity Grouping;
5. Entity Ranking by a BiLSTM Ranker.

Below, we describe each step in turn.

3.1 Pre-training LM and Word Embeddings from Unlabelled Data

This embedding step is necessary since our sequence tagging utilises TagLM. To pre-train LM and word embeddings, we use unlabelled product descriptions that are separate from our small labelled data set, as we shall describe in Sect. 4.1. For word embedding, we employed CBOW (Continuous Bag of Words) word2vec [10]. As for LM embedding, we employed CNN-BIG-LSTM [6], following the work of Peters *et al.* on TagLM [11].

3.2 Sequence Tagging by TagLM

Sequence tagging takes an original product description as the input, and tags each word with an entity type. For example, given an input word sequence ⟨Tokyo, Osaka, 4, /, 5, day, family, travel⟩, we aim to convert it into an entity type sequence ⟨$C, C, Sch, Sch, Sch, Sch, T, T$⟩ where C means "City," Sch means "Schedule," and T means "travel Type." We employ TagLM [11] with two BiL-STM layers for this task, by leveraging the LM and word embeddings to represent each word in the input description, as illustrated in Fig. 2. More details are given below.

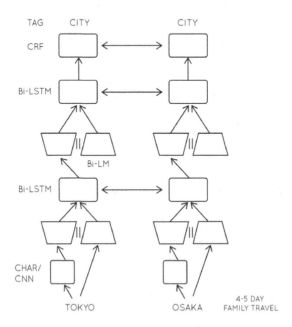

Fig. 2. Our TagLM architecture

Let $t_1, \ldots, t_k \ldots, t_N$ be an input sequence of tokens (i.e., words). For each token t_k, we form its representation x_k by concatenating c_k, the character-based representation, and w_k, the CBOW word embedding:

$$c_k = C(t_k; \theta_c), \tag{1}$$

$$w_k = W(t_k; \theta_w), \tag{2}$$

$$x_k = [c_k; w_k]. \tag{3}$$

Here, c_k is trained by a model $C(\cdot, \theta_c)$ with parameter θ_c, and w_k is represented by a CBOW word2vec model $W(\cdot, \theta_w)$ with parameter θ_w. The x_k thus formed is used as the input of the first LSTM layer.

We then incorporate pre-trained LM embedding into our model to form context sensitive representations. Our first-layer BiLSTM is constructed as follows.

$$\overrightarrow{h}_{k,1} = \overrightarrow{LSTM}_1(x_k, \overrightarrow{h}_{k-1,1}, \theta_{\overrightarrow{LSTM}_1}), \tag{4}$$

$$\overleftarrow{h}_{k,1} = \overleftarrow{LSTM}_1(x_k, \overleftarrow{h}_{k-1,1}, \theta_{\overleftarrow{LSTM}_1}), \tag{5}$$

$$h_{k,1} = [\overrightarrow{h}_{k,1}; \overleftarrow{h}_{k,1}; h_k^{LM}], \tag{6}$$

where $\overrightarrow{LSTM}_1$ and $\overleftarrow{LSTM}_1$ are forward and backward first-layer LSTMs, and $\theta_{\overrightarrow{LSTM}_1}, \theta_{\overleftarrow{LSTM}_1}$ are the corresponding parameters, and h_k^{LM} is the pretrained bidirectional LM embedding representation of t_k.

The output $h_{k,1}$ of the first BiLSTM layer is the input to the second-layer BiLSTM. Unlike the first layer, the output of the second layer does not involve concatenation of the LM embedding:

$$\overrightarrow{h}_{k,2} = \overrightarrow{LSTM}_2(h_{k,1}, \overrightarrow{h}_{k-1,2}, \theta_{\overrightarrow{LSTM}_2}), \tag{7}$$

$$\overleftarrow{h}_{k,2} = \overleftarrow{LSTM}_2(h_{k,1}, \overleftarrow{h}_{k-1,2}, \theta_{\overleftarrow{LSTM}_2}), \tag{8}$$

$$h_{k,2} = [\overrightarrow{h}_{k,2}; \overleftarrow{h}_{k,2}]. \tag{9}$$

The final CRF layer [5] predicts entity type tag scores for each token as follows.

$$y_k = CRF(h_{k,2}, H_2), \tag{10}$$

where H_2 is a sequence of $h_{k,2}$ context vectors.

3.3   Brand Name Tag Correction (for Fashion Only)

This step applies to the fashion domain only. In the fashion domain, it is known that brand names are important in advertising. We have a list of 1,538 fashion brand names, and it is relatively stable over time. Since sequence tagging without explicit knowledge of brand names can be limited in accuracy and the brand name list is already available, we utilise the list to correct the output of sequence tagging wherever necessary. While this is technically trivial, such a step is very important for ensuring accuracy in real commercial services.

3.4 Entity Grouping

Recall that our sequence tagging step simply converts a sequence of input words such as ⟨Tokyo, Osaka, 4, /, 5, day, family, travel⟩ into an entity type sequence such as ⟨$C, C, Sch, Sch, Sch, Sch, T, T$⟩. In this step, we simply merge consecutive entities tagged with the same entity type, to try to ensure that the final shortened text is cohesive. For example, the above entity type sequence would be further converted into ⟨C, Sch, T⟩. While this means that multiple entities of the same type are treated as one entity (e.g., "Tokyo Osaka"), it is actually often desirable to retain all of them in the final output (e.g. We want to see "Tokyo Osaka (travel)," not just "Tokyo" or "Osaka.").

3.5 Entity Ranking by a BiLSTM Ranker

Given a sequence of entities, entity ranking provides assigns a probability to each entity, so that we can include as many entities as possible given a character length limit. The final output of our system is a shortened description, which is actually a sequence of entities selected to be included in the description. For example, given the input ⟨Tokyo Osaka, 4/5 day, family travel⟩ tagged with ⟨C, Sch, T⟩ (See Sect. 3.4), our entity ranker generates an inclusion probability for each of these three tags.

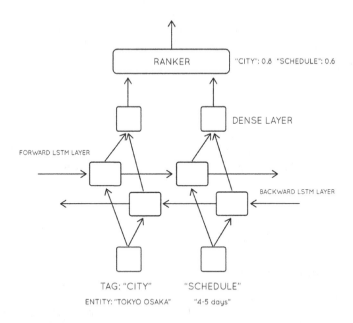

Fig. 3. BiLSTM ranker architecture.

We implemented our entity ranker using a BiLSTM, as illustrated in Fig. 3. Given a sequence of entities $e_1, e_2 \ldots e_k$ and their corresponding entity type tags, where the vector representation of the k-th entity type tag is given by tag_k (which is initialised as a random vector as there is no pretraining step), our BiLSTM ranker operates as follows.

$$\overrightarrow{h}_{k,1} = \overrightarrow{LSTM}_1(tag_k, \overrightarrow{h}_{k-1,1}, \theta_{\overrightarrow{LSTM}_1}), \tag{11}$$

$$\overleftarrow{h}_{k,1} = \overleftarrow{LSTM}_1(tag_k, \overleftarrow{h}_{k-1,1}, \theta_{\overleftarrow{LSTM}_1}), \tag{12}$$

$$h_{k,1} = [\overrightarrow{h}_{k,1}; \overleftarrow{h}_{k,1}], \tag{13}$$

$$y_k = \text{Sigmoid}(h_{k,1}), \tag{14}$$

where y_k is the inclusion probability for the k-th entity.

4   Offline Experiments

This section describes our offline experiments for evaluating our sequence tagging and entity type ranking methods.

4.1   Data

For our evaluation, we selected fashion and travel domains based on our observation that the traditional truncation approach is often highly inadequate for the product descriptors from these domains. According to reasons we mentioned in Sect. 1, for each of these two domains, we constructed a small data set containing 1,200 original Korean product descriptions. For each product, an annotator manually constructed a shortened version of the product description; this is our gold data for the entity type classification task (Sect. 4.3). Furthermore, each product descriptor was manually tagged with entity types, in order to provide the gold data for our sequence tagging subtask (Sect. 4.2). We devised different entity types for each domain as shown in Tables 1 and 2, based on the viewpoint that some entity types (within the context of other entity types) should be kept in the shortened description while others should not be.

Each of the above two data sets were split into training and test data by a 9:1 ratio; hence each of our test data contains 120 products. Moreover, in addition to these labelled data, we utilised a total of 98,852 and 80,066 unlabelled descriptors for fashion and travel domains, respectively, to pre-train LM and word embeddings (See Sect. 3.1).

4.2   Evaluation of TagLM-Based Sequence Tagging

In this section, we evaluate our sequence tagging component. Recall that the input to sequence tagging is a textual product description, and that the output is a sequence of entity types tagged to the input words. For comparison, we also evaluate a standard LSTM-CRF model (Sect. 2) as a baseline.

We evaluate the task by examining whether a correct entity type is assigned to each input word. To be more specific, for each description, we compute the

Table 1. Entity types used for the fashion domain.

Entity type	Description
BRAND	Brand name of clothe, for example: VANS, GUCCI and etc.
USER	Target user type, for example: unisex, male, female and etc.
STYLE	Clothe style, for example: sporty, lite, slim and etc.
CAT	Clothe category, for example: coat, jeans and etc.
Material	Clothe materials, for example: mink, fur and etc.
Color	Clothe color
O	Other

Table 2. Entity types used for the travel domain.

Entity type	Description
AREA	(Fist level of location) Continent, Sea, etc.
NT	(Second level of location) Nation
CITY	(Third level of location) City, Province, States, Island
AOI	Area Of Interest. Popular place such as museum, restaurant, mountain, building, park, etc.
ACC	Accommodation. Hotel, resort, etc.
SCH	Schedule of travel
COND	Condition. For example, No shopping, No option, Special promotion, Discount
TYPE	Type of travel package. For example, Honeymoon, Free travel, Family travel and Cruise tour
EVENT	Certain event included, such as hot spring, massage, ski, golf, seeing sunrise
TR	Transportation, such as airplane, train, bus, etc.
O	Other

accuracy, defined as the proportion of input words tagged with the correct entity (as defined by the manually prepared gold data). We then compute the mean accuracy over the test data (120 product descriptions).

Table 3 shows the results of our sequence tagging experiments. It can be observed that while the gain over the LSTM-CRF baseline is not quite statistically significant at $\alpha = 0.05$ for the fashion domain, the gain is substantial and statistically highly significant for the travel domain. To be more specific, whereas LSTM-CRF performs poorly for travel, TagLM performs almost equally effectively for both domains. By manually checking our sequence tagging results, we observed that travel domain entity types tend to correspond to complex phrases rather than single words: for example, "3 days/4 days" could be tagged as SCH (Schedule of travel), and "eastern Europe" could be tagged as AREA by TagLM.

Table 3. Sequence tagging evaluation results (sample size: 120).

	Model	Mean accuracy	Paired t-test p-value
Fashion	LSTM-CRF	0.831	
	TagLM	0.866	0.073
Travel	LSTM-CRF	0.511	
	TagLM	0.814	3.49e−25

It is possible that this caused problems for LSTM-CRF, as it relies on the surface words rather than entity types.

4.3 Evaluation of BiLSTM-Based Entity Ranking

In this section, we evaluate the entity ranking subtask. Recall that the input to entity ranking is a sequence of entities, and the output is a ranking of entities sorted by the inclusion probability for the final shortened description. Since the cap on the output length is given as a constraint (set to 15 characters in the present experiment), we can use the ranking to include as many entities as possible until the cap is reached. Hence, the evaluation should be done at the binary classification level, i.e., whether an entity is preserved in the shortened text or not.

Since the gold data for the above binary classification task has been manually prepared for each product in the form of manually shortened texts, we can compute the recall and precision of entities for each product, as well as the F_1 measure. Finally, the evaluation measures can be averaged over the test data.

In addition to our BiLSTM ranker, we also evaluated two baselines: LambdaMART [2] and Random Forest [1]. Unlike our BiLSTM ranker, these require manually extracted features. We therefore used the following features with the two baselines:

- Entity type (represented as an integer; let us denote it by T) of the entity to be ranked;
- Position of the entity in the entity sequence;
- Proportion of the number of words in the entity to the total number of words in the description;
- Proportion of the number of characters in the entity to the total number of characters in the description;
- Proportion of the number of entities tagged with T in the entity sequence.

All features are normalised so that their ranges are $[0, 1]$.

Table 4 compares our BiLSTM entity ranker with the two baselines in terms of mean recall, precision and F_1; Table 5 shows the significance test results based on Tukey HSD tests [12]. Given the significance level of $\alpha = 0.05$, the results can be summarised as follows.

Table 4. Entity type ranking evaluation results (sample size: 120).

	Model	Mean F_1	Mean recall	Mean precision
Fashion	LambdaMART	0.845	0.842	0.860
	RandomForest	0.856	0.851	0.873
	BiLSTM Ranker	0.889	0.880	0.911
Travel	LambdaMART	0.640	0.695	0.613
	RandomForest	0.763	0.735	0.821
	BiLSTM Ranker	0.807	0.806	0.835

Table 5. Tukey HSD test results for Mean F_1 scores.

	System 1	System 2	Mean diff $(1-2)$	Lower	Upper	p value
Fashion	BiLSTM Ranker	LambdaMART	0.044	0.007	0.082	0.016
	RandomForest	LambdaMART	0.011	−0.026	0.049	0.762
	RandomForest	BiLSTM Ranker	−0.032	−0.070	0.005	0.099
Travel	BiLSTM Ranker	LambdaMART	0.170	0.104	0.237	0.000
	RandomForest	LambdaMART	0.124	0.057	0.190	0.001
	RandomForest	BiLSTM Ranker	−0.046	−0.113	0.020	0.232

- In both domains, our BiLSTM ranker statistically significantly outperforms LambdaMART;
- In the travel domain, RandomForest statistically significantly outperforms LambdaMART.

In short, our BiLSTM ranker performs best despite the fact that it does not require manual selection of features as the two baselines do.

A manual inspection of the low-F_1 cases with our method suggests that some of our shortened descriptors are arguably as good as the gold data; although we manually constructed one gold text per product, this is a highly subjective process, and there in fact could be multiple possible shortened descriptors that may be acceptable to the human eye, just as there can be multiple gold summaries of the same original document in textual summarisation. However, as our objective is to increase the CTR and not to explore which shortened descriptors "look acceptable," the present offline experiment probably suffices when viewed as a preliminary checking step before the online A/B testing (Sect. 5).

4.4   Case Studies

Figure 4 provides a few examples from both successful and unsuccessful cases in our experiments. Case (a) is successful: our method manages to remove adjectives like "premium" and "light-weight" while retaining the product type "supply bags." Note that "supply bags" would have been lost by the traditional truncation method. In contrast, Case (b) is not successful as the product type

(a) [빈폴 키즈(ONLINE)] 블랙 프리미엄 모던 경량 보조가방
[Beanpole Kids (ONLINE)] Black Premium Modern Light-weight Supply Bags
→빈폴 키즈 블랙 모던 경량 보조가방
Beanpole Kids Black Modern Supply Bags
(b) [빈폴골프] [NDL 라인] 여성 블루 저지 풀오버
[Beanpole Golf] [NDL Line] Woman Blue Jersey Pullover
→빈폴골프 여성 블루
Beanpole Golf Woman Blue
(c) [가족愛발견] 하노이/하롱베이/옌뜨 고품격 가족여행
[Discovering Love of Family] Hanoi/Ha Long Bay/Yen Tu High-quality Family Tour
→하노이/하롱베이/옌뜨 가족여행
Hanoi/Ha Long Bay/Yen Tu Family Tour
(d) [긴일정 스테디셀러] 서유럽 4/6개국 완전일주
[Long term Steady Seller] Trip Around Western Europe 4/6 Countries
→긴일정 서유럽
Long term Western Europe

Fig. 4. Successful (blue) and unsuccessful (red) cases from the fashion ((a)(b)) and travel ((c)(d)) domains: the original texts are in Korean, so English translations are also provided here. (Color figure online)

"pullover" is actually lost. Similarly, Case (c) successfully removes abstract phrases such as "love of family" from the travel ad description, whereas in Case (d), the crucial information "4/6 countries" is lost and hence specificity is hurt. Clearly, there is a lot of room for improvement.

5   Online A/B Testing

Having verified that our sequence tagging and entity classification methods achieve reasonable performances, we verified whether our approach improves the CTR over the traditional truncation approach in a real online advertising environment by means of A/B testing. First, we sampled original Korean product descriptions that are more than 25 characters in length, and we set our output length cap to 20 characters. After filtering out some noisy output (such as extremely short output and output with repetitive words) using simple heuristics, we obtained 2,072 pairs of original and shortened descriptors. The average lengths were 31.01 and 15.97 characters, respectively. According to our observation over three days (April 26–28, 2019), our CTR improved by 34.1% compared to the truncation approach in the desktop PC environment. Although this experiment is preliminary, the result suggests that our work will have a practical and commercial impact.

6   Conclusions and Future Work

We proposed a pipeline model for summarising a short textual product description for inclusion in an online advertisement banner. Our objective is to improve the users' click through rate (CTR) when compared to the traditional fixed-length truncation approach, given very little training data. In our offline experiments with Korean data from travel and fashion domains, our TagLM sequence tagger outperformed an LSTM-CRF baseline, and our BiLSTM entity ranker outperformed LambdaMART and RandomForest baselines. More importantly, in our online A/B testing where the proposed method was compared to the simple truncation approach, the CTR improved by 34.1% in the desktop PC environment.

Our future work includes extending our work to the mobile online advertising environment, where the banners on the smartphone screens are small and therefore it is more challenging to improve the CTR. Moreover, we would like to apply our approaches to domains other than travel and fashion.

References

1. Breiman, L.: Random forests. Mach. Learn. **45**(1), 5–32 (2001). https://doi.org/10.1023/A:1010933404324
2. Burges, C.J.C.: From RankNet to LambdaRank to LambdaMART: an overview. Technical report. Microsoft Research (2010)
3. Graves, A., Schmidhuber, J.: Framewise phoneme classification with bidirectional LSTM and other neural network architectures. Neural Netw. Off. J. Int. Neural Net. Soc. **18**, 602–610 (2005)
4. Hochreiter, S., Schmidhuber, J.: Long short-term memory. Neural Comput. **9**(8), 1735–1780 (1997)
5. Huang, Z., Xu, W., Yu, K.: Bidirectional LSTM-CRF models for sequence tagging. CoRR (2015), http://arxiv.org/abs/1508.01991
6. Józefowicz, R., Vinyals, O., Schuster, M., Shazeer, N., Wu, Y.: Exploring the limits of language modeling. CoRR (2016). http://arxiv.org/abs/1602.02410
7. Lafferty, J.D., McCallum, A., Pereira, F.C.N.: Conditional random fields: probabilistic models for segmenting and labeling sequence data. In: Proceedings of ICML 2001, pp. 282–289. Morgan Kaufmann Publishers Inc., San Francisco, CA, USA (2001)
8. Ma, X., Hovy, E.H.: End-to-end sequence labeling via bi-directional LSTM-CNNs-CRF. CoRR (2016). http://arxiv.org/abs/1603.01354
9. McCallum, A., Freitag, D., Pereira, F.C.N.: Maximum entropy Markov models for information extraction and segmentation. In: Proceedings of ICML 2000, pp. 591–598. Morgan Kaufmann Publishers Inc., San Francisco, CA, USA (2000)
10. Mikolov, T., Chen, K., Corrado, G., Dean, J.: Efficient estimation of word representations in vector space. CoRR (2013). http://arxiv.org/abs/1301.3781
11. Peters, M.E., Ammar, W., Bhagavatula, C., Power, R.: Semi-supervised sequence tagging with bidirectional language models. CoRR (2017). http://arxiv.org/abs/1705.00108
12. Sakai, T.: Laboratory Experiments in Information Retrieval: Sample Sizes, Effect Sizes, and Statistical Power. Springer, Heidelberg (2018). https://doi.org/10.1007/978-981-13-1199-4
13. Sun, F., Jiang, P., Sun, H., Pei, C., Ou, W., Wang, X.: Multi-source pointer network for product title summarization. CoRR (2018). http://arxiv.org/abs/1808.06885

Experiments with Cross-Language Speech Retrieval for Lower-Resource Languages

Suraj Nair[1]([envelope]), Anton Ragni[2], Ondrej Klejch[3], Petra Galuščáková[1], and Douglas Oard[1]

[1] University of Maryland, College Park, MD 20742, USA
{srnair,petra,doug}@umd.edu
[2] University of Cambridge, Cambridge CB2 1TN, UK
ar527@cam.ac.uk
[3] University of Edinburgh, Edinburgh EH8 9YL, UK
ondrej.klejch@gmail.com

Abstract. Cross-language speech retrieval systems face a cascade of errors due to transcription and translation ambiguity. Using 1-best speech recognition and 1-best translation in such a scenario could adversely affect recall if those 1-best system guesses are not correct. Accurately representing transcription and translation probabilities could therefore improve recall, although possibly at some cost in precision. The difficulty of the task is exacerbated when working with languages for which limited resources are available, since both recognition and translation probabilities may be less accurate in such cases. This paper explores the combination of expected term counts from recognition with expected term counts from translation to perform cross-language speech retrieval in which the queries are in English and the spoken content to be retrieved is in Tagalog or Swahili. Experiments were conducted using two query types, one focused on term presence and the other focused on topical retrieval. Overall, the results show that significant improvements in ranking quality result from modeling transcription and recognition ambiguity, even in lower-resource settings, and that adapting the ranking model to specific query types can yield further improvements.

1   Introduction

The problem of Cross-Language Information Retrieval (CLIR) involves finding relevant documents in one language for a given query in different language. For example, one straightforward approach to CLIR is to use a Machine Translation (MT) system for translating queries into the document language and performing the retrieval in the document language. In the case of cross-language speech retrieval, the system must also determine which words were spoken in each speech "document." This might, for example, be done by transcribing the speech using Automatic Speech Recognition (ASR). If ASR and MT were perfect, we would expect this approach to yield retrieval results that are about as good as could be achieved by monolingual text retrieval. Neither process is perfect, however, and

© Springer Nature Switzerland AG 2020
F. L. Wang et al. (Eds.): AIRS 2019, LNCS 12004, pp. 145–157, 2020.
https://doi.org/10.1007/978-3-030-42835-8_13

moreover fairly good ASR and MT systems are available for only a few dozen of the world's thousands of languages. ASR and MT errors arise from two causes: (1) Out-Of-Vocabulary (OOV) errors in which words that are not known to the system aren't correctly handled, and (2) selection errors, in which the system could have selected the correct transcription or translation, but failed to do so. Modern ASR and MT systems learn to minimize both types of errors by training on large corpora. When large training corpora are not available, as is still the case for the vast majority of the world's languages, both types of errors increase. Those errors can adversely affect cross-language speech retrieval results.

These challenges are well understood, and methods have been developed for mitigating the effects of OOV and selection errors in CLIR and in monolingual speech retrieval. In early dictionary-based CLIR research, pre-translation query expansion helped to mitigate the effect of translation OOV errors by augmenting the query with related terms that may be translatable [13]. Today, dictionaries are often used together with translation lexicons learned from parallel (i.e., translation-equivalent) corpora [8]. Such an approach allows alternative translations to be weighted using translation probability weights learned from corpus statistics [25]. In speech retrieval, similar approaches can be used to mitigate the effect of transcription errors, again with reliance on transcription probabilities to limit the effect of selection errors [1].

In this paper, we leverage two new test collections to study error mitigation techniques for cross-language speech retrieval with English queries and spoken content in either Tagalog (a Philippine language) or Swahili (an African language). Section 2 introduces related work on CLIR, speech retrieval and cross-language speech retrieval. Section 3 describes our test collections, and Sect. 4 then introduces our CLIR and speech retrieval techniques and how those techniques are used together for cross-language speech retrieval. Section 5 presents our experiment design, results, and discussion of those results. Finally, we conclude the paper with some remarks on future work.

2   Related Work

Our approach to cross-language speech retrieval draws on three lines of research that we summarize in this section.

2.1   Cross-Language Information Retrieval

Much early work on CLIR involved replacing query terms with dictionary translations and then searching with that set of translations as a document-language query. Using multiple dictionary translations can help to avoid selection errors, but at the risk of considerably lower precision than a correct single selection could have produced. Pirkola [17] is generally credited with having been the first to introduce the idea of a "structured query" method for CLIR, although the idea has antecedents in Hull's work a year earlier [6]. In this method, term frequency statistics for alternative translations of the same query term are used differently from term frequency statistics for different languages in order to limit selection error effects. This idea was subsequently extended to incorporate translation probabilities by Darwish in an approach that is now known as Probabilistic Structured Queries (PSQ) [4], although this idea too had an antecedents in the work of Xu [29] three years earlier. Subsequently the PSQ method was extended by Wang [25] to leverage evidence for meaning equivalence constructed from bidirectional translation probabilities. We use Wang's method in our experiments.

2.2 Speech Retrieval

A good deal of the early work on retrieval of spoken content involved cascading the output of an ASR system to a text retrieval system [2,9–11,24,27]. This works fairly well when ASR transcription accuracy is high, but at word error rates above about 30% the adverse effect on recall becomes severe. This happens because ASR systems typically do best on common words, but the Inverse Document Frequency statistic used by many query-document matching methods (including the BM25 scores used in our experiments) gives the most weight to the least common query words. In early work, OOV terms that were not known to the ASR system explained some of the failures to correctly transcribe less common terms, but as the vocabularies of ASR systems have grown, selection errors have clearly emerged as the most common cause for the transcription errors. In other words, ASR systems trained for lower-resource languages often make mistakes on less common words, but when they do it is because they guessed wrong, not because they didn't know the word. ASR systems typically do, however, generate internal representations of the alternative words that might plausibly have been spoken (e.g., as a word lattice), and probabilities for these alternative hypotheses can be estimated from acoustic model, language model and pronunciation probabilities. When word error rates are relatively high, as is the case for ASR systems that are trained to recognize speech in lower-resource languages, these transcription probabilities can be used to compute expected term counts in a manner that is strikingly similar to the term frequency estimation in PSQ [1,22]. We use expected term counts in our experiments.

There has also been considerable work on speech recognition and keyword spotting for lower-resource languages, including Tagalog [3,7,12,19,26]. With one recent exception [30], all of this work has focused on monolingual applications. The one exception, Zbib's SIGIR 2019 paper, also uses MATERIAL test collections, but with different retrieval models than we use.

2.3 Evaluation of Cross-Language Speech Retrieval

There has been far less work on cross-language speech retrieval than on CLIR for text, in part because ASR for speech is far more expensive computationally than is the corresponding process (tokenization) for text, and in part because cross-language speech retrieval test collections have until now been rather rare.

The first widely available cross-language speech retrieval test collections were produced for the Topic Detection and Tracking (TDT) evaluations between 1999 and 2004. In TDT, the closest task to retrieval was a filtering task known as "topic tracking" in which between 1 and 4 news stories formed an example-based query, and the system's goal was to find all future stories addressing the same event (or its closely connected consequences). TDT included English text and speech from the outset, with Chinese text and speech added in 1999, and Arabic text and speech added in 2002 [5]. It thus became possible to use TDT collections for cross-language speech retrieval, but only using by-example queries in which one or more examples implicitly specify the content that is sought.

The first cross-language speech retrieval test collections to use more traditional Web-like ("ad hoc") queries were created for the Cross Language Evaluation Forum (CLEF) Cross-Language Speech Retrieval (CL-SR) evaluations between 2005 and 2007 [14,16,28]. Two document collections were built, one in English (with 96 topics) and one in Czech (with 113 topics). For the English test collection, queries were available in six languages (Czech, Dutch, French, German, Spanish, and, for comparison, English). For the Czech test collection, only English and Czech queries were available. One limitation of the CLEF CL-SR test collections is that all of the experimentation with that test collection at CLEF was based on ASR transcripts (and associated metadata) that were provided by the organizers; at the time this precluded experimentation with techniques based on indexing alternative plausible transcriptions.

After a decade-long hiatus in CL-SR research, the Intelligence Advanced Research Projects Activity (IARPA) began the MATERIAL program in 2017[1] with the goal of accelerating work on cross-language retrieval of text and speech in lower-resource languages. To date, MATERIAL has produced test collections for Bulgarian, Lithuanian, Somali, Swahili and Tagalog; test collections for several more languages are expected over the next few years. Like the CLEF CL-SR test collections, these MATERIAL test collections include relevance judgments for ad hoc queries (all of which are available only in English), but in MATERIAL there are two broad types of ad hoc queries: (1) topical queries, which like the queries in most information retrieval test collections ask for content on a topic, and (2) lexical queries, which ask for content in which some translation of a specific query term was spoken.[2] Some MATERIAL queries are also formed as a Boolean conjunction of two lexical queries, or of one conceptual and one lexical query. As we show below, these different query types can benefit from different ranking functions. Unlike the CLEF CL-SR test collections, speech processing for the MATERIAL collections is done directly on the audio rather than on automatic transcriptions provided by the organizers. In this paper we report on experiments using the spoken content in two of these collections, for Swahili as

---

[1] Material is an acronym for Machine Translation for English Retrieval of Information in Any Language [21].

[2] In the MATERIAL program these are referred to as *conceptual* and *simple queries*, but we prefer to refer to them as topical and lexical in keeping with the way those terms are used in information retrieval and natural language processing, respectively. Some topical and lexical queries also contain additional clues (e.g., synonyms or hypernyms) to guide the interpretation of query terms, but we do not make use of these additional clues in our experiments.

a development setting, and for Tagalog as a second application of the retrieval approach that we first developed on the larger Swahili test collection.

3   Test Collections

Table 1 lists the details of the Swahili and Tagalog speech collections. For Swahili, the Validation (Val) collection is the union of the MATERIAL DEV, ANALYSIS1 and ANALYSIS2 sets. The Evaluation (Eval) collection is the union of the MATERIAL EVAL1, EVAL2 and EVAL3 sets. For Tagalog, the single test collection is the union of the MATERIAL ANALYSIS1 and ANALYSIS2 sets. The larger EVAL sets for Tagalog have not yet been released by IARPA, and restricting ourselved to the ANALYSIS sets in the case of Tagalog allows us to additionally report results on manual transcriptions and manual translations (both of which are available only for the ANALYSIS sets). As Table 1 summarizes, these audio files were obtained from three types of sources: news broadcasts, topical broadcasts (e.g., podcasts), and conversational telephone speech.

Table 1. Document counts (and duration) for MATERIAL speech collections.

	Swahili		Tagalog
	Val	Eval	
News broadcast	173 (5 h)	1,327 (48 h)	131 (4 h)
Topical broadcast	157 (12 h)	1,343 (115 h)	130 (11 h)
Conversational	153 (3 h)	597 (29 h)	54 (0.5 h)

Table 2. MATERIAL query statistics.

	Swahili		Tagalog
	Val	Eval	
Lexical queries	71	352	199
Topical queries	17	29	67
Conjunctive queries	38	319	121

We use only queries that have at least one relevant document in the collection being searched. For Val we use MATERIAL Swahili query set Q1 and for Eval we use query sets Q2 and Q3. Val and Eval thus have disjoint queries and documents. For Tagalog we use MATERIAL Tagalog query sets Q1, Q2 and Q3. As Table 2 shows, there are many more lexical queries than topical queries.

4   Methods

This section introduces the specific methods that we use in our experiments.

4.1 Keyword Spotting

In the technique we refer to as Keyword Spotting (KWS), we use the posterior probability of each term to compute the expected counts [22]. For word k and document d, the expected count is:

$$\mathbb{E}(k|d) = \sum_{u \in d} \sum_{a:l(a)=k} P\left(a|O^{(u)}\right) \qquad (1)$$

where a is a lattice arc, $l(a)$ is a term label associated with a, u is a segment of document audio and $O(u)$ are associated observations used by an ASR system to yield posterior probabilities.

4.2 Translation Probabilities

We follow the approach of [25] for estimating the probability of meaning equivalence $p(s \leftrightarrow t)$ for a word s in one language and a word t in another language from the bidirectional translation probabilities $p(s|t)$ and $p(t|s)$. Translation probabilities in each direction are generated using Giza++ [15]. These probabilities are multiplied and then normalized to sum to one, an approach that has the effect of suppressing translations that are not well attested in one of the two directions.

4.3 Probabilistic Structured Queries

Following Darwish, we compute the expected term frequency in the query language (English) based on document language statistics as follows:

$$TF_j(Q_i) = \sum_{\{k|D_k \in T(Q_i)\}} [TF_j(D_k) \times P(D_k \leftrightarrow Q_i)] \qquad (2)$$

where Q_i is a query term, D_k is a document term (in our case, a transcribed term in the spoken content), $TF_j(Q_i)$ is the term frequency of Q_i in document j, $T(Q_i)$ is the set of translation-equivalent English terms for document-language term Q_i, $TF_j(D_i)$ counts the number of times term i occurs in document j, and $P(D_k \leftrightarrow Q_i)$ is the translation probability of D_k given the query term Q_i [4]. Darwish also estimated the Inverse Document frequency (IDF) that is used to model query term specificity in the BM25 formula in a similar way, but the combination of small collections sizes and the presence of transcription ambiguity would make that a questionable choice for our speech retrieval task. Instead, we estimated IDF directly from a side collection in English, the New York Times corpus[3]. In practice we can get the IDF from any sufficiently large and sufficiently representative collection. So although the New York Times is perhaps less representative of language use in our task than the actual collections being searched would be, its much larger size makes it a reasonable choice in this case.

---

[3] https://catalog.ldc.upenn.edu/LDC2008T19.

4.4 Combined Approach

To glue the two pieces together, all we need to do is to modify the term frequency given in Eq. (2) by using the posterior probability in Eq. (1). The updated term frequency computation is:

$$TF_j(Q_i) = \sum_{\{k|D_k \in T(Q_i)\}} [\mathbb{E}(k|j) \times P(D_k \leftrightarrow Q_i)] \qquad (3)$$

where $\mathbb{E}(k|j)$ is the expected count of the term computed by using the posterior probabilities as denoted in Eq. (1).

5 Experiments

In this section we present our experiment design and our results.

5.1 KWS

Along with news, topical broadcast and conversational telephone speech (CTS) audio released for CLIR evaluation, the National Institute of Standards and Technology (NIST) released limited quantities of manually transcribed CTS data exclusively for training and evaluating ASR systems. We augmented this CTS training data with additional content read from scripts that had been previously created for the IARPA Babel program.[4] As Table 3 shows, a total of 96 h of training data were available for Swahili, and a total of 194 h for Tagalog. The use of limited amounts of CTS and read speech for training ASR systems results in relatively high word error rates on the news and topical broadcasts in the test collection, both of which were recorded at a higher sampling rate [18]. As Table 3 shows, word error rates are generally above 30%.

Table 3. ASR statistics.

Training data (hours)		
	Swahili	Tagalog
Scripted (read)	14	33
Conversational	82	161

Word error rate		
	Swahili	Tagalog
News broadcast	28.6%	31.1%
Topical broadcast	42.2%	38.9%
Conversational	32.8%	38.7%

Lattices produced by the ASR system for spoken content were indexed by converting them to a time-factored representation amenable to efficient indexing. Before that, acoustic and language model scores for each lattice arc were combined into a single arc score by scaling down the acoustic score to adjust the dynamic range mismatch. Arc scores were additionally scaled down, as that had

---

[4] https://www.iarpa.gov/index.php/research-programs/babel.

been found beneficial for spoken term detection in the Babel program. Optimal scaling factors in both cases were determined on a portion of the Swahili Val set.

For the methods that use keyword search output, all output terms provided by the KWS system, even those with temporal overlap, were used. Low probability terms were not filtered, based upon the evidence using the Val set. However, terms longer than 20 characters were removed from the index.

5.2 Translation

The parallel text used for training Giza++ includes aligned sentences from MATERIAL "build pack" for each language, LORELEI,[5] GlobalVoices[6] and CommonCrawl[7]. Lexicons downloaded from Panlex[8] and Wiktionary[9] were additionally used as training data. The data was lowercased and cleaned to remove punctuations and diacritics. Table 4 details the statistics of the training data.

Table 4. Giza++ training data.

	Unit	Swahili	Tagalog
MATERIAL	Sentences	37.0k	65.9k
LORELEI	Sentences	–	32.9k
GlobalVoices	Sentences	30.3k	2.5k
CommonCrawl	Sentences	8.9k	18.2k
Panlex+Wiktionary	Words	190.1k	107.2k

5.3 CLIR

Our experiments were run using the Okapi BM25 ranking function, with the default parameter values of $b = 0.75$ and $k1 = 1.2$ [20]. We used Indri [23] to index each document collection, but the rankings are computed using PSQ with BM25 outside Indri. Our baseline ranking model uses PSQ with 1-best ASR output (PSQ+ASR). It is compared against a model that uses the KWS index in place of 1-best ASR (PSQ+KWS). For conjunctive queries, both parts of the query are scored separately and the scores are then combined using either an arithmetic, geometric or harmonic mean.

The MATERIAL test collections contain some content that is spoken entirely in a different language that were intended to measure the effect of spoken language identification, but that is outside the scope of our experiments for this paper. We therefore used test collection metadata to filter out those documents

---

[5] https://www.darpa.mil/program/low-resource-languages-for-emergent-incidents.

[6] https://globalvoices.org/.

[7] http://commoncrawl.org/.

[8] https://panlex.org/.

[9] https://en.wiktionary.org/wiki/Wiktionary:Main_Page.

from our result sets prior to evaluation. Additionally, in the MATERIAL test collections each query is labeled with a domain, and relevance judgments are available only for documents that are labeled with the same domain (e.g. Military, Sports, Government, Business, Law). The system used in our experiments has no domain-specific processing. This has the effect of scoring some otherwise-relevant documents as not relevant if the domain does not match. The effect is, however, consistent across systems, and thus comparisons made under this condition remain informative.

5.4 Swahili Results

This section details the effect of different retrieval methods for Swahili, using Mean Average Precision (MAP) as the evaluation measure. Note, however, that MAP is equivalent to Mean Reciprocal Rank when only one relevant document exists, as is often the case for the Val collection in which about half (64) of the 126 queries that have any relevant documents have just one.

The effect of the two retrieval methods, PSQ+ASR and PSQ+KWS, is shown by query type (for non-conjunctive queries) in Table 5. MAP for lexical queries increases significantly when using KWS over that of 1-best ASR. For topical queries, gains are apparent on the Val set, but MAP is essentially unchanged on the larger Eval set. We therefore conclude that PSQ+KWS is the preferred approach for both basic query types.

Table 5. MAP scores of different query types for Swahili test collection

	Val		Eval	
	Lexical	Topical	Lexical	Topical
PSQ+ASR	0.367	0.146	0.157	0.145
PSQ+KWS	0.394	0.163	0.160	0.144

Computing BM25 scores for each part of a query separately and then combining those scores using a geometric or a harmonic mean consistently results in higher MAP than simply treating the query as a flat bag of words (which is the arithmetic mean condition in Table 6) for both the Swahili Val and Eval sets. As that table shows, substantial improvements are observed in both the baseline PSQ+ASR condition and in the PSQ+KWS system. Moreover, the geometric mean seems to have a slight edge in the PSQ+KWS condition, which comports well with our intuition (since the geometric mean models an independence assumption between the two parts of the query). We therefore use the geometric mean for conjunctive queries in the remainder of our experiments.

Table 6. MAP for conjunctive queries with three types of means, Swahili.

	Val			Eval		
	Arithmetic	Geometric	Harmonic	Arithmetic	Geometric	Harmonic
PSQ+ASR	0.202	0.329	0.329	0.177	0.181	0.181
PSQ+KWS	0.196	0.349	0.341	0.179	0.184	0.181

Table 7 summarizes the overall improvements on the two Swahili test collections. We observe that switching from ASR to KWS yields a statistically significant improvement, and that then adding conjunction processing using the geometric mean yields a further statistically significant improvement. Moreover, the net improvement from the combination of these two changes is substantial: 12% (relative) on the larger Eval collection, and 21% on the small Val collection.

Table 7. MAP for all queries. x, y and z denote statistical significant improvements over ASR, KWS and ASR+GeoMean, respectively, using a two-tailed Wilcoxon signed rank test with $p < 0.05$

	Swahili Val	Swahili Eval	Tagalog
PSQ+ASR	0.288	0.165	0.388
PSQ+KWS	0.303x	0.168	0.406x
PSQ+ASR+GeoMean	0.329x	0.181x	0.417x
PSQ+KWS+GeoMean	0.349xyz	0.184xyz	0.458xyz
PSQ+Manual Transcription			0.485
Manual Translation & Transcription			0.512
Manual Translation & Transcription+GeoMean			0.513

5.5   Tagalog Results

We do not have separate Val and Eval sets for Tagalog, but as Table 7 also shows, we can observe the same trends on the one relatively small Tagalog collection. Statistically significant improvements result from each change, and the net improvement from the two together is 18% (relative). We therefore conclude that the choices that we made on Swahili seem to be reasonable choices for Tagalog as well. About two-thirds (250) of the 387 Tagalog queries that have any relevant documents at all have only one relevant document. Our best Tagalog result (a MAP of 0.458) corresponds roughly to typically placing a single relevant document at rank 2 (since the Mean Reciprocal Rank for a system that always placed the first relevant document at rank 2 would be 0.5). This seems like a credible performance for a lower-resource language (noting that the comparable value for our similarly-sized Swahili Val set equates to roughly rank 3, which is also potentially good enough to be useful in practical applications).

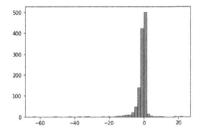

Fig. 1. Difference between expected and actual term count.

For the Tagalog test collection we also have manual 1-best transcription and manual 1-best translation available. As Table 7 shows, using these 1-best manual processes yields a MAP of 0.513 for Tagalog, which is only 12% (relative) above our best present Tagalog result. While we note that 1-best transcription and translation are not an upper bound on what systems with good modeling of translation ambiguity could achieve, we find this small gap to be further confirmation that our Tagalog system is yielding credible results. As Fig. 1 shows, one possible source of this difference is that the expected term count more often underestimates than overestimates the correct term count (as measured on the one-best translation). Averaging over all terms in the collection, the mean absolute error of the expected counts is 1.727.

6 Conclusion and Future Work

We have presented an approach to mitigate some of the errors that arise from cascading of ASR and MT systems. First, we have shown that using word lattices from ASR to generate multiple hypothesis can be useful for cross-language speech retrieval, even in lower-resource languages. We have also shown that further substantial improvements can be obtained using specialized handing for conjunctive queries in the MATERIAL test collection. We have shown that these techniques are synergistic, each contributing to statistically significant improvements on two lower-resource languages.

A productive direction for future work would be to replicate the results for additional MATERIAL test collections. Another possible direction would be to explore the impact of using a retrieval model that is specifically designed for the term-presence condition that lexical queries seek to find, such as the approach described in [30]. A third possibility would be to explore whether query and document expansion techniques can yield further improvements when used together with the methods in this paper. While much remains to be done, it does seem that with these new test collections we can expect to see a renaissance of cross-language speech retrieval research.

References

1. Can, D., Saraclar, M.: Lattice indexing for spoken term detection. IEEE Trans. Audio Speech Lang. Process. **19**(8), 2338–2347 (2011)
2. Chelba, C., et al.: Retrieval and browsing of spoken content. IEEE Signal Process. Mag. **25**(3), 39–49 (2008)
3. Chen, G., et al.: Using proxies for OOV keywords in the keyword search task. In: ASRU, pp. 416–421 (2013)
4. Darwish, K., Oard, D.: Probabilistic structured query methods. In: SIGIR, pp. 338–344 (2003)
5. Fiscus, J., Doddington, G.: Topic detection and tracking evaluation overview. In: Allan, J. (ed.) Topic Detection and Tracking. The Information Retrieval Series, vol. 12, pp. 17–31. Springer, Boston (2002)
6. Hull, D.: Using structured queries for disambiguation in cross-language information retrieval. In: AAAI Symposium on Cross-Language Text and Speech Retrieval (1997)
7. Karakos, D., et al.: Score normalization and system combination for improved keyword spotting. In: ASRU, pp. 210–215 (2013)
8. Kim, S., et al.: Combining lexical and statistical translation evidence for cross-language information retrieval. JASIST **66**(1), 23–39 (2015)
9. Lee, L.S., Chen, B.: Spoken document understanding and organization. IEEE Signal Process. Mag. **22**(5), 42–60 (2005)
10. Lee, L.S., Pan, Y.C.: Voice-based information retrieval—how far are we from the text-based information retrieval? In: ASRU, pp. 26–43 (2009)
11. Makhoul, J., et al.: Speech and language technologies for audio indexing and retrieval. Proc. IEEE **88**(8), 1338–1353 (2000)
12. Mamou, J., et al.: Developing keyword search under the IARPA Babel program. In: Afeka Speech Processing Conference (2013)
13. McNamee, P., Mayfield, J.: Comparing cross-language query expansion techniques by degrading translation resources. In: SIGIR, pp. 159–166 (2002)
14. Oard, D.W., et al.: Overview of the CLEF-2006 cross-language speech retrieval track. In: Peters, C., et al. (eds.) CLEF 2006. LNCS, vol. 4730, pp. 744–758. Springer, Heidelberg (2007). https://doi.org/10.1007/978-3-540-74999-8_94
15. Och, F., Ney, H.: A systematic comparison of various statistical alignment models. Comput. Linguist. **29**(1), 19–51 (2003)
16. Pecina, P., Hoffmannová, P., Jones, G.J.F., Zhang, Y., Oard, D.W.: Overview of the CLEF-2007 cross-language speech retrieval track. In: Peters, C., et al. (eds.) CLEF 2007. LNCS, vol. 5152, pp. 674–686. Springer, Heidelberg (2008). https://doi.org/10.1007/978-3-540-85760-0_86
17. Pirkola, A.: The effects of query structure and dictionary setups in dictionary-based cross-language information retrieval. In: SIGIR, pp. 55–63 (1998)
18. Ragni, A., Gales, M.: Automatic speech recognition system development in the 'wild'. In: ICSA, pp. 2217–2221 (2018)
19. Riedhammer, K., et al.: A study on LVCSR and keyword search for tagalog. In: INTERSPEECH, pp. 2529–2533 (2013)
20. Robertson, S.: Okapi at TREC-7: automatic ad hoc, filtering, VLC and interactive track. In: TREC (1998)
21. Rubino, C.: IARPA MATERIAL program (2016). https://www.iarpa.gov/index.php/research-programs/material/material-baa

22. Saraclar, M., Sproat, R.: Lattice-based search for spoken utterance retrieval. In: NAACL (2004)

23. Strohman, T., et al.: Indri: a language model-based search engine for complex queries. In: International Conference on Intelligence Analysis (2005)

24. Tur, G., De Mori, R.: Spoken Language Understanding: Systems for Extracting Semantic Information from Speech. Wiley, New York (2011)

25. Wang, J., Oard, D.: Matching meaning for cross-language information retrieval. Inf. Process. Manag. **48**(4), 631–653 (2012)

26. Wegmann, S., et al.: The TAO of ATWV: probing the mysteries of keyword search performance. In: ASRU, pp. 192–197 (2013)

27. Weintraub, M.: Keyword-spotting using SRI's DECIPHER large-vocabulary speech-recognition system. In: ICASSP, vol. 2, pp. 463–466 (1993)

28. White, R.W., Oard, D.W., Jones, G.J.F., Soergel, D., Huang, X.: Overview of the CLEF-2005 cross-language speech retrieval track. In: Peters, C., et al. (eds.) CLEF 2005. LNCS, vol. 4022, pp. 744–759. Springer, Heidelberg (2006). https://doi.org/10.1007/11878773_82

29. Xu, J., Weischedel, R.: Cross-lingual information retrieval using hidden Markov models. In: EMNLP, pp. 95–103 (2000)

30. Zbib, R., et al.: Neural-network lexical translation for cross-lingual IR from text and speech. In: SIGIR (2019)

Weighted N-grams CNN for Text Classification

Zequan Zeng[1], Yi Cai[1(✉)], Fu Lee Wang[2], Haoran Xie[3], and Junying Chen[1]

[1] South China University of Technology, Guangdong, China
zengzequan_scut@foxmail.com, {ycai,jychense}@scut.edu.cn
[2] The Open University of Hong Kong, Kowloon, Hong Kong SAR
pwang@ouhk.edu.hk
[3] Lingnan University, New Territories, Hong Kong SAR
hrxie2@gmail.com

Abstract. Text categorization can solve the problem of information clutter to a large extent, and it also provides a more efficient search strategy and more effective search results for information retrieval. In recent years, Convolutional Neural Networks have been widely applied to this task. However, most existing CNN models are difficult to extract longer n-grams features for the reason as follow: the parameters of the standard CNN model will increase with the increase of the length of n-grams features because it extracts n-grams features through convolution filters of fixed window size. Meanwhile, the term weighting schemes assigning reasonable weight values to words have exhibited excellent performance in traditional bag-of-words models. Intuitively, considering the weight value of each word in n-grams features may be beneficial in text classification. In this paper, we proposed a model called weighted n-grams CNN model. It is a variant of CNN introducing a weighted n-grams layer. The parameters of the weighted n-grams layer are initialized by term weighting schemes. Only by adding fixed parameters can the model generate any length of weighted n-grams features. We compare our proposed model with other popular and latest CNN models on five datasets in text classification. The experimental results show that our proposed model exhibits comparable or even superior performance.

Keywords: Text classification · Weighted n-grams features · CNN model

1 Introduction

Text classification (TC) is a fundamental and traditional topic for natural language processing (NLP), in which one needs to assign predefined categories to unlabeled sentences or documents. It is an important technology in many applications such as sentiment analysis and web searching. In recent years, deep learning models have been popularly used in this task, including Neural Bag-of-Words models (NBOW) [16,21], Recurrent Neural Networks

© Springer Nature Switzerland AG 2020
F. L. Wang et al. (Eds.): AIRS 2019, LNCS 12004, pp. 158–169, 2020.
https://doi.org/10.1007/978-3-030-42835-8_14

(RNNs) [19,20], Recursive Neural Networks [17] and Convolutional Neural Networks (CNNs) [2,6,11,22,23,27]. In particular, inspired by the great success of CNN in computer vision, CNN has also been significantly applied to NLP applications such as text classification. Most existing CNN models employ multiple convolution filters of fixed size. Convolution filter is a fixed-size window sliding from the beginning to the end of a text to generate features maps, which is equivalent to extract fixed-size n-grams features. [29] shows that the optimal filter region size will be set large when the average length of all sentences in dataset is long. For example, when the average length of all sentences in dataset is more than 100, the optimal filter region size may be 30 or larger. However, the longer n-grams features is extracted in this way, the more parameters of the standard CNN model will increase. Therefore, the standard CNN usually sets the filter region size from three to five because it is computationally expensive for CNN model to capture longer n-grams features.

Meanwhile, thanks to powerful effectiveness of Neural Bag-of-Words models [16,21], it is significant to generate continuous word representation by simple mathematical operations of word embedding, such as addition and averaging. Though most NBOW models directly generate the sentence or document representations, the SWEM-hier [16] has extracted n-grams features through averaging operation over word embedding as a transition step and has exhibited comparable or even superior performance in text classification. Most importantly, any length of n-grams features generated in this way does not add any more parameters. Therefore, in order to capture longer n-grams features without adding more parameters and capture deep feature information from embedding, we utilize the sum of embedding to represent the n-grams information and the convolution filters over n-grams representation.

Utilizing the sum-of-embedding method to generate the n-grams representations takes every word in context as equally important. However, the different words have different important degree in one sentence and the same word may also has different important degree in different sentences or in different corpus in text classification task. For example, the words 'thoughtful', 'provocative', 'humanizing' in the sentence 'a thoughtful, provocative, insistently humanizing film' are more important than the words 'a', 'insistently', 'film' and the punctuation ',' in sentiment classification. Note that word embeddings cannot explicitly reflect the important degree of words in text classification. Therefore, it is reasonable to consider the weight of different words when extracting n-grams information. For this reason, we introduce the weight to sum-of-embedding called weighted sum-of-embedding. The weight value of weighted sum-of-embedding will be initialized by term weighting schemes because of their significant improvements over raw Bag-Of-Words representation in text classification [12,24].

In this work, we propose a variant of CNN model called weighted n-grams CNN. It introduces the weighted n-grams layer after the input layer and before the convolution layer. We simply describe the weighted n-grams layer. Firstly, it will be based on the input layer of each word embedding to generate the forward n-grams features and backward n-grams features using weighted sum-of-embedding. Then it will combine the word embedding with its two n-grams features embeddings to obtain max-embedding and sum-embedding by max-pooling and addition-pooling respectively. Finally it will concatenate the max-embedding and sum-embedding as the integrated embedding for each word embedding.

The rest of our paper is organized as follows: Sect. 2 introduces the related work about deep learning in text classification. Section 3 details some concepts, term weighting schemes and our proposed model. Section 4 analyzes experimental results from accuracy, parameter of convolution two aspects to verify the effectiveness of our model. Finally, a conclusion is described in Sect. 5.

2   Related Work

Bag-of-Words (BoW) models were mainly used in traditional text classification. They treated each word in the text as an independent token, which represented the sentence as a high-dimension sparse vector. The most critical problem of BoW models was that it ignored the fact that texts were essentially sequential data [15]. Thus, the models could not consider word-order and syntax information. Due to the advantages of being effective and robust, they were still widely used in various kinds of NLP tasks such as information retrieval, question answering and text classification [10]. Term weighting schemes were usually used to obtain better performance in Bag-of-Words models in traditional text classification. They were good strategies to measure the important degree of words in the sentence or in the corpus. According to whether the label information of the sentence was used, term weighting schemes could be divided into unsupervised weighting schemes and supervised weighting schemes. The most common unsupervised weighting schemes were TF, IDF, and TF·IDF [4] and the most common supervised weighting schemes were RF [7], BDC [25]. Currently, term weighting schemes had been successfully applied in bag-of-words models, but they were still seldom used in neural models. To the best of our knowledge, there was a few works in combining term weighting schemes with neural models [10,30]. [10] exploited term weighting schemes and n-grams in objective function based on the Paragraph Vector (PV) model [9].

In recent years, many deep neural models were proposed and had achieved impressive results. In particular, CNN had also been significantly applied to NLP applications such as text classification. [1] first used CNN with pre-trained word embedding for text classification. [6] further explored CNN by using multi-channel embedding. [27] proposed a variant of Convolutional Neural Network treating text as a kind of raw signal at character level, which was the temporal (one-dimensional) ConvNets. [11] proposed a variant of Convolutional Neural Network encoding semantic features into initialize the convolutional filters which helped the model focus on learning useful features at the beginning of the training. [23] proposed a variant of Convolutional Neural Network equipped with dense connections between convolutional layers and with a multi-scale feature attention mechanism, which was able to adaptively select multi-scale features for

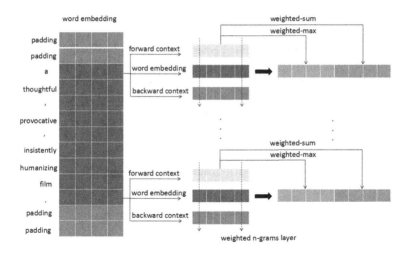

Fig. 1. The weighted n-grams layer

text classification. [2] proposed a deep Convolutional Neural Network with 29 layers of convolution on top of word vectors which was able to learn hierarchical representations of whole sentences, jointly with the task.

3 Model

In order to consider the important degree of each word in n-grams features and be easier to capture longer n-grams features for text classification with Convolutional Neural Network, we add a weighted n-grams layer after the input layer and before the convolutional layer in Convolutional Neural Network. The overall architecture of the weighted n-grams layer is shown in Fig. 1.

In this section, we first introduce the weighted sum-of-embedding to represent the n-grams features. Then we introduce term weighting schemes which initialize the weight value in the weighted n-grams layer. Finally we introduce the weighted n-grams layer. For convenience, we define the mathematical symbols shown in Table 1.

Table 1. The description of some mathematical symbols

Symbol	Description
$X = (x_1, x_2, ..., x_L)$	A text sequence
$x_i (i \in [1, L])$	The ith token in X
L	The number of tokens in X
$V = (v_1, v_2, ..., v_L)$	A word embedding sequence
$v_i \in R^m (i \in [1, L], m \in Z^+)$	The word embedding of ith word x_i
$w_i (i \in [1, L])$	The weight value of ith word x_i

3.1 Weighted Sum-of-Embedding

In recent years, word embedding has become popular and powerful [16]. Inspired by the effectiveness of Neural Bag-Of-Words models [16,21], we also take each token $x_i (i \in [1, L])$ in the text sequence $X = (x_1, x_2, ..., x_L)$ as independent and generate n-grams representation by weighted averaging over the word embedding v_i, called weighted sum-of-embedding shown in Fig. 2.

$$v_{i,n} = v_{i-n} * w_{i-n} + ... + v_i * w_i \tag{1}$$

where $v_{i,n}$ represents the weighted n-grams features of word x_i. The w_i here is the important degree of the word in n-grams representation. The higher weight value, the more important degree of the word in n-grams representation.

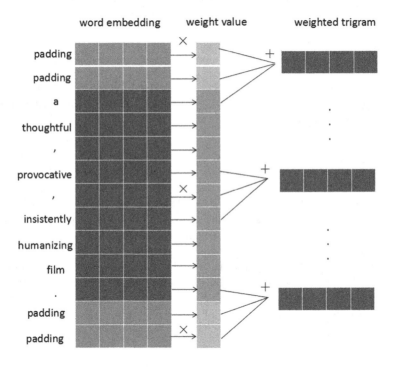

Fig. 2. Weighted sum-of-embedding

3.2 Term Weighting Schemes

In the text classification task, different word has different important degree in one sentence and the same word may also has different important degree in different sentences or in different corpus. In order to initialize the weight value when generating the weighted n-grams, we utilize term weighting schemes. Term weighting schemes are good strategies to measure the important degree of words in one sentence or in the corpus. According to whether the label information of the sentence is used, term weighting schemes can be divided into unsupervised weighting schemes and supervised weighting schemes. The most common unsupervised weighting schemes are TF, IDF, and TF·IDF [4] and the most common supervised weighting schemes are RF [7], BDC [25]. In this paper, we utilize BDC scheme to initialize the weight value because of its effectiveness [25]. BDC scheme is based on information theory and measures the discriminating power of a token based on its global distributional concentration in the categories of a corpus [25]. More details are described below.

$$bdc(t) = 1 - \frac{BH(t)}{log(|C|)} = 1 + \frac{\sum_{i=1}^{|C|} f(t|c_i)logf(t|c_i)}{log(|C|)} \tag{2}$$

$$f(t|c_i) = \frac{p(t|c_i)}{\sum_{i=1}^{|C|} p(t|c_i)} \tag{3}$$

$$p(t|c_i) = \frac{num(t|c_i)}{num(c_i)}, i \in [1, |C|] \tag{4}$$

where $|C|$ represents the number of the categories, $num(t|c_i)$ represents the frequency of the token t in category c_i and $num(c_i)$ represents the frequency sum of all term in the category c_i. The value of $bdc(t)$ ranges from zero to one, which the more important degree of the token, the higher weight value.

3.3   Weighted N-grams Layer

In the weighted n-grams layer as shown in Fig. 1, we first utilize weighted sum-of-embedding to obtain the forward n-grams features of word x_i and the backward n-grams features of word x_i, as shown in Eqs. (5) and (6).

$$v_{f,n,i} = v_{i-n} * w_{i-n} + \ldots + v_i * w_i \tag{5}$$

$$v_{b,n,i} = v_i * w_i + \ldots + v_{i+n} * w_{i+n} \tag{6}$$

where $v_{f,n,i}$ represents the forward n-grams features of word x_i and $v_{b,n,i}$ represents the backward n-grams features of word x_i. Both $v_{f,n,i}$ and $v_{b,n,i}$ are dense vectors with $|m|$ real value elements, which have the same number of dimension comparing with the word embedding v_i. For example, in Fig. 1, forward n-grams features encodes the semantics of the context 'padding padding a' based on word 'a' and backward n-grams features encodes the semantics of the context 'a thoughtful,' based on word 'a'.

Then we leverage a max-pooling operation directly over the word embedding v_i, forward n-grams features $v_{f,n,i}$ and backward n-grams features $v_{b,n,i}$ to select its most salient features as shown in Eq. (7). We also leverage a sum operation directly over the word embedding v_i, forward n-grams features $v_{f,n,i}$ and backward n-grams features $v_{b,n,i}$ to select its comprehensive features as shown in

Eq. (8). Note that both $v_{i,max}$ and $v_{i,sum}$ are dense vectors with $|m|$ real value elements, which also have the same number of dimension comparing with the word embedding v_i.

$$v_{i,max} = ((max(v_{f,n,i,0}, v_0, v_{b,n,i,0}), ..., \\ max(v_{f,n,i,m}, v_m, v_{b,n,i,m}))) \tag{7}$$

$$v_{i,sum} = (v_{f,n,i,0} + v_0 + v_{b,n,i,0}, ..., \\ v_{f,n,i,m} + v_m + v_{b,n,i,m}) \tag{8}$$

Finally we generate the weighted n-grams representation based on word x_i by concatenating vector $v_{i,max}$ and $v_{i,sum}$ as shown in Eq. (9).

$$v_{i,cat} = v_{i,max} \oplus v_{i,sum} \tag{9}$$

After the weighted n-grams layer, each word in the text sequence from the input layer is transformed to a vector. The vector combines the word embedding information and the n-grams features. Then the changed vector matrix will be fed to convolutional layer and classifier layer to obtain the prediction label.

4   Experiments

4.1   Experiment Setting

We conducted the experiments on five datasets to evaluate the effectiveness of our proposed model. In the experiments, we used Google 300-dimensional word2vec to initialize the word embedding in all datasets [13]. Out-of-Vocabulary (OOV) words were initialized from a uniform distribution with range $[-0.05, 0.05]$. The word embedding was of size 300. The model was implemented using Tensorflow and was trained on GTX 1080Ti. The hyper-parameter settings of the neural network were as follows:

(1) We trained our model's parameters through stochastic gradient descent over shuffled mini-batches with the Adadelta update rule [28] and mini-batch size was 50.
(2) For datasets without a standard train/test split, we used 10-fold cross-validation.
(3) The number of n-grams was selected from the set [3, 4, 5, 6].
(4) For all datasets we used rectified linear units and dropout rate of 0.5. For AG datasets, we used filter windows of 1, 2, 3 with 100 feature maps each. For MPQA, Subj, MR, SST-2 datasets, we used filter windows of 1, 2 with 200, 100 feature maps respectively.
(5) For all datasets we padded the input text to a fixed length - maxlen, where maxlen was chosen 36 for MPQA, 56 for MR, 100 for AG, 120 for subj and 53 for SST-2 respectively.

4.2   Datasets

We evaluate our proposed model on the five commonly used datasets and use accuracy as the metric. The summary statistics of the datasets is shown in Table 2 and the simple descriptions of each dataset are shown as follows.

Table 2. Summary statistics of datasets. Classes: Number of classes. Train: Train set size. Test: Test set size (CV means there was no standard train/test split and thus 10-fold CV was used)

Datasets	Classes	Train	Test
MR	2	10,662	cv
Subj	2	10,000	cv
AG	4	120,000	7,600
SST-2	2	9,613	1,821
MPQA	2	10,606	cv

Movie Reviews[1] (MR): This dataset is a movie reviews dataset consisting of 5331 positive and 5331 negative movie-review snippets (one sentence per review) [14]. The task is sentiment classification to classify a sentence as being positive or negative.

Subjectivity Dataset[2] (Subj): Subjectivity dataset is a corpus consisting of 5000 subjective and 5000 objective processed sentence. The task is seen as a dichotomous problem to classify a sentence as being subjective or objective.

AG News[3] (AG): AG is obtained from more than 1 million Internet news articles [3]. News articles have been gathered from more than 2000 news sources. Each article consists of news title and the description fields. We only use Word, Entertainment, Sports and Business four topics from this corpus for classification. Each topics contains 30000 samples of train set and 1900 of test set.

Stanford Sentiment Treebank[4] (SST-2): SST-2 is an extension of MR but with train/dev/test splits provided [18]. Follow the setting of [6], the data is actually provided at the phrase-level and hence we train the model on both phrases and sentences but only score on sentences at test time, as in [5,8,18]. The task is sentiment classification to classify a sentence as being positive or negative.

MPQA[5]: This corpus contains news articles from a wide variety of news sources manually annotated for opinions and other private states (i.e., beliefs, emotions, sentiments, speculations, etc.) [26]. It contains 10606 sentences of opinion. The task is a opinion polarity detection to classify a sentences as being positive or negative.

---

[1] https://www.cs.cornell.edu/people/pabo/movie-review-data/.
[2] http://www.cs.cornell.edu/home/llee/data/search-subj.html.
[3] http://www.di.unipi.it/~gulli/AG_corpus_of_news_articles.html.
[4] http://nlp.stanford.edu/sentiment/.
[5] http://www.cs.pitt.edu/mpqa.

4.3   Results and Discussion

We analyze the advantages of our model from two aspects. They are accuracy analysis and parameter analysis of convolution.

Table 3. Accuracy of all the models on the five datasets. The results marked with * are re-printed from the references. The results marked with ♮ are re-printed from [23]. The results marked with – are lacking from the references.

Model	MPQA	Subj	MR	SST-2	AG
SWEM-concat* [16]	–	93.0	78.2	84.3	92.66
CNN-non-static* [6]	89.5	93.4	81.5	87.2	91.6♮
CharCNN* [27]	–	–	77.0	–	78.27
Densely connected CNN	–	–	80.1	–	92.9
+Multi-scale feature attention* [23]	–	–	81.5	–	93.6
VD-CNN* [2]	–	–	–	–	91.3
Weighted n-grams CNN	**90.5**	**93.7**	**81.6**	**88.3**	**93.84**

Accuracy Analysis

The results of all datasets on all models are shown in Table 3. Compared with the proposed models, we can see that our model Weighted n-grams CNN gets highest accuracy on MPQA, Subj, AG, SST-2 four datasets and comparable accuracy on MR datasets. We believed that the weighted n-grams layer generating the longer n-grams representations and considering the important degree of the word in sentence is beneficial for text classification.

Compared with SWEM-concat, our model gets better results on all datasets. Although the direct mathematical combination over word embedding is simple and effective, it is beneficial to extract the deep features with the Convolutional Neural Network in text classification. Compared with CNN-non-static, our model also gets better results on all datasets. It demonstrates the effectiveness of the weighted n-grams layer for capturing the longer n-grams features in text classification task.

Table 4. The numbers of parameters and n-grams for Subj dataset on two models

CNN-non-static		Weighted n-grams CNN	
param	n-grams	param	n-grams
360000	5	120000	24
720000	24	120000	30

Parameter Analysis of Convolution

We compare the numbers of parameters to the convolution on Subj dataset between the standard CNN model and our weighted n-grams CNN model shown in Table 4. The standard CNN model uses filter windows of 3, 4, 5 with 100 feature maps each. The number of parameters related to convolution is 360,000. Our weighted n-grams CNN model uses filter windows of 1, 2 with 200 and 100 features respectively. The numbers of parameters to convolution are 120,000. Note that our model can be easier to capture 24-grams features or even longer n-grams features without extra parameters, when parameters of the standard CNN model increasing with the increase of context length. For example, when the standard CNN model captures 24-grams features, it needs a filter window of 24 with 100 features maps and the numbers of parameters will be 720,000. On the contrary, weighted n-grams CNN model can capture 30-grams features without extra parameters. Therefore, our model can be easier to capture longer n-grams features and achieve comparative or even better performance in text classification.

5   Conclusion

In this paper, we propose a weighted n-grams CNN which considers the important degree of each word in the n-grams features and is easier to capture longer n-grams features for text classification. It is a variant of Convolutional Neural Network adding a weighted n-grams layer after the input layer and before the convolutional layer in Convolutional Neural Network. According to our experimental results, we find that our proposed model exhibits comparable or even superior performance in the text classification compared with other variants of CNN. Our future work will focus on taking more term weighting schemes into consideration and addressing the huge computation problem in long sentence or document classification.

Acknowledgements. This work was supported by the Fundamental Research Funds for the Central Universities, SCUT (No. 2017ZD048, D2182480), the Science and Technology Planning Project of Guangdong Province (No. 2017B050506004), the Science and Technology Programs of Guangzhou (No. 201704030076, 201707010223, 201802010027, 201902010046).

References

1. Collobert, R., Weston, J., Bottou, L., Karlen, M., Kavukcuoglu, K., Kuksa, P.P.: Natural language processing (almost) from scratch. J. Mach. Learn. Res. **12**, 2493–2537 (2011). http://dl.acm.org/citation.cfm?id=2078186
2. Conneau, A., Schwenk, H., Barrault, L., LeCun, Y.: Very deep convolutional networks for natural language processing. CoRR abs/1606.01781 (2016). http://arxiv.org/abs/1606.01781
3. Del Corso, G.M., Gulli, A., Romani, F.: Ranking a stream of news. In: Proceedings of the 14th International Conference on World Wide Web, pp. 97–106. ACM (2005)

4. Jones, K.S.: A statistical interpretation of term specificity and its application in retrieval. J. Doc. **60**(5), 493–502 (2004). https://doi.org/10.1108/00220410410560573
5. Kalchbrenner, N., Grefenstette, E., Blunsom, P.: A convolutional neural network for modelling sentences. arXiv preprint arXiv:1404.2188 (2014)
6. Kim, Y.: Convolutional neural networks for sentence classification. arXiv preprint arXiv:1408.5882 (2014)
7. Lan, M., Tan, C.L., Su, J., Lu, Y.: Supervised and traditional term weighting methods for automatic text categorization. IEEE Trans. Pattern Anal. Mach. Intell. **31**(4), 721–735 (2009). https://doi.org/10.1109/TPAMI.2008.110
8. Le, Q., Mikolov, T.: Distributed representations of sentences and documents. In: International Conference on Machine Learning, pp. 1188–1196 (2014)
9. Le, Q.V., Mikolov, T.: Distributed representations of sentences and documents. In: Proceedings of the 31st International Conference on Machine Learning, ICML 2014, Beijing, China, 21–26 June 2014, pp. 1188–1196 (2014). http://jmlr.org/proceedings/papers/v32/le14.html
10. Li, B., Zhao, Z., Liu, T., Wang, P., Du, X.: Weighted neural bag-of-n-grams model: new baselines for text classification. In: 26th International Conference on Computational Linguistics, Proceedings of the Conference: Technical Papers, COLING 2016, Osaka, Japan, 11–16 December 2016, pp. 1591–1600 (2016). http://aclweb.org/anthology/C/C16/C16-1150.pdf
11. Li, S., Zhao, Z., Liu, T., Hu, R., Du, X.: Initializing convolutional filters with semantic features for text classification. In: Proceedings of the 2017 Conference on Empirical Methods in Natural Language Processing, EMNLP 2017, Copenhagen, Denmark, 9–11 September 2017, pp. 1884–1889 (2017). https://aclanthology.info/papers/D17-1201/d17-1201
12. Martineau, J., Finin, T.: Delta TFIDF: an improved feature space for sentiment analysis. In: Proceedings of the Third International Conference on Weblogs and Social Media, ICWSM 2009, San Jose, California, USA, 17–20 May 2009 (2009). http://aaai.org/ocs/index.php/ICWSM/09/paper/view/187
13. Mikolov, T., Sutskever, I., Chen, K., Corrado, G.S., Dean, J.: Distributed representations of words and phrases and their compositionality. In: Advances in Neural Information Processing Systems 26: 27th Annual Conference on Neural Information Processing Systems 2013. Proceedings of a Meeting Held at Lake Tahoe, Nevada, USA, 5–8 December 2013, pp. 3111–3119 (2013). http://papers.nips.cc/paper/5021-distributed-representations-of-words-and-phrases-and-their-compositionality
14. Pang, B., Lee, L.: Seeing stars: exploiting class relationships for sentiment categorization with respect to rating scales. In: Proceedings of the 43rd Annual Meeting on Association for Computational Linguistics, pp. 115–124. Association for Computational Linguistics (2005)
15. Pang, B., Lee, L., Vaithyanathan, S.: Thumbs up? Sentiment classification using machine learning techniques. In: Proceedings of the 2002 Conference on Empirical Methods in Natural Language Processing, EMNLP 2002, Philadelphia, PA, USA, 6–7 July 2002 (2002). https://aclanthology.info/papers/W02-1011/w02-1011
16. Shen, D., et al.: Baseline needs more love: on simple word-embedding-based models and associated pooling mechanisms. arXiv preprint arXiv:1805.09843 (2018)
17. Socher, R., Lin, C.C., Ng, A.Y., Manning, C.D.: Parsing natural scenes and natural language with recursive neural networks. In: Proceedings of the 28th International Conference on Machine Learning, ICML 2011, Bellevue, Washington, USA, 28 June–2 July 2011, pp. 129–136 (2011)

18. Socher, R., et al.: Recursive deep models for semantic compositionality over a sentiment treebank. In: Proceedings of the 2013 Conference on Empirical Methods in Natural Language Processing, pp. 1631–1642 (2013)
19. Sutskever, I., Vinyals, O., Le, Q.V.: Sequence to sequence learning with neural networks. In: Advances in Neural Information Processing Systems 27: Annual Conference on Neural Information Processing Systems 2014, Montreal, Quebec, Canada, 8–13 December 2014, pp. 3104–3112 (2014). http://papers.nips.cc/paper/5346-sequence-to-sequence-learning-with-neural-networks
20. Tai, K.S., Socher, R., Manning, C.D.: Improved semantic representations from tree-structured long short-term memory networks. In: Proceedings of the 53rd Annual Meeting of the Association for Computational Linguistics and the 7th International Joint Conference on Natural Language Processing of the Asian Federation of Natural Language Processing, ACL 2015, Beijing, China, 26–31 July 2015, Long Papers, vol. 1, pp. 1556–1566 (2015). http://aclweb.org/anthology/P/P15/P15-1150.pdf
21. Wang, G., et al.: Joint embedding of words and labels for text classification (2018)
22. Wang, J., Wang, Z., Zhang, D., Yan, J.: Combining knowledge with deep convolutional neural networks for short text classification. In: Proceedings of the Twenty-Sixth International Joint Conference on Artificial Intelligence, IJCAI 2017, Melbourne, Australia, 19–25 August 2017, pp. 2915–2921 (2017). https://doi.org/10.24963/ijcai.2017/406
23. Wang, S., Huang, M., Deng, Z.: Densely connected CNN with multi-scale feature attention for text classification. In: Proceedings of the Twenty-Seventh International Joint Conference on Artificial Intelligence, IJCAI 2018, Stockholm, Sweden, 13–19 July 2018, pp. 4468–4474 (2018). https://doi.org/10.24963/ijcai.2018/621
24. Wang, S.I., Manning, C.D.: Baselines and bigrams: simple, good sentiment and topic classification. In: The 50th Annual Meeting of the Association for Computational Linguistics, Proceedings of the Conference, Jeju Island, Korea, 8–14 July 2012, Short Papers, vol. 2, pp. 90–94 (2012). http://www.aclweb.org/anthology/P12-2018
25. Wang, T., Cai, Y., Leung, H., Cai, Z., Min, H.: Entropy-based term weighting schemes for text categorization in VSM. In: 27th IEEE International Conference on Tools with Artificial Intelligence, ICTAI 2015, Vietri sul Mare, Italy, 9–11 November 2015, pp. 325–332 (2015). https://doi.org/10.1109/ICTAI.2015.57
26. Wiebe, J., Wilson, T., Cardie, C.: Annotating expressions of opinions and emotions in language. Lang. Resour. Eval. **39**(2–3), 165–210 (2005)
27. Xiang, Z., Zhao, J., LeCun, Y.: Character-level convolutional networks for text classification (2015)
28. Zeiler, M.D.: ADADELTA: an adaptive learning rate method. arXiv preprint arXiv:1212.5701 (2012)
29. Zhang, Y., Wallace, B.: A sensitivity analysis of (and practitioners' guide to) convolutional neural networks for sentence classification. arXiv preprint arXiv:1510.03820 (2015)
30. Ren, H., Zeng, Z.Q., Cai, Y., Du, Q., Li, Q., Xie, H.: A weighted word embedding model for text classification. In: Li, G., Yang, J., Gama, J., Natwichai, J., Tong, Y. (eds.) DASFAA 2019. LNCS, vol. 11446, pp. 419–434. Springer, Cham (2019). https://doi.org/10.1007/978-3-030-18576-3_25

Semantics

Detecting Emerging Rumors
by Embedding Propagation Graphs

Dang-Thinh Vu and Jason J. Jung[✉]

Department of Computer Engineering, Chung-Ang University,
84 Heukseok-ro, Dongjak-gu, Seoul, Korea
vudangthinh@gmail.com, j2jung@gmail.com

Abstract. In this paper, we propose a propagation-driven approach to discover newly emerging rumors which are spreading on social media. Firstly, posts and their responsive ones (i.e., comments, sharing) are modeled as graphs. These graphs will be embedded using their structure and node's attributes. We then train a classifier to predict from these graph embedding vectors rumor labels. In addition, we also propose an incremental training method to learn embedding vectors of out-of-vocabulary (OOV) words because newly emerging rumor regularly contains new terminologies. To demonstrate the actual performance, we conduct an experiment by using a real-world dataset which is collected from Twitter. The result shows that our approach outperforms the state-of-the-art method with a large margin.

Keywords: Rumor detection · Propagation graph · Centrality · PageRank · Word embedding

1 Introduction

Facebook and Twitter are popular websites for spreading and updating breaking news in our society [8]. However, there exists a large amount of news published without any verification. This leads to the spread of improper information which can cause bad effects towards individuals or organizations. These damage can be avoided if we can debunk rumors from spreading.

Allport and Postman [3] have defined a rumor is a story or a statement whose truth value is unverified and quickly spreads from person to person. This means that a rumor is a piece of information which can eventually be true or false. Furthermore, there are two categories of rumor which are discriminated by temporal characteristic, namely long-standing rumors and newly emerging rumors (breaking news rumors) [25].

- **Long-standing rumors:** which are discussed for long periods of time. For instance, a rumor that is ubiquitous on the internet and still being discussed is that Albert Einstein was a bad student with low academic performance.

© Springer Nature Switzerland AG 2020
F. L. Wang et al. (Eds.): AIRS 2019, LNCS 12004, pp. 173–184, 2020.
https://doi.org/10.1007/978-3-030-42835-8_15

– **Newly emerging rumors:** which are spawned during fast-paced events such as breaking news; therefore, this kind of rumors have not been observed or discussed before.

Rumor detection is the task of determining which pieces of information spreading in the social media have unverifiable truth values at the time of posting [2]. In case of detecting long-standing rumors, we can train a classifier based on historical discussions of the rumors, because the vocabulary is less likely to differ. In contrast, detecting newly emerging rumors task is confronted with more challenges. Firstly, this kind of rumors normally mentions newly topics or events which may not exist before; thus, these ones also not exist in the training dataset. This challenge requires to build a general model which has ability to predict unseen data well. Secondly, the content of newly emerging rumors usually includes out-of-vocabulary (OOV) words, e.g., new terminology, new hashtag or new entity names that do not exist in the training dataset. The issue of OOV is a challenge when building a word embedding model. Using pre-trained word embedding or training embedding on only training data cannot address this problem because of the new terms that have not been observed before. Most of researches in this field only concentrate on detecting long-standing rumors. By contrast, we focus on the problem of detecting newly emerging rumors on social media and propose an approaches to deal with difficulties of this task.

When a user has a post on social media such as Twitter and Facebook, it will be propagated over the network by many shares or retweets. Each post also contains many information itself such as its content, the number of likes, owner user features, and so on [16]. For these reasons, we modeled a post and its propagation as a graph. Each source post and its responsive ones are presented as nodes, and edges represent relations between them. The properties of each node represent the information of each post.

When modeling a post as a graph, the task of detecting rumor becomes a graph classifying problem. Therefore, we propose an algorithm that has abilities to embed a graph from its structure and node's properties, then classify it. Firstly, we vectorize each node based on its attributes. Table 1 illustrates several features we can build from properties of a node [26]. Secondly, we create graph vector by combining all node vectors. This combined vector is a representation of a graph. There are various ways to combine a set of vectors to only one vector. For example, we can concatenate or average them. In this paper, given a set of vectors, we propose a linear combination method based on the importance of nodes, which is also known as node centrality. More specifically, we use temporal information and expand PageRank algorithm for calculating the node centrality [4,17]. Finally, we classify the graph vectors by applying traditional machine learning algorithms. In this way, our model can learn both from attributes of posts and propagation structure of a post.

The second issue of classifying newly emerging rumor is the out-of-vocabulary problem. There are several popular methods to deal with this issue, e.g., using morphological similarity [6], Hybrid Word-Character Models [12]. In order to solve this challenge (i.e., embedding new terminologies), we extend the word embedding model (e.g., Word2Vec [15]) to incrementally training newly emerging rumor content.

We evaluated our proposed model on a real-world dataset. The experimental results proved that our model outperformed the state-of-the-art rumor detection model with a large margin. The main contribution of our works are summarized as:

- We introduced a novel algorithm to model a post and its responsive ones as a graph and combine both of post's content and propagation structure for learning. To the best of our knowledge, this is the first study that proposes a method to integrate both graph structure and node's properties based on centrality to resolve the problem of debunking newly emerging rumors in social media.
- We proposed a training strategy to mitigate the OOV issue by updating embedding for vocabularies which appeared in newly emerging rumors.

The rest of the paper is organized as follows. Section 2 covers some related works. Section 3 describes our approach for rumor detection issue. Then, we carefully evaluate our study in Sect. 4. Finally, Sect. 5 gives some conclusions and future works.

2   Related Work

The rumor detection issue have attracted many researches in recent years. A group of traditional feature-based approaches was proposed by [1,5,11,18,22], they extracted a set features from content, user profile, propagation structure, and so on to train a supervised model for classifying. However, feature engineering likely to biased and labor intensive. Zhao et al. [23] manually defined a curated list of regular expression to explore a pattern in the content of rumor. This method heavy depends on predefined regular expressions, so it is impossible to capture new patterns in newly emerging rumors.

A sequential classifier model based on the Conditional Random Fields (CRF) was proposed by Zubiaga et al. [26], where CRF was used to leverages context learned during an event. Similarly, Kwon and Cha suggested an approach based on the diffusion pattern of rumors by claiming that rumor's temporal shape has multiple peaks over time and longer life span than non-rumors [9]. These approaches are not efficient at the initial propagation phase due to lack of diffusion pattern and content.

Moreover, some kernel-based methods were applied to exploit the propagation structure of rumor. For example, Wu et al. [20] introduced a graph-kernel based hybrid SVM classifier which captures the propagation patterns and semantic features for detecting rumors on Sina Weibo. Ma et al. [13] proposed a new tree-kernel function to learn the similarity between propagation trees, then apply kernel SVM for classifying. The drawback of these kernel methods is their computation is memory and time consuming.

Recently, Deep Learning techniques also are used to deal with this issue. Alkhodair et al. [2] introduced a Long Short-Term Memory (LSTM) model for classifying rumor by learning from source post content. Ma et al. [14] introduced the Tree-structured Recursive Neural Networks which based on the structure of Recursive Neural Networks [19] to learn a representation of a rumor based on propagation structure.

However, none of these works considered the role of responses when a rumor spreading over social media. In addition, most of them only focus on detecting long-standing rumors rather than new rumors of emerging topics. In this paper, we introduced a method to measure the importance of each response and tackle the difficulties of detecting newly emerging rumors.

Table 1. Content-based and social-based features of a tweet on Twitter.

Category	Features
Content-based	*Word vectors*: embedding vector of post content
	Part-of-speech tags: vector of part-of-speech (POS) tags
	Capital ratio: ratio of capital letters
	Question marks: number of question marks in the post
	Exclamation marks: number of exclamation marks used
	Period marks: number of period marks in the post
	Word count: number of words in the post
Social-based	*Tweet count*: number of tweets written by the author
	Listed count: number of lists that include the author's account
	Follow ratio: the following ratio of the author's account
	Age: the age of the author's account
	Verified: whether the account of the author is verified or not

3   Rumor Detection via Propagation Graph Embedding

3.1   Problem Statement

The problem of detecting newly emerging rumor on social media can be defined as follows: for a given post regarding specific information, the task is to determine if it is a rumor or non-rumor. Let $G = \{G_1, G_2, ..., G_N\}$ is a set of graph, where each graph $G_i = \langle V_i, E_i \rangle$ corresponds to a representation of a source post. V_i refers to a set of nodes in graph G_i, each representing a source post or its responsive ones. E_i is a set of directed edges corresponding to the relationship between source post and its responsive ones. N is the number of tweets in the dataset.

Each node in the graph is represented by a vector $v \in V$ which is built from content-based and social-based features of a post. Content-based features are created based on text content of a post, and social-based features are metadata associated with the author of the post and the post itself. Table 1 illustrates some of content-based and social-based features which yielded the state-of-the-art performance in the study by Zubiaga et al. [26].

3.2   Propagation Graph Embedding

Our task is classifying graphs which are representations of conversations (the source post and its responsive ones) in social media. The problem is that most of classifying algorithms such as Linear Regression, Random Forest are not designed for graphs. Therefore, before applying classifying algorithms, we need to model each graph as a vector. In this study, we propose a method to embed a graph based on node centrality. Firstly, we calculate the centrality of each node in a graph. Let w_{ij} is the centrality value of node v_{ij} in the graph G_i. Then, the vector of graph G_i is formulated as:

$$g_i = \sum_{j=0}^{n_i} w_{ij} v_{ij}, \tag{1}$$

where g_i denotes i-th graph vector and n_i is the number of nodes in the graph i. After creating graph vector, we can apply different algorithms for classifying graphs such as Logistic Regression, SVM, Random Forest, and so on. In this study, we applied Random Forest to classify graph vectors. To calculate node centrality, we propose three different methods which are based on temporal and propagation structure as follows.

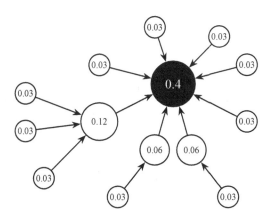

Fig. 1. PageRank of each node in a graph representing a conversation. The black node denotes the source-tweet, white nodes denote responsive posts (comments or retweets). The numbers in each node represent the PageRank value of a node. Node size denotes the importance of each node based on PageRank value. Directed edges start from responsive posts to the source post.

Temporal Centrality. We have an assumption that in normal conversations, people are likely to be distracted from the main topic over a long conversation, so they are probably discussing problems which are unrelated to the main one. Similarly, when a post is spreading, its responsive posts are very likely to be out of focus over time, so their contribution to the main topic in the source post will be reduced. Therefore, we built a temporal centrality metric which decreases the role of a post if the time lag between it and the source post increases. We call t_0 is the posting time of a source post and t_i is the posting time of a responsive post. We assign the importance of the source post $w_0 = 1$; therefore, the importance of a responsive one is formulated as:

$$w_i = \frac{1}{\log(t_i - t_0)}. \tag{2}$$

PageRank. To utilize the propagation structure of a conversation, we applied the PageRank algorithm to calculate weight of each node in the graph, so which node has higher PageRank will has higher contribution to the graph vector.

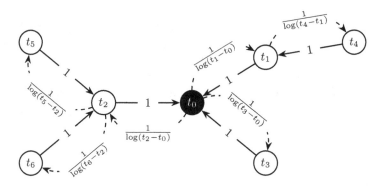

Fig. 2. The graph of a conversation in Temporal PageRank. The black node denotes the source post, and white nodes denote responsive posts. Labels in the nodes are posting time of corresponding posts. Labels in edges are weights of them.

Figure 1 gives an example of the PageRank value of each node in the graph. If a responsive post is posted, we can think that it includes a reference to the source post, so the edge direction will start from the responsive post to the source post. This is similar to how a graph of web pages is built. In addition, the original idea of creating PageRank is to rank pages on the web-graph, also known as ranking nodes in the graph. The property of PageRank is that it will give high rank to the pages that received many in-coming links from high-rank web pages. Therefore, if we apply PageRank to calculate the importance of each node in a graph of a post, the source post will always have the highest rank, and if a responsive post has more responsive ones, it will have a higher rank than a responsive post which has less responsive ones. This properties of PageRank algorithms makes it is suitable to measure the importance of each post in the graph of a conversation. The more important node will have more contribution to the graph vector. With this reason, we used the PageRank value of each node to weight the contribution of information in each node to graph vector.

Temporal PageRank. To incorporate both temporal and propagation structure, we suggest the Temporal PageRank method. The problem of traditional PageRank is that it cannot consider temporal attribute of nodes for ranking; therefore, it will give equal rank if two nodes have the same in-link structure. In the Temporal PageRank method, we applied the temporal information of each node for ranking. Therefore, when two nodes have the same in-link structure but having different posting time, which node has lower time lag will have higher PageRank. To utilize temporal information, we design graph structure like Fig. 2, instead of only creating edges from responsive posts to their direct source posts, we also add reverse edges from posts to their responsive ones. We assign the weight of edges which start from responsive posts to their direct source posts to 1, and modeling weights of reverse edges as:

$$w_{ij} = \frac{1}{\log(t_j - t_i)}, \tag{3}$$

where w_{ij} is weight of an edge from node i to node j, t_i and t_j are posting time of node i and j respectively. We then apply the Weighted PageRank algorithm [21] to calculate rank of each node in the graph. This allows us to learn the importance of a node both from graph structure and temporal information.

3.3   Word Embedding for Newly Emerging Rumor

The problem of classifying newly emerging rumor is that it often covers topics and event that we may not find in the training dataset. Therefore, this kind of rumor is very likely to contain new words which do not exist in the training dataset. To address this challenge, we propose training word embedding model incrementally with new rumors before making a prediction. When posts about a new topic spreading in social media, we will build a new corpus with tokens extracted from the content of these posts. After that, we update the parameters of the pre-trained embedding model by training this model on this new corpus. In this way, the embedding of existing words will be updated. Furthermore, we can learn the embedding of new terminologies.

4   Experiments and Results

In this section, we describe the dataset and our experimental settings. Next, we compare our approach with different baselines and the state-of-the-art approach.

Table 2. The numbers of rumor and non-rumor tweets in the PHEME dataset.

Event	Rumors	Non-rumors	Total
Charlie Hebdo	458	1,621	2,079
Ferguson	284	859	1,143
Germanwings Crash	238	231	469
Ottawa Shooting	470	420	890
Sydney Siege	522	699	1,221
Total	1,972	3,830	5,802

4.1 Datasets

In our experiments, we used PHEME dataset [24]. This dataset provides breaking news about five real-life events, namely Ferguson unrest, Ottawa shooting, Sydney siege, Charlie Hebdo shooting, Germanwings plane crash. Table 2 gives statistic about the numbers of rumor and non-rumor tweets in each event [26]. For each conversation thread, the PHEME dataset provides source-tweet information, responsive tweets information and structure of conversations.

4.2 Experimental Settings

To evaluate our model, we compared it against the following baselines:

- Naive Bayes (NB): a traditional machine learning algorithm which detect rumors based on content-based and social-based features.
- Conditional Random Fields (CRF) [10]: using CRF as a structured classifier to model sequences of tweets as observed in the timelines of breaking news.

With each of the classifier, we made comparisons based on content-based features, and the combination of content-based and social-based features. The set of content-based and social-based features are described in Table 1.

In this experience, we used Word2Vec model for learning word embedding, and the dimensionality of a word vector is 300. A node vector is the concatenation of its content vector and additional features which are described in Table 1. The node content vector is created by averaging embeddings of words in the content. To illustrate our model performance in the scenario of newly emerging rumor, we simulated this by training our model on four breaking news stories and keep the fifth one for evaluation. Therefore, the news used for evaluation was not presented in the training dataset. In addition, we performed 5-fold cross validation with each fold is one event, then averaging accuracy, precision, recall, and F1-score to evaluate model performance.

4.3 Experimental Results

Table 3 compares the proposed model with the existing ones in terms of accuracy, precision, recall and F1-score based on content-based and social-based features.

In this table, the performance of existing models we get from the study by Zubiaga et al. [26]. In addition, we also evaluate our model performance on using only word vectors. Even though the Naive Bayes method gives the best result in terms of recall, our model outperforms other models in terms of precision and F1-score. Based on only word vectors, the Temporal PageRank model gives the highest accuracy, precision, and F1-score. Based on content-based features, the Temporal PageRank model outperforms others in terms of accuracy and F1-score, but Temporal Centrality gives slightly better precision than others. Finally, the PageRank model outperforms others in terms of accuracy, precision, and F1-score based on the combination of content-based and social-based features. Surprisingly, using content-based features gives lower performance than using only word vectors in the Temporal Centrality, PageRank, and Temporal PageRank model. This is caused by most of features which are content-based are created by handcrafted process. This process is likely to create noisy features, which can bias the model.

Table 3. Comparing performance of different models in the rumor detection task.

Classifier	Features	Accuracy	Precision	Recall	F1
Naive Bayes [26]	Content-based	–	0.309	**0.723**	0.433
	Content-based + Social-based	–	0.310	**0.723**	0.434
CRF [26]	Content-based	–	0.683	0.545	0.606
	Content-based + Social-based	–	0.667	0.556	0.607
Temporal centrality	Word vectors	0.779	0.699	0.607	0.640
	Content-based	0.779	**0.701**	0.596	0.635
	Content-based + Social-based	0.781	0.706	0.601	0.641
PageRank	Word vectors	0.779	0.692	0.613	0.639
	Content-based	0.777	0.697	0.598	0.633
	Content-based + Social-based	**0.783**	**0.704**	0.616	**0.647**
Temporal PageRank	Word vectors	**0.782**	**0.702**	0.614	**0.644**
	Content-based	**0.780**	0.700	0.614	**0.643**
	Content-based + Social-based	0.779	0.698	0.607	0.639

In addition, we also made a comparison between our model and other node ranking methods in the graph, namely Degree Centrality, Closeness Centrality, Betweenness Centrality, Average Centrality and Second Order Centrality [7]. Table 4 compares performance between centrality methods when using only word vectors as feature of nodes. It shows that Temporal PageRank is the most efficient method for measuring the importance of each post in a rumor thread. In addition, Temporal Centrality and PageRank also outperform other centrality measurements. In general, our model outperforms other models because it can exploit both the propagation structure and other properties of a rumor.

Table 4. Comparing performance of our approach and different centrality algorithms.

Centrality	Accuracy	Precision	Recall	F1
Degree centrality	0.773	0.690	0.602	0.631
Closeness centrality	0.772	0.688	0.609	0.630
Betweenness centrality	0.757	0.692	0.536	0.585
Average centrality	0.761	0.681	0.513	0.579
Second order centrality	0.725	0.634	0.421	0.501
Temporal centrality	0.779	0.699	0.607	0.640
PageRank	0.779	0.692	0.613	0.639
Temporal PageRank	**0.782**	**0.702**	**0.614**	**0.644**

5   Conclusion and Future Work

We have introduced a novel approach which leveraging the post's properties and its propagation structure to resolve the rumor detection issue in social media. Our idea based on representing a rumor propagation as a growing graph. From that we can learn the importance of each post in propagating process, then classify the source post by modeling its propagation process as a vector. By doing experiments in a dataset which includes tweets about five breaking events, our proposed approach has proven to outperform the state-of-the-art classifier as well as other baseline classifiers in terms of precision and F1-score. In the future, we will focus on improving the rumor detection by applying propagation graph kernels which measure the similarity between graphs to detect rumors in social media.

Acknowledgments. This work was supported by the National Research Foundation of Korea (NRF) grant funded by the Korea government (MSIP) (2017R1A2B4010774, 2017R1A4A1015675).

References

1. Al-Khalifa, H.S., Al-Eidan, R.M.B.: An experimental system for measuring the credibility of news content in twitter. Int. J. Web Inf. Syst. **7**(2), 130–151 (2011)
2. Alkhodair, S.A., Ding, S.H., Fung, B.C., Liu, J.: Detecting breaking news rumors of emerging topics in social media. Inf. Process. Manag. **57**, 102018 (2019)
3. Allport, G., Postman, L.: The Psychology of Rumor. Russell & Russell, New York (1965)
4. Berkhout, J.: Google's pagerank algorithm for ranking nodes in general networks. In: 13th International Workshop on Discrete Event Systems, WODES 2016, pp. 153–158. IEEE (2016)
5. Castillo, C., Mendoza, M., Poblete, B.: Information credibility on twitter. In: Proceedings of the 20th International Conference on World Wide Web, WWW 2011, Hyderabad, India, pp. 675–684. ACM (2011)

6. Cotterell, R., Schütze, H.: Morphological word-embeddings. In: Proceedings of the 2015 Conference of the North American Chapter of the Association for Computational Linguistics: Human Language Technologies, Denver, Colorado, pp. 1287–1292. Association for Computational Linguistics (2015)
7. Das, K., Samanta, S., Pal, M.: Study on centrality measures in social networks: a survey. Social Netw. Anal. Min. **8**(1), 13 (2018)
8. Hoang Long, N., Jung, J.J.: Privacy-aware framework for matching online social identities in multiple social networking services. Cybern. Syst. **46**(1–2), 69–83 (2015)
9. Kwon, S., Cha, M.: Modeling bursty temporal pattern of rumors. In: Proceedings of the 8th International Conference on Weblogs and Social Media, ICWSM 2014, pp. 650–651 (2014)
10. Lafferty, J., McCallum, A., Pereira, F.C.: Conditional random fields: probabilistic models for segmenting and labeling sequence data. In: Proceedings of the Eighteenth International Conference on Machine Learning, pp. 282–289. Morgan Kaufmann Publishers Inc., San Francisco (2001)
11. Liu, X., Nourbakhsh, A., Li, Q., Fang, R., Shah, S.: Real-time rumor debunking on twitter. In: Proceedings of the 24th ACM International on Conference on Information and Knowledge Management, CIKM 2015, Melbourne, Australia, pp. 1867–1870. ACM (2015)
12. Luong, M.T., Manning, C.D.: Achieving open vocabulary neural machine translation with hybrid word-character models. In: Proceedings of the 54th Annual Meeting of the Association for Computational Linguistics, ACL 2016, Berlin, Germany, pp. 1054–1063. Association for Computational Linguistics (2016)
13. Ma, J., Gao, W., Wong, K.: Detect rumors in microblog posts using propagation structure via kernel learning. In: Proceedings of the 55th Annual Meeting of the Association for Computational Linguistics, ACL 2017, Vancouver, Canada, pp. 708–717. Association for Computational Linguistics (2017)
14. Ma, J., Gao, W., Wong, K.: Rumor detection on twitter with tree-structured recursive neural networks. In: Proceedings of the 56th Annual Meeting of the Association for Computational Linguistics, ACL 2018, Melbourne, Australia, pp. 1980–1989. Association for Computational Linguistics (2018)
15. Mikolov, T., Sutskever, I., Chen, K., Corrado, G., Dean, J.: Distributed representations of words and phrases and their compositionality. In: Proceedings of the 26th International Conference on Neural Information Processing Systems, NIPS 2013, Lake Tahoe, Nevada, USA, pp. 3111–3119. Curran Associates Inc. (2013)
16. Nguyen, H.L., Jung, J.J.: Social event decomposition for constructing knowledge graph. Future Gen. Comput. Syst. **100**, 10–18 (2019)
17. Nguyen, T.T., Jung, J.J.: Exploiting geotagged resources to spatial ranking by extending HITS algorithm. Comput. Sci. Inf. Syst. **12**(1), 185–201 (2015)
18. Qazvinian, V., Rosengren, E., Radev, D.R., Mei, Q.: Rumor has it: identifying misinformation in microblogs. In: Proceedings of the 2011 Conference on Empirical Methods in Natural Language Processing, EMNLP 2011, pp. 1589–1599. Association for Computational Linguistics, John McIntyre Conference Centre, Edinburgh (2011)
19. Socher, R., Lin, C.C.Y., Ng, A.Y., Manning, C.D.: Parsing natural scenes and natural language with recursive neural networks. In: Proceedings of the 28th International Conference on International Conference on Machine Learning, ICML 2011, pp. 129–136. Omnipress, Bellevue (2011)

20. Wu, K., Yang, S., Zhu, K.Q.: False rumors detection on Sina Weibo by propagation structures. In: 31st IEEE International Conference on Data Engineering, ICDE 2015, Seoul, South Korea, pp. 651–662 (2015)
21. Xing, W., Ghorbani, A.: Weighted pagerank algorithm. In: Proceedings of the Second Annual Conference on Communication Networks and Services Research, CNSR 2004, pp. 305–314. IEEE (2004)
22. Yang, F., Liu, Y., Yu, X., Yang, M.: Automatic detection of rumor on Sina Weibo. In: Proceedings of the ACM SIGKDD Workshop on Mining Data Semantics, MDS 2012, Beijing, China, pp. 13:1–13:7. ACM (2012)
23. Zhao, Z., Resnick, P., Mei, Q.: Enquiring minds: early detection of rumors in social media from enquiry posts. In: Proceedings of the 24th International Conference on World Wide Web, WWW 2015, pp. 1395–1405. International World Wide Web Conferences Steering Committee, Florence (2015)
24. Zubiaga, A., Hoi, G.W.S., Liakata, M., Procter, R.: PHEME dataset of rumours and non-rumours (2016)
25. Zubiaga, A., Aker, A., Bontcheva, K., Liakata, M., Procter, R.: Detection and resolution of rumours in social media: a survey. ACM Comput. Surv. **51**(2), 1–36 (2018)
26. Zubiaga, A., Liakata, M., Procter, R.: Learning reporting dynamics during breaking news for rumour detection in social media. CoRR abs/1610.07363 (2016)

Improving Arabic Microblog Retrieval with Distributed Representations

Shahad Alshalan[1], Raghad Alshalan[1(✉)], Hend Al-Khalifa[2], Reem Suwaileh[3], and Tamer Elsayed[3]

[1] Imam Abdulrahman Bin Faisal University, Dammam, Saudi Arabia
{ssalshalan,rsalshaalan}@iau.edu.sa
[2] King Saud University, Riyadh, Saudi Arabia
hendk@ksu.edu.sa
[3] Qatar University, Doha, Qatar
{rs081123,telsayed}@qu.edu.qa

Abstract. Query expansion (QE) using pseudo relevance feedback (PRF) is one of the approaches that has been shown to be effective for improving microblog retrieval. In this paper, we investigate the performance of three different embedding-based methods on Arabic microblog retrieval: Embedding-based QE, Embedding-based PRF, and PRF incorporated with embedding-based reranking. Our experimental results over three variants of *EveTAR* test collection showed a consistent improvement of the reranking method over the traditional PRF baseline using both MAP and P@10 evaluation measures. The improvement is statistically-significant in some cases. However, while the embedding-based QE fails to improve over the traditional PRF, the embedding-based PRF successfully outperforms the baseline in several cases, with a statistically-significant improvement using MAP measure over two variants of the test collection.

Keywords: Twitter · Arabic · Query expansion · Word embeddings

1 Introduction

Ad-hoc search on microblogging platforms such as Twitter is a challenging task due to the unique characteristics of the tweets. For example, the *limited length* of posts and the *noisy* nature of the stream increase the risk of the lexical gap between queries and tweets, which causes the so-called "query-document mismatch" problem. This problem does not only cause the missing of many relevant tweets, but could also negatively affect their ranking [30].

The problem is more profound with the Arabic language, given its high degree of ambiguity at the lexical, morphological, and syntactic levels. Furthermore, Arabic tweets show a special linguistic phenomenon that makes the retrieval problem even more complex, which is the high diversity of dialectal Arabic used by Arabic users on Twitter compared to Modern standard Arabic (MSA). Using

© Springer Nature Switzerland AG 2020
F. L. Wang et al. (Eds.): AIRS 2019, LNCS 12004, pp. 185–194, 2020.
https://doi.org/10.1007/978-3-030-42835-8_16

dialectal Arabic complicates the retrieval problem because of the lack of spelling and grammar standards, which in turn increases the severity of query-document mismatch problem.

Several techniques have been proposed in the literature to improve microblog retrieval, e.g., query expansion (QE) [8,9,24], document expansion [7,12], and reranking [30]. Most of the QE approaches rely on pseudo relevance feedback (PRF) and show a noticeable improvement [8,9,13].

Recently, few studies have utilized the *distributed word representations* (or *embeddings*) to improve the performance of different retrieval tasks [26] such as document ranking [11,25], terms re-weighting [28,32], and short text similarity [16]. Particularly, word embedding models have been successfully employed as a global source to expand queries using the most similar words induced from the word embedding pre-trained models [6,17,18]. Other studies empirically explored the effectiveness of embedding-based QE with PRF [10,31] or integrating the word embedding similarity into PRF models [10]. In this work, we propose a similar approach that incorporates embedding-based scores into PRF for query expansion, yet using different weighting scheme with a special focus on microblogs and Arabic language. We also propose an embedding-based reranking approach integrated with traditional PRF.

In this paper, our goal is to study the performance of different word embedding-based methods against traditional PRF on Arabic microblog retrieval. We first propose an embedding-based query expansion method that utilizes the semantic representations captured by word embeddings to expand the query. We also explore approaches that integrate word embeddings with PRF. We propose two methods on that track. First, we propose an embedding-based PRF which incorporates similarity scores obtained from word embeddings to weight the additional query terms. Second, we propose an embedding-based reranking to rerank the top documents retrieved by PRF. Finally, we study the impact of Arabic linguistic diversity in social media on the performance of our proposed methods. Specifically, we aim to investigate if the retrieval performance is different on dialect vs. MSA tweets.

In summary, we tackle the following research questions in the context of Arabic microblog retrieval:

- **RQ1.** Is word embedding-based query expansion superior to traditional PRF?
- **RQ2.** Does incorporating word embedding representations into traditional PRF model improve the retrieval performance?
- **RQ3.** Is there a difference in the performance of word-embedding-based methods over dialectal vs. MSA tweets?

We evaluated the proposed methods using three variants of *EveTAR* test collection [14]. The results show that the proposed embedding-based query expansion method under-performs the baseline (PRF) (RQ1). However, the embedding-based reranking method when incorporated with PRF query expansion outperforms the baseline and other approaches in all settings, and significantly in some cases (RQ2). The results also show that the embedding-based PRF led to performance improvement over the baseline in most cases, with a statistically-significant improvement in MAP measure over two variants of the test collection (RQ2). Finally, there were noticeable differences in the retrieval performance of embedding-based reranking method on dialect vs. MSA tweets in terms of P@10. This shows that the linguistic variations between the diverse forms of Arabic language impact their semantic representations in the embedding space (RQ3).

The contribution of this paper is twofold:

1. We investigate the performance of different embedding-based methods against traditional PRF method on Arabic microblog retrieval over different test collections.
2. We study the impact of the variations of the Arabic language on the retrieval performance of the proposed methods.

The remainder of the paper is organized as follows. Section 2 describes our proposed methods. Section 3 presents experiments and results. Finally, Sect. 4 concludes and discusses future work.

2   Proposed Approach

In this section, we describe our proposed methods in detail: (1) developing semantic representation, which is obtained by training a word embedding model on domain-specific collection (Sect. 2.1), and (2) leveraging word embeddings in query expansion or documents reranking (Sect. 2.2).

2.1   Learning Distributed Representation

The word representations are trained over a domain-specific collection (i.e., tweets) using the *Continuous Bag of Words* (CBOW) architecture of Word2Vec model proposed by Mikolov et al. [19,20]. Prior to training, text pre-processing, a core step in building any effective retrieval system, is performed. It is particularly important for Arabic retrieval, however, as the Arabic language is morphologically and orthographically rich, resulting in huge lexical variations between semantically similar words. Another challenge arises from the nature of the tweets, which are mostly noisy and frequently contain misspelled words or non-Arabic letters. To handle these issues, several steps are applied to clean the tweets and reduce both orthographic and morphological variations. This includes typical pre-processing steps such as cleaning, normalization, and stemming.

2.2   Embedding-Based Methods

We propose three different methods for incorporating the distributed word embeddings in ad-hoc retrieval task. In this section, we describe these methods in detail. We implemented our basic ad-hoc retrieval system over Lucene search library.[1]

---

[1] lucene.apache.org/core/7_0_1/index.html.

Embedding-Based Query Expansion (EQE). This method aims to expand a query with semantically-related terms online, during the retrieval phase. Given the original query Q that consists of m terms $\{q_1, q_2, \ldots q_M\}$, the goal is to expand it with semantically-related terms $Q_{exp} = \{t_1, t_2, \ldots t_N\}$ that are extracted from the vocabulary space based on their semantic similarity to all query terms in the embedding space. The final expanded query Q_{final} is then constructed as $Q_{final} = Q \cup Q_{exp}$. To score the terms and construct the Q_{exp} set, the centroid vector Q_c of Q is first constructed as follows [22]:

$$Q_c = \frac{1}{|Q|} \sum_{q_i \in Q} \overrightarrow{q_i} \tag{1}$$

where $\overrightarrow{q_i}$ is the distributed vector representation of the query term q_i. We then select the top N terms in the embedding space based on their similarity to Q_{cent}. We use *Cosine similarity* to estimate their closeness. The expanded query is eventually used (as a free-text query) to retrieve relevant tweets.

Embedding-Based PRF (EPRF). In this method, we extract expansion terms from terms that appear in potentially-relevant tweets rather than the entire vocabulary space. This is traditionally called Pseudo-Relevance Feedback (PRF). Given the pseudo relevant results of the original query Q, we extract a set of candidate terms from the top k results, R_k. Alternative to the common *tf-idf* scoring function, we score each term by computing the cosine similarity between its embedding vector and the query centroid vector Q_c (Eq. 1). The top N terms are then selected to construct the Q_{exp} set, which expands the original query.

PRF with Embedding-Based Reranking (PRF+ERerank). We also propose a reranking approach that leverages a pre-trained embedding model to rerank the pseudo relevant documents. We represent the query and the documents in the embedding space as centroid vectors of their constituent words using Eq. 1. After the initial retrieval, we apply the standard PRF-based query expansion with *tf-idf* scoring function to retrieve a new ranked list of documents. The top retrieved documents are then *reranked* based on two possible scoring methods:

1. **PRF+ERerank$_{ES}$:** pseudo-relevant documents are represented in the embedding space and reranked by their cosine similarity to the query centroid vector.
2. **PRF+ERerank$_{ES+PRF}$:** pseudo documents are scored similar to the above scoring scheme (in PRF+ERerank$_{ES+PRF}$) but their absolute scores from the first PRF retrieval phase are also added to their similarity scores to the query in the embedding space.

3   Experimental Evaluation

In this section, we describe the experimental setup and present and discuss the evaluation results thoroughly.

3.1   Experimental Setup

Test Collections. We evaluated the proposed methods using *EveTAR* test collection [14]. *EveTAR* is a test collection of Arabic tweets that was built to support multiple retrieval tasks, and designed around popular events. It contains 50 topics along with their relevance judgments, all in MSA form. We used three variants of *EveTAR*, all released besides the full collection: (1) *EveTAR*-S, which is a random sample of *EveTAR*, (2) *EveTAR*-S.m, which is a subset of *EveTAR*-S that includes only MSA tweets, and (3) *EveTAR*-S.d, which is a subset of *EveTAR*-S that includes only dialectal tweets. Table 1 shows detailed statistics of *EveTAR* upon our own crawl of the tweets.

Table 1. Test collections statistics.

	EveTAR-S	*EveTAR*-S.m	*EveTAR*-S.d
# accessible tweets	9.5M	5.5M	4M
# accessible qrels	46,873	36,791	11,961
Avg. rel tweets/topic	381	335	45
# tokens	5.1M	3.1M	3,1M

Pre-processing. Before indexing the test collections and building the Word2Vec models, we applied a pipeline of preprocessing steps on the collections. The steps include removing noisy characters (such as URLs, emojis, and emoticons), tokenization, normalization, and stemming using Farasa stemmer [1]. The same preprocessing steps are applied on queries.

Word2Vec Models. We trained two Word2Vec models using the Continuous Bag of Words (CBOW) training algorithm [19]. We used Gensim tool[2] in python. Each model was trained over a different collection. The first model was trained over target (local) collection, which is *EveTAR*-S collection. The second model was trained using external (global) collection that is a subset of *AraVec* tweets dataset [29].

As for the hyper-parameters of the models, we selected a contect window of size 3, since the length of tweets is generally small [29]. We set the vector dimensions to 300, as studies showed that the best accuracy is achieved at this

---

[2] https://radimrehurek.com/gensim/.

dimensional space and there is no dramatic improvement beyond it [19]. We set the other hyper-parameters to their defaults.

Motivated by Mitra et al. [23], we keep both input (IN) and output (OUT) embeddings learned by the Word2Vec model. We first experimented using the regular single embedding space (SES), in which the query and target documents/terms are both mapped into the *IN* space. We also experimented using the dual embedding space (DES), in which we map the query into the *IN* space and the target document/terms into the *OUT* space. Our preliminary experiments showed that using DES has positive impact on the effectiveness of the proposed methods over SES[3].

Baseline and Parameter Tuning. As for the baseline, we implemented query expansion with PRF since it has been shown to be effective for microblog retrieval [9,13,24]. We specifically used a PRF with *tf-idf* scoring function, where the query is expanded using the n top-scored terms that are extracted from the pseudo-relevant results R_k. We tuned all parameters for each method independently using 2-fold cross validation and over MAP measure. Table 2 presents all parameters alongside the values we experimented with.

Table 2. Values of tuned parameters.

Parameter	Values
Dirichlet parameter (μ)	1000, 1500, 2000, 2500
Expansion terms weight (α)	0.3, 0.4, 0.5
# expansion terms in PRF (n)	5, 10, 15
# pseudo results (k)	5, 10, 15, 20
# reranked docs (r)	15, 30
# expansion terms in EQE (N)	5, 10, 15, 20
Similarity threshold	0.6

3.2   Results and Discussion

In Table 3, we summarize the results of the different tuned models: embedding-based query expansion (EQE), embedding-based PRF (EPRF), and PRF with embedding-based reranking (PRF+ERerank) with the two scoring schemes.

It is clear that EQE model under-performs the baseline consistently using $P@10$ and MAP evaluation measures. To investigate the reasons behind such behavior, we conducted query-by-query failure analysis and found that approximately only 50% of the queries were expanded due to the strict term selection criteria in EQE method (threshold and N). Moreover, although EQE manages

---

[3] Due to the space constraints, we solely report the DES results.

Table 3. The results of proposed methods against the baselines. The best result in each column is grey shaded. The second-best result is boldfaced. A star (*) indicates statistically-significant improvement over the baseline.

Method	WE model	*EveTAR*-S		*EveTAR*-S.m		*EveTAR*-S.d	
		P@10	MAP	P@10	MAP	P@10	MAP
PRF (baseline)	NA	0.846	0.329	0.820	0.426	0.556	0.466
EQE	Local	0.760	0.322	0.750	0.423	0.566	0.474
EQE	Global	0.794	0.312	0.782	0.404	0.550	0.444
EPRF	Local	0.838	0.370*	0.822	0.488*	0.574	0.488
EPRF	Global	0.834	**0.361***	0.840	**0.473***	0.586	**0.479**
PRF+ERerank$_{ES+PRF}$	Local	**0.868**	0.332	0.834	0.429	0.642*	0.471
PRF+ERerank$_{ES+PRF}$	Global	0.856	0.330	0.824	0.427	**0.632**	0.478
PRF+ERerank$_{ES}$	Local	0.870	0.332	0.836	0.429	0.630	0.473
PRF+ERerank$_{ES}$	Global	0.862	0.330	**0.838**	0.428	**0.632***	0.473

to extract semantically-related expansion terms for a relatively good number of queries, it causes topic drift for others.

Our analysis indicates that the notion of similarity learned by Word2Vec models, even when utilizing *IN* and *OUT* embeddings [23], leans towards the *Typical* similarity more than *Topical* similarity when trained over a short window size (short text) [21]. Practically, this is not aligned with the ultimate objective of most retrieval tasks that model the notion of relevance as *Topical* similarity.

Having established the required definition of similarity for retrieval tasks, we think that exploiting the learned embeddings in more local, query-dependant context may alleviate the drift issue. Thus, we examined the EPRF method in which the expansion terms are selected from the *query's initial R_k results*, based on their semantic similarity to the query. The result shows that EPRF method improves P@10 over the baseline in several cases, with being statistically-significant in terms of MAP over both *EveTAR*-S and *EveTAR*-S.m collections.

Additionally, PRF+ERerank method performs better than the baseline consistently using both P@10 and MAP measures. PRF+ERerank achieves the best results over the *EveTAR*-S.d test collection, where it exhibits statistically-significant improvement over the baseline.

In *EveTAR*'s three variants, all queries and almost all relevant tweets are written in MSA. However, *EveTAR*-S.d collection includes mostly dialectal tweets. This fact might make word embedding models more effective in boosting relevant MSA tweets over irrelevant dialectal tweets for the reranking in *EveTAR*-S.d collection compared to *EveTAR*-S and *EveTAR*-S.m collections, where most of tweets are written in MSA. Generally, these differences in the performance among test collections articulate the impact of linguistic variations between MSA and dialectal text.

Finally, the experimental results demonstrate no major differences in the performance among the local and global word embedding models in all proposed methods. Although this is not expected, it can be attributed to the fact that both models are trained on Arabic tweets data that share similar characteristics.

4   Conclusion

In this work, we investigated the performance of different embedding-based methods against traditional PRF method for the task of Arabic microblog retrieval. Our results showed that using word embeddings for query expansion negatively affects the retrieval performance compared to traditional PRF. However, word embeddings can lead to a significant improvement when integrated with PRF.

We also observed some differences in the performance between the MSA vs. dialectal test collections, which we impute to the effect of the linguistic variations between MSA and dialects. Furthermore, our analysis suggests taking into consideration the learning objective of word embeddings in the context of microblogs, which is not aligned perfectly with the objective of most of the retrieval tasks.

For future work, we aim at investigating the proposed methods over English Tweets test collections to perform a comparative evaluation. We also plan to experiment our methods with other embedding models that are more aligned with short text (e.g., tweet2vec) [5] and tools such as ELMo [27], BERT [4], Infersent [3], FastText [15], and the Universal Sentence Encoder (USE) [2].

References

1. Abdelali, A., Darwish, K., Durrani, N., Mubarak, H.: Farasa: a fast and furious segmenter for Arabic. In: Proceedings of the 2016 Conference of the North American Chapter of the Association for Computational Linguistics: Demonstrations, pp. 11–16 (2016)
2. Cer, D., et al.: Universal sentence encoder. arXiv preprint arXiv:1803.11175 (2018)
3. Conneau, A., Kiela, D., Schwenk, H., Barrault, L., Bordes, A.: Supervised learning of universal sentence representations from natural language inference data. arXiv preprint arXiv:1705.02364 (2017)
4. Devlin, J., Chang, M.W., Lee, K., Toutanova, K.: BERT: pre-training of deep bidirectional transformers for language understanding. arXiv preprint arXiv:1810.04805 (2018)
5. Dhingra, B., Zhou, Z., Fitzpatrick, D., Muehl, M., Cohen, W.: Tweet2Vec: character-based distributed representations for social media. In: Proceedings of the 54th Annual Meeting of the Association for Computational Linguistics (Volume 2: Short Papers), pp. 269–274. Association for Computational Linguistics, Berlin, August 2016. http://anthology.aclweb.org/P16-2044
6. Diaz, F., Mitra, B., Craswell, N.: Query expansion with locally-trained word embeddings. In: Proceedings of the 54th Annual Meeting of the Association for Computational Linguistics (Long Papers), pp. 367–377. Association for Computational Linguistics, Berlin (2016)

7. Efron, M., Organisciak, P., Fenlon, K.: Improving retrieval of short texts through document expansion. In: Proceedings of the 35th International ACM SIGIR Conference on Research and Development in Information Retrieval (SIGIR), pp. 911–920. ACM (2012)

8. El-Ganainy, T., Magdy, W., Gao, W., Wei, Z.: QCRI at TREC 2013 microblog track. In: Proceedings of the 22nd Text Retrieval Conference (TREC) (2013)

9. El-Ganainy, T., Magdy, W., Rafea, A.: Hyperlink-extended pseudo relevance feedback for improved microblog retrieval. In: Proceedings of the First International Workshop on Social Media Retrieval and Analysis (SoMeRA 2014), pp. 7–12. ACM Press, Gold Coast (2014)

10. El Mahdaouy, A., El Alaoui, S.O., Gaussier, E.: Word-embedding-based pseudo-relevance feedback for Arabic information retrieval. J. Inf. Sci. **45**(4), 429–442 (2018)

11. Ganguly, D., Roy, D., Mitra, M., Jones, G.: Representing documents and queries as sets of word embedded vectors for information retrieval. In: ACM SIGIR Workshop on Neural Information Retrieval (Neu-IR) (2016)

12. Han, Z., Li, X., Yang, M., Qi, H., Li, S., Zhao, T.: HIT at TREC 2012 microblog track. In: Proceedings of the 21st Text Retrieval Conference (TREC), vol. 12, p. 19 (2012)

13. Hasanain, M., Elsayed, T.: QU at TREC-2014: online clustering with temporal and topical expansion for tweet timeline generation. In: Proceedings of the 23rd Text Retrieval Conference (TREC) (2014)

14. Hasanain, M., Suwaileh, R., Elsayed, T., Kutlu, M., Almerekhi, H.: EveTAR: building a large-scale multi-task test collection over Arabic tweets. Inf. Retr. J. **21**(4), 307–336 (2018)

15. Joulin, A., Grave, E., Bojanowski, P., Mikolov, T.: Bag of tricks for efficient text classification. arXiv preprint arXiv:1607.01759 (2016)

16. Kenter, T., De Rijke, M.: Short text similarity with word embeddings. In: Proceedings of the 24th ACM International Conference on Information and Knowledge Management (CIKM), pp. 1411–1420. ACM (2015)

17. Kuzi, S., Carmel, D., Libov, A., Raviv, A.: Query expansion for email search. In: Proceedings of the 40th International ACM SIGIR Conference on Research and Development in Information Retrieval, SIGIR 2017, pp. 849–852. ACM (2017)

18. Kuzi, S., Shtok, A., Kurland, O.: Query expansion using word embeddings. In: Proceedings of the 25th ACM International on Conference on Information and Knowledge Management - CIKM 2016, pp. 1929–1932. ACM Press, Indianapolis (2016)

19. Mikolov, T., Chen, K., Corrado, G., Dean, J.: Efficient estimation of word representations in vector space. arXiv:1301.3781 [cs], January 2013

20. Mikolov, T., Sutskever, I., Chen, K., Corrado, G.S., Dean, J.: Distributed representations of words and phrases and their compositionality. In: Advances in Neural Information Processing Systems, pp. 3111–3119 (2013)

21. Mitra, B., Craswell, N.: Neural models for information retrieval. arXiv preprint arXiv:1705.01509 (2017)

22. Mitra, B., Craswell, N., et al.: An introduction to neural information retrieval. Found. Trends® Inf. Retr. **13**(1), 1–126 (2018)

23. Mitra, B., Nalisnick, E., Craswell, N., Caruana, R.: A dual embedding space model for document ranking. arXiv preprint arXiv:1602.01137 (2016)

24. Miyanishi, T., Seki, K., Uehara, K.: Improving pseudo-relevance feedback via tweet selection. In: Proceedings of the 22nd ACM International Conference on Information & Knowledge Management, pp. 439–448. ACM (2013)

25. Nalisnick, E., Mitra, B., Craswell, N., Caruana, R.: Improving document ranking with dual word embeddings. In: Proceedings of the 25th International Conference Companion on World Wide Web, pp. 83–84. International World Wide Web Conferences Steering Committee (2016)
26. Onal, K.D., et al.: Neural information retrieval: at the end of the early years. Inf. Retr. J. **21**(2–3), 111–182 (2018)
27. Peters, M.E., et al.: Deep contextualized word representations. arXiv preprint arXiv:1802.05365 (2018)
28. Rekabsaz, N., Lupu, M., Hanbury, A., Zamani, H.: Word embedding causes topic shifting; exploit global context! In: Proceedings of the 40th International ACM SIGIR Conference on Research and Development in Information Retrieval, pp. 1105–1108. ACM (2017)
29. Soliman, A.B., Eissa, K., El-Beltagy, S.R.: AraVec: a set of Arabic word embedding models for use in Arabic NLP. Procedia Comput. Sci. **117**, 256–265 (2017)
30. Wei, Z., Gao, W., El-Ganainy, T., Magdy, W., Wong, K.F.: Ranking model selection and fusion for effective microblog search. In: Proceedings of the First International Workshop on Social Media Retrieval and Analysis (SoMeRA 2014), pp. 21–26. ACM Press, Gold Coast (2014)
31. Zamani, H., Croft, W.B.: Embedding-based query language models. In: Proceedings of the 2016 ACM International Conference on the Theory of Information Retrieval, pp. 147–156. ACM (2016)
32. Zheng, G., Callan, J.: Learning to reweight terms with distributed representations. In: Proceedings of the 38th International ACM SIGIR Conference on Research and Development in Information Retrieval, pp. 575–584. ACM (2015)

LODeDeC: A Framework for Integration of Entity Relations from Knowledge Graphs

Sini Govindapillai[1], Lay-Ki Soon[2(✉)], and Su-Cheng Haw[1]

[1] Persiaran Multimedia, Multimedia University, 63100 Cyberjaya, Selangor, Malaysia
sinisanjay@gmail.com, sucheng@mmu.edu.my
[2] School of Information Technology, Monash University Malaysia,
Jalan Lagoon Selatan, 47500 Bandar Sunway, Selangor, Malaysia
soon.layki@monash.edu

Abstract. Large knowledge graphs (KGs), which are part of Linked Open Data (LOD) serve as the primary source for retrieving structured data in many Semantic Web applications. In order for machines to efficiently process the data for different data mining, entity linking and information retrieval tasks, it is always beneficial to have as many reliable facts from KGs as possible. But none of the KGs is complete on its own with respect to the number of relations describing an entity. Moreover, large KGs like DBpedia, YAGO and Wikidata appear similar in nature, but do not fully merge in terms relations of the entities from different domains. The complementary nature of different KGs can be utilized to expand the coverage of relations of the an entity. In order to achieve this, a framework for integration of entity information from different KGs using LOD, semantic similarity approaches and RDF reification is proposed in this paper.

Keywords: Knowledge Graphs · Entity information integration · Linked Open Data

1 Introduction

The vision of the Semantic Web is that machines are able to query and process the information on the Web like humans. In order to exhibit intelligent behavior by machines, knowledge should be available in machine-readable format. Knowledge Graphs (KGs) serve as the primary source of structured information. Machines process semantically rich queries with KGs as the backbone of their applications. Semantic search, question-answering, machine translation and named entity recognition are some of the applications of KGs. Linked Open Data (LOD), interconnects these KGs and acts as a global data space [1].

© Springer Nature Switzerland AG 2020
F. L. Wang et al. (Eds.): AIRS 2019, LNCS 12004, pp. 195–201, 2020.
https://doi.org/10.1007/978-3-030-42835-8_17

The volume and accuracy of data in these KGs plays an important role in performing the above tasks efficiently. But current KGs are noisy and incomplete due to the humongous data and the complex extraction process and sometimes, even due to error from the source [2,3]. There are a number of KG refinement approaches for completion and error detection, addressing different targets like entity types, relations and literals. Most of these approaches addresses only one target and is specific to one or two KGs only. However, it is very challenging to achieve completion and correctness at the same time [2].

There are a number of attempts to increase the coverage of relations of KGs. In order to establish the fact that relations of a KG are not complete on its own, an empirical study on DBpedia, YAGO and Wikidata has been conducted [6]. From the outcome, it can be concluded that relations of an entity have different coverage in different KGs. Based on the outcome, a hypothesis such that integration of the same entity information from different KGs can contribute to completeness of relations of an entity is thus formulated. To the best of our knowledge, integration of entity information from different KGs to increase the coverage of KGs has not been addressed before [2].

In this paper, a framework which integrates entity information from different cross-domain knowledge graph is proposed and presented. The main aim of the framework is to enable the retrieval of complete entity relations. The approach employs the concept of LOD together with different similarity measures, such as string and semantic similarity for the integration. The remainder of this paper is organized as follows: Sect. 2 discusses the background study, which explores different KGs and its complimentary nature. Section 3 proposes the methodology while Sect. 4 describes the work done thus far and concludes the paper.

2   Background Study

2.1   Knowledge Graphs

The idea behind **DBpedia**[1] is to make the information in Wikipedia available in structured form. Therefore, main source of information in DBpedia is the infoboxes of the articles in Wikipedia[2]. DBpedia is also the hub of LOD as it contains links to many datasets. **YAGO**[3] is a large ontology derived from Wikipedia and combined with taxonomy of WordNet. YAGO schema does not contain many distinct relations, but have abstract relation like *created* and relations composed of different words like *wasBornIn*, *hasWonPrize*. The abstract relations make it difficult to infer the meaning, most of the time, need to consider domain and range to do so. **Wikidata**[4] is community-created and is imported from other primary datasets. In Wikidata facts are stored as statements together

---

[1] http://dbpedia.org.

[2] https://www.wikipedia.org/.

[3] https://www.mpi-inf.mpg.de/departments/databases-and-information-systems/ research/yago-naga/yago/.

[4] https://www.wikidata.org.

with provenance information and temporal information. Wikidata uses RDF reification extensively. Wikidata classes and relations are community controlled and more complete.

2.2 Analysis of Different KGs

KGs appear to contain equivalent information. But in reality, they do not. Ringler and Paulheim in their work [5], discusses the major five cross-domain KGs DBpedia, YAGO, Wikidata, NELL and OpenCyc. The authors illustrate that even though these KGs appear similar, they are complimentary in nature and have their own advantage and disadvantages. They analyze these KGs and conclude that merging KGs may show a 5% increase in coverage of entities. Abián et al. in his work [4] has done a comparison between the DBpedia and Wikidata in order to identify the differences between the two, particularly in terms of the data quality. They have analyzed the KGs along different categories of data quality dimensions, namely intrinsic, contextual, representational and accessibility. Three KGs, namely DBpedia, YAGO and Wikidata have been empirically studied, focusing on the completeness of relations of a KG with respect to relations of an entity, timeliness of the data and accessibility of the KGs [6]. While [6] analyzes the coverage of relations of the same entity in different KGs, [5] analyzes the coverage of instance in different KGs.

3 Proposed Approach

In this paper, a framework named LODeDeC (*LOD*-based Approach for *E*rror *D*etection and *C*orrection) is proposed. The framework aims to integrate the relations of an entity from different KGs. For the purpose of the experiments, three KGs have been selected, which are DBpedia, YAGO and Wikidata. However, the framework is not limited to these three selected KGs, it can be extended to as many KGs as possible. Public SPARQL is used to extract the data in order to ensure that the latest data is always available for integration. LOD and different similarity measures for integration of triples are applied in the proposed framework. Figure 1 illustrates the data flow diagram of the proposed framework.

Initially, one of the KGs is chosen as the master KG. Integrated entity information will follow the ontology of this KG. Among the three selected KGs, DBpedia is chosen as the master KG since this is hub of linked data and has a stable ontology. Next, data extraction from different KGs will be carried out. In this step, data is extracted with selected entity as subject and object of the triples from each KG. Prior to the integration, segregation of entity relations and literals are done for each KGs. At this stage, only relations are integrated for the purpose of this research.

As shown in Fig. 1, for the integration, the predicates and related entities which describe the same fact about the entity from various KGs should be identified. First, it is checked whether the defined domain or range of the object triple

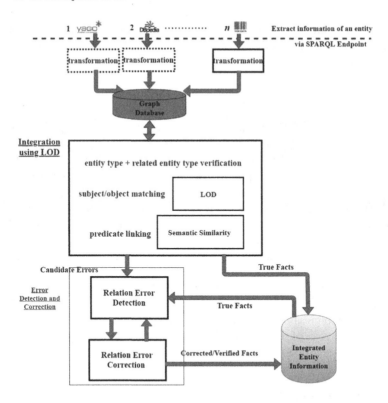

Fig. 1. Data flow diagram for LODeDec

is the same as the actual entity type of the related entity. Next, Using LOD inter-links, the set of triples from other KGs are retrieved and correct triples will be linked for integration purpose. For the predicate matching, semantic similarity is used. Predicates are composed of different words. Examples from DBpedia are *birthPlace* and *doctoralStudent*. Weightage will be given to triples with prove-nance information attached to it.

There are few possible scenarios when integrating triples from different KGs, as illustrated in Fig. 2. In the first scenario, scenario (1), triples are available in all the KGs. In this case, predicates are semantically matched in all the KGs with related entity as subject/object. This is considered as true facts. Remain-ing triples are considered as candidate errors and further computation is needed before integration. These triples are then passed to error detection module for checking whether these are true facts or errors. Table 1 provides examples of different scenarios of integration. The examples serve as preliminary results obtained from integrating the three selected KGs.

Algorithm 1 gives an overview of true facts identification from candidate errors in LODeDeC. Let E denotes set of entities, C denotes set of classes or entity types and P denotes set of properties of a KG. Entity to be integrated, $e \in E$, is accepted as input to the algorithm. Triples for this entity is retrieved

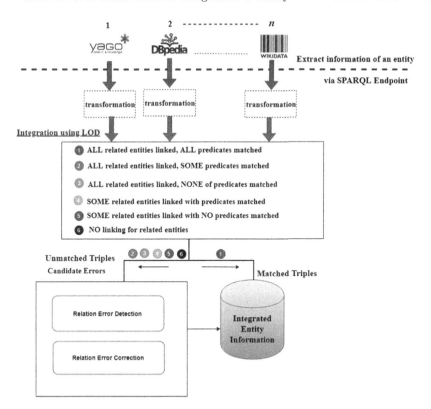

Fig. 2. Potential scenarios for integration

from KGs and processed to get the integrated result. Subscripts d, y and w are used to represent the data from KGs DBpedia, YAGO & Wikidata respectively. Therefore, $e_d \in E_d$, $e_y \in E_y$ and $e_w \in E_w$ represent the same entity from DBpedia, YAGO & Wikidata respectively. Using interlinking nature of LOD, e_y and e_w are retrieved from DBpedia. Next, set of triples, $T_{ds}(e_d, p_d, re_d)$ with the entity e_d as subject is retrieved from DBpedia. In the triples, $re_d \in E_d$ represent the entities related to e_d using properties $p_d \in P_d$.

For each triple $T_{dsi}(e_d, p_{di}, re_{di}) \in T_{ds}(e_d, p_d, re_d)$, where i represents a positive integer, the following steps are performed. Corresponding entities of re_{di} is retrieved from YAGO ($re_y \in E_y$) and Wikidata ($re_w \in E_w$) using LOD. In line 8, set of all triples T_{ys} with the entity e_y as subject is retrieved from YAGO. In line 9, set of all triples T_{yo} with the entity e_y as object is retrieved from YAGO. This is done to ensure that all the relations involving this entity are obtained from KGs. Candidate entities T_{yc} for integration are obtained by merging these 2 sets. In line 11, semantic similarity of T_{yc} to DBpedia triple T_{dsi} is computed. From this, the triple with highest semantic similarity and which is above the threshold is filtered out. This triple T_y is considered as the equivalent triple of T_{dsi} in YAGO. Above steps (7–12 line numbers) are performed for Wikidata and

T_w is obtained. If equivalent triples are available in YAGO and Wikidata, this is considered as a true fact.

In similar manner, equivalent triples for T_{do} is also computed from YAGO and Wikidata. The set of triples which are complement to the set of *truefacts* are considered as candidate errors for further computation.

Algorithm 1: True Fact Identification Algorithm

Data: entity for integration
Result: True Facts, Equivalent triples from all KGs
1   **Function** *getTrueFacts(entity)* :
2     $e_y \leftarrow$ getEntityUsingLOD(e_d,Yago)
3     $e_w \leftarrow$ getEntityUsingLOD(e_d,Wikidata)
4     $T_ds \leftarrow$ getTriplesWithEntityAsSubject(e_d,DBpedia)
5     $T_do \leftarrow$ getTriplesWithEntityAsObject(e_d,DBpedia)
6   **while** $T_{dsi}(e_d$, p_{di}, $re_{di}) \in T_{ds}$ *and domainRangeVerified(T_{dsi})* **do**
7       $re_y \leftarrow$ getEntityUsingLOD(re_{di},Yago)
8       $T_{ys} \leftarrow$ getTriples(e_y, re_y,Yago)
9       $T_{yo} \leftarrow$ getTriples(re_y, e_y,Yago)
10      $T_{yc} \leftarrow T_ys \cup T_yo$
11      $T_{yc}, score_sim \leftarrow$ getSemanticSimilarity(T_{dsi}, T_{yc})
12      $T_y \leftarrow$ highest($T_{yc}, score_{sim}$) $\wedge$ ($score_{sim} > sem_{thresh}$)
13      $re_w \leftarrow$ getEntityUsingLOD(re_{di},Wikidata)
14      $T_{ws} \leftarrow$ getTriples(e_w, re_w,Wikidata)
15      $T_{wo} \leftarrow$ getTriples(re_w, e_w,Wikidata)
16      $T_{wc} \leftarrow T_{ws} \cup T_{wo}$
17      $T_{wc}, score_{sim} \leftarrow$ getSemanticSimilarity(T_{dsi}, T_{wc})
18      $T_w \leftarrow$ highest($T_wc, score_{sim}$) $\wedge$ ($score_{sim} > sem_{thresh}$)
19   **if** *(T_y) $\wedge$ (T_w)* **then**
20   truefacts $\leftarrow$ addToTrueFacts($T_{ds}i, T_y, T_w$)
21   **end**
22   **end**
23   **while** $T_{doj}(re_{dj}$, p_{dj}, $e_d) \in T_{do}$ **do**
24   ....
25   **end**
26   canderrors $\leftarrow$ addToCandidateErrors($truefacts^c$)
27 **end**

Table 1. Sample triples of integration

Scenario	Subject - Object	DBpedia	YAGO	Wikidata
1, 2 or 3	Bill Gates - Seattle	birthPlace	wasBornIn	P19 (place of birth)
	Bill Gates - Microsoft	board	created	P1830 (owner of)
	Stephen Hawking - Bruce Allen	doctoralStudent	linksTo	P185 (doctoral student)
4 or 5	Bill Gates - Bill & Melinda Gates Foundation	–	created	P108 (employer)
	Bill Gates - Corbis	–	owns	P 1830 (Owner of)
	Bill Gates - Mary Maxwell Gates	parent	–	P25 (mother)
6	Bill Gates - GAMCO Investors	–	owns	–
	Xavier Naidoo - Brothers Keepers	associatedBand	–	–
	Xavier Naidoo - Germany	–	–	P27 (country of citizen)

An error detection module which identifies potential errors by using the concept of LOD, semantic similarity, RDF reification and entity disambiguation is incorporated in the proposed LODeDec. Currently, the work on error detection and correction after the integration is ongoing.

4 Conclusion

The development of Linked Open Data is tremendous and fast due to its ability in connecting and linking different data sets into one global KG. In this paper, a framework named LODeDec is proposed for integrating entity relations of the same entity from different KGs using LOD, semantic similarity and RDF reification. The framework includes processes for the integration of entity relations together with error detection and correction. This framework can be used as the basis for strengthening the construction and refinement approaches of different KGs. The main contribution of LODeDeC is that it uses the existing information from LOD to increase the completeness of relations of an entity. Algorithms for performing error detection and correction of the proposed framework will be incorporated once the existing experiments on error detection are completed. Holistic evaluation of the proposed framework will be presented in future publication.

Acknowledgements. This work is partially funded by Fundamental Research Grant Scheme (FRGS) by Malaysia Ministry of Higher Education (Ref: FRGS/2/2013/ICT07/MMU/02/2).

References

1. Bizer, C., Heath, T., Berners-Lee, T: Linked data - the story so far. Int. J. Semant. Web Inf. Syst. **5**(3), 1–22. https://doi.org/10.4018/jswis.2009081901
2. Paulheim, H.: Knowledge graph refinement: a survey of approaches and evaluation methods. Semant. Web **8**(3), 489–508 (2017). https://doi.org/10.3233/SW-160218
3. Melo, A., Paulheim, H.: Detection of relation assertion errors in knowledge graphs. In: Proceedings of the 9th International Conference on Knowledge Capture. ACM (2017). https://doi.org/10.1145/3148011.3148033
4. Abián, D., Guerra, F., Martínez-Romanos, J., Trillo-Lado, R.: Wikidata and DBpedia: a comparative study. In: Szymański, J., Velegrakis, Y. (eds.) IKC 2017. LNCS, vol. 10546, pp. 142–154. Springer, Cham (2018). https://doi.org/10.1007/978-3-319-74497-1_14
5. Ringler, D., Paulheim, H.: One knowledge graph to rule them all? Analyzing the differences between DBpedia, YAGO, Wikidata & co. In: Kern-Isberner, G., Fürnkranz, J., Thimm, M. (eds.) KI 2017. LNCS (LNAI), vol. 10505, pp. 366–372. Springer, Cham (2017). https://doi.org/10.1007/978-3-319-67190-1_33
6. Pillai, S.G., Soon, L.-K., Haw, S.-C.: Comparing DBpedia, Wikidata, and YAGO for web information retrieval. In: Piuri, V., Balas, V.E., Borah, S., Syed Ahmad, S.S. (eds.) Intelligent and Interactive Computing. LNNS, vol. 67, pp. 525–535. Springer, Singapore (2019). https://doi.org/10.1007/978-981-13-6031-2_40

Author Index

Printed in the United States
By Bookmasters